CAMBRIDGE TEXTS IN THE
HISTORY OF PHILOSOPHY

———

AQUINAS

Disputed Questions on the Virtues

CAMBRIDGE TEXTS IN THE
HISTORY OF PHILOSOPHY

Series editors

KARL AMERIKS
Professor of Philosophy, University of Notre Dame

DESMOND M. CLARKE
Professor of Philosophy, University College Cork

The main objective of Cambridge Texts in the History of Philosophy is to expand the range, variety, and quality of texts in the history of philosophy which are available in English. The series includes texts by familiar names (such as Descartes and Kant) and also by less-well-known authors. Wherever possible, texts are published in complete and unabridged form, and translations are specially commissioned for the series. Each volume contains a critical introduction together with a guide to further reading and any necessary glossaries and textual apparatus. The volumes are designed for student use at undergraduate and postgraduate level and will be of interest not only to students of philosophy but also to a wider audience of readers in the history of science, the history of theology, and the history of ideas.

For a list of titles published in the series, please see end of book.

Thomas Aquinas
Disputed Questions on the Virtues

EDITED BY

E. M. ATKINS
Trinity and All Saints College, Leeds

THOMAS WILLIAMS
University of Iowa

TRANSLATED BY

E. M. ATKINS

CAMBRIDGE
UNIVERSITY PRESS

CAMBRIDGE UNIVERSITY PRESS
Cambridge, New York, Melbourne, Madrid, Cape Town,
Singapore, São Paulo, Delhi, Mexico City

Cambridge University Press
The Edinburgh Building, Cambridge CB2 8RU, UK

Published in the United States of America by Cambridge University Press, New York

www.cambridge.org
Information on this title: www.cambridge.org/9780521776615

First published 2005

A catalogue record for this publication is available from the British Library

Library of Congress Cataloguing in Publication Data
Thomas, Aquinas, Saint, 1225?–1274.
[Selections. English. 2005]
Aquinas : disputed questions on the virtues / edited by
E. M. Atkins, Thomas Williams; translated by E. M. Atkins.
p. cm. (Cambridge texts in the history of philosophy)
Includes bibliographical references and index.
ISBN 0 521 77225 7 – ISBN 0 521 77661 9 (pbk.)
1. Ethics, Medieval. 2. Christian ethics – Early works to 1800. 3. Virtues – Early works to 1800.
I. Atkins, E. M. (E. Margaret) II. Williams, Thomas, 1967– III. Title. IV. Series.
B765.T51 2005
179.9 – dc22   2004062845

ISBN 978-0-521-77225-9 Hardback
ISBN 978-0-521-77661-5 Paperback

This volume is dedicated to friends in the Order of Preachers

Contents

Preface

The translation, Translator's note on the text, and Glossary are the work
of Margaret Atkins. The Introduction and Further reading are the work
of Thomas Williams. Both editors contributed to the annotations, and
each of us read and commented extensively on the work of the other.

Margaret Atkins would like to thank her colleagues at Trinity and All
Saints, and above all Geoffrey Turner, for making possible the year's
leave in which this translation was largely completed, and Alison and Bob
Samuels for their unfailingly warm welcome on visits to Oxford. The hos-
pitality of the President and Fellows of Magdalen College, Oxford, and of
the Rector and Professors of the Pontifical University of St Thomas,
Rome, made this an extremely pleasant and fruitful year. She would
also like to thank many friends and colleagues for advice and help with
Thomistic questions, and in particular Kevin Flannery, SJ, for guidance in
matters Aristotelian, especially with reference to *On the Cardinal Virtues*,
article 3.

Thomas Williams is grateful for the superbly capable help of his
research assistant, Brett Gaul, in tracking down references, indexing,
and preparing the typescript for publication.

Introduction

The basic procedure was simple. The topic would be announced in advance so that everyone could prepare an arsenal of clever arguments. When the faculty and students had gathered, the professor would offer a brief introduction and state his thesis. All morning long an appointed graduate student would take objections from the audience and defend the professor's thesis against those objections. (And if the graduate student began to flounder, the professor was allowed to help him out.) A secretary would take shorthand notes. The next day the group would reassemble. This time it would be the professor's job to summarise the arguments on both sides and give his own response to the question at issue. The whole thing would be written up, either in a rough-and-tumble version deriving from the secretary's notes or in a more carefully crafted and edited version prepared by the professor himself. Records of such academic exercises have come down to us under the title 'disputed questions'.

The present text offers translations of some disputed questions on ethical topics presided over by Thomas Aquinas (1224/6–74), probably during the period of 1271–2, when he was for the second time the Dominican Regent Master in theology at the University of Paris. They examine the nature of virtues in general; the fundamental or 'cardinal' virtues of practical wisdom, justice, courage, and temperateness; the divinely bestowed virtues of hope and charity; and the practical question of how, when, and why one should rebuke a 'brother' for wrongdoing. Whether these were formal public disputations of the sort I have described, or a more low-key version adapted for use in Aquinas's own classroom, is not altogether clear. What is certainly undeniable is that they show Aquinas using the disputed-question format with characteristic brilliance, as we can see by contrasting the *Disputed Questions on the Virtues* with discussions of the same topics in the second part of the *Summa theologiae*, which dates from roughly the same period of Aquinas's career. The articles of the *Summa theologiae* follow a truncated disputed-question format, suited perhaps to the 'beginners' for whom he intended that great work. They typically include three opposing arguments for each thesis, and Aquinas's 'determinations' (the 'My reply' or 'I answer that' sections) are ordinarily a couple of paragraphs. In the *Disputed Questions on the Virtues* the determinations run much longer, and there are (on average) fifteen or sixteen opposing arguments. This more expansive treatment, though initially somewhat challenging for the present-day reader, allows Aquinas to offer more supporting examples, tease out more nuances, draw more helpful distinctions, and guard against a wider variety of possible misunderstandings than in the *Summa*.

These *Disputed Questions* focus on virtue. But is a close look at Aquinas's account of virtue really the best way into his ethics? Many historians of philosophy see Aquinas principally as a defender of natural law theory. Others regard his account of happiness, his analysis of human action, or his theory of practical reasoning as the cornerstone of his ethics. One need only look at some recent titles of books on Aquinas's ethics to see the differing emphases: *The Recovery of Virtue, Aquinas's Theory of Natural Law, Aquinas on the Twofold Human Good, Aquinas on Human Action, Right Practical Reason*. Some scholars argue that their favoured discussion has at least *expository* priority: in other words, that in laying out Aquinas's ethics one must talk about that area first, and only then can one understand other areas properly. Some go still further and argue for something stronger, which we might call *logical* priority: that their favoured area is the real heart of Aquinas's ethics, and other areas are at best mere appendages and at worst regrettable excrescences. There has been a particular rivalry between interpreters who focus on natural law theory and those who focus on the doctrine of virtue.

In an introduction to a set of questions on virtue one might expect to find a defence of the centrality of virtue in Aquinas's ethical thought. But in fact I think it is a mistake to describe his theory of virtue as any more or less central than his accounts of happiness, the natural law, practical reasoning, and responsible action. Aquinas's ethics is so thoroughly systematic that one cannot adequately understand any of these accounts without drawing heavily on all the others; to talk in anything like sufficient detail about any one of them requires one to talk about all of them. Since the doctrines of natural law and virtue have been regarded as particularly remote from each other, I can best make my case for the systematic unity of Aquinas's moral theory, and illustrate the place of virtue within it, by beginning from the theory of natural law and showing how it leads inevitably to the discussion of virtue.

From natural law to virtue

A good place to start is with the first appearance of what will become a standing analogy in the so-called *Treatise on Law*: the analogy between the functioning of speculative reason (the sort of thinking that aims simply at knowing the truth) and the functioning of practical reason (the sort of thinking that aims at making or doing something). Aquinas writes:

> Now in speculative reason, what comes first is the definition, then the proposition, and then the syllogism or argument. And since practical reason also makes use of a syllogism of sorts having to do with possible actions . . . we need to find something in practical reason that bears to actions the same relation that the proposition in speculative reason bears to conclusions. Such universal propositions of practical reason ordered to actions have the character of law.
>
> (*ST* 1a2ae 90.1 ad 2)

We can think of Aquinas as setting forth an analogy with all the points of comparison filled in but one:

	Speculative reason	*Practical reason*
Starts from	propositions (aka first principles)	?
Proceeds by way of	theoretical argument/syllogism	practical argument/syllogism
Until it reaches	a conclusion	a particular act

His proposal is that we give the name 'natural law' to those universal principles in practical reason that function in a way analogous to principles in speculative reason.

Now Aquinas does not think that anyone who engages in speculative reasoning is actually thinking about first principles in every single argument she makes; in fact, unless she is a philosopher, she may well *never* think about first principles. Nevertheless, those principles are operative in her reasoning, even though they may not be actively before her mind. When someone has a bit of knowledge in this way, Aquinas says that she has that knowledge 'dispositionally' (*habitualiter*). The disposition of the speculative intellect in virtue of which it grasps first principles is called *intellectus*. Since there are analogous principles – the natural law – operative in practical thinking, even if the thinker is not at the moment attending to them (or indeed has never attended to them), we can expect that there is an analogous disposition in the practical intellect. That disposition is called *synderesis*. *Synderesis* 'is the disposition containing the precepts of the natural law, which are the first principles of human acts' (1a2ae 94.1 ad 2).

Aquinas continues his development of the analogy by noting that in the speculative realm there is one principle that is absolutely first: the principle of non-contradiction. In the practical realm the analogous principle is that 'good is to be done and pursued, and evil is to be avoided' (1a2ae 94.2). Both first principles are indemonstrable: that is, they cannot be proved. But they are not the only indemonstrable principles in their respective realms. Principles in the speculative realm are all indemonstrable; even though some of them are of less generality than others, they do not depend on others in the sense of being deducible from them. For example, the principle that the whole is greater than the (proper) part is – in a sense that turns out to be very difficult to pin down – of less generality than the law of non-contradiction, but it cannot be deduced from the law of non-contradiction. We find the same sort of relationship among principles in the practical realm. The most general principles are hierarchically ordered, but they are not deduced from the very first principle or from each other.[1]

As I have said, the first precept of the natural law is that good is to be done and pursued, and evil is to be avoided. The most general precepts of the natural law will be more substantive principles that point out specific goods that are to be pursued. Aquinas identifies these goods by appealing to a general metaphysical theory of goodness and a philosophical

[1] In fact, being indemonstrable is part of the definition of 'principle'. Keep in mind that the Latin word for 'principle' is *principium*, a beginning or starting point. Principles are the starting points of arguments, not conclusions of arguments.

anthropology that goes hand in hand with that theory. According to the general metaphysical theory of goodness, a thing is good to the extent to which it lives up to the standards of its specific nature. Like any good Aristotelian, Aquinas holds that there are internal dynamisms in every substance that are naturally directed towards the specific perfections of that substance. Those internal dynamisms are called 'appetite' or 'desire'. Here we have the fundamental sense in which Aquinas believes that 'all things seek the good': there is in all things a desire for their proper specific perfection, and that perfection is what it is for those things to be good.[2]

In the case of human beings, that specific perfection is complicated. Aquinas tells us in 1a2ae 94.2 that it involves three broad types of good, hierarchically arranged. As it is for every creature, it is a good for us to maintain ourselves in existence. As it is for every animal, it is a good for us to reproduce ourselves and to care for our offspring. But for us alone among all animals it is also a good to exercise the powers of rational thought, and (consequently) to live in society and to know God. These three goods are not three independent, coordinate goods. They are arranged both hierarchically, so that our unique good is the best of these three goods, and inclusively, so that our unique good subsumes the other two without superseding them.

In keeping with the general Aristotelian view about desires, Aquinas must then posit desires corresponding to each of these goods. The two lower-level goods are aimed at by the sensory desire, which has two aspects: the aspect that desires what is pleasant and what is conducive to survival and reproduction, and shuns the opposite of these (the sensual part); and the aspect that fights against threats to what is desirable (the aggressive part). The highest good is aimed at by the intellectual desire or will, which is a natural inclination to choose what reason takes to be good.

Both the hierarchy and the inclusiveness of which I have spoken are important for Aquinas's conception of the human good. The hierarchy is important because it tells us that the good of the human being is, in a sense, rational activity itself. The inclusiveness is important because it tells us that the specifically human rational activity that constitutes our good is not theoretical but practical reasoning. It is reasoning about how

---

[2] Note, then, that 'desire' (*appetitus*) has a broader extension in Aquinas's philosophy than in our ordinary usage of the term. We would not ordinarily speak of plants, for example, as having desires; but they do have *appetitus*, since they have internal dynamisms by which they tend towards achieving their characteristic good.

to achieve our specific perfection – at every level – in our action. In other words, the *aim* of rational activity is the good of the person as a whole integrated system that includes a variety of inclinations; it is not the good of the reason itself.

Three reasons we need the virtues

Now we can see how this works out in the doctrine of the virtues. Virtues are dispositions by which we appropriate our specific good effectively. The other animals do not need virtues because their desires direct them spontaneously to their specific perfection. But because our specific perfection involves reason, it can only be attained through rational choice, and our desires alone do not suffice for fully rational choice. Why not? There are three reasons, each of which exposes the need for a certain type of virtue if we are to attain our good as discerned by reason. The first reason is that the sensory desire is by its nature aimed at only a *part* of our good, the part that we share with the lower animals. It can therefore come into conflict with what reason discerns as good for the person as a whole integrated system. As a result, 'When . . . someone has to deal with the objects of the sensory desire, he needs, in order to do this well, a kind of tendency or completeness in the sensory desire that will enable it to obey reason easily. That is what we call virtue' (*DQVirtGen* 4 rep.). Temperateness is the virtue that perfects the sensual part, and courage is the virtue that perfects the aggressive part.

So the sensory desire needs virtue in order to follow reason easily and reliably. The will, however, does not. Its very nature is to be a rational desire: that is, to incline to whatever reason presents to it as a good. Nonetheless, even rational desire is not sufficient for us to lead the life of reason, because it is aimed only at our individual good (*DQVirtGen* 5 rep.). But our individual good is open-ended in a certain crucial way: part of the human good is to live in society, but life in society requires certain relations to other people that go beyond narrow considerations of our individual perfection (even if they don't actually *contravene* our individual perfection). The will therefore needs to be perfected by justice, by which an individual conforms her own pursuit of the rationally apprehended good to the larger good of the community, whose well-being and institutional integrity provide the context in which she can pursue her own good.

Thus far we have seen two reasons why our appetitive inclinations are not by themselves enough to enable us to attain our characteristic human good. The first concerned the sensory desire: since on its own it can come into conflict with reason, it requires the virtues of temperateness and courage if it is to be properly disposed to the human good as discerned by reason. The second concerned the rational desire: since the will is directed to the good of the individual, it requires the virtue of justice if it is to be properly disposed to the good of others. There is a third reason, which concerns desire in general. Aquinas explains that animals 'engage in a limited number of activities' and their good is fixed and unchanging. So they need only what he calls 'natural judgement' – a kind of recognition of what is good that does not involve intellectual discernment – and a natural appetite for their fixed and unchanging good. Human beings, by contrast, 'engage in many diverse activities'. Their 'good comes in many varieties, and what is good for human beings comprises many different things. Therefore there could not be a natural desire in human beings for a determinate good that suited all the conditions needed for something to be good for them.' Nor is natural judgement adequate for our attainment of this varied and multifaceted human good. Human beings therefore need reason, 'which is capable of comparing different things, to discover and discern their own distinctive good, determined in the light of all relevant circumstances, as it should be sought at this time and in this place' (*DQVirtGen* 6 rep.). The virtue that enables reason to do this easily and reliably is practical wisdom.

To summarise the argument thus far: Aquinas's natural law theory is an account of the most general forms of human flourishing. From that account we learn precisely why temperateness, courage, justice, and practical wisdom are necessary for human flourishing. What I want to do now is to discuss Aquinas's account of those virtues and their relation to each other, and show how even the specific details of his conception of virtue and practical reasoning depend upon the general account of human flourishing established in the discussion of the natural law.

Natural law and the virtues: affective virtues

The doctrine of the affective virtues – temperateness and fortitude, which modify not only our actions but our emotions – is part of an explanation of how we go about achieving the end that is set forth in the theory of natural law. As we have seen, the most general principles of practical reason (or, in other words, the precepts of the natural law) prescribe that certain broadly conceived goods be pursued in action. Those goods are arranged both hierarchically and inclusively. So according to the natural law, a life well lived is one in which reason governs every level of human functioning so that it makes its proper contribution to the overall human good. If we are to live such a life, we must re-educate our emotions so that they spontaneously aim us at our proper end. A life in which we are constantly having to struggle against contrary desires, in which reason is always having to put down insurrections in order to maintain its sway, is not a good life. The affective virtues help ensure that we act consistently, not just haphazardly, in the pursuit of our end, and that we do so in a way that befits a creature endowed with reason.

This overview of the place of temperateness and fortitude in Aquinas's moral theory shows how natural law theory motivates the doctrine of the affective virtues. I now want to point out how natural law theory also supplies part of the content of that doctrine. I shall focus on temperateness. In 2a2ae 141.6, Aquinas explains the 'standard of temperateness' (*regula temperantiae*), and he does so by appealing to the natural law considerations I have already sketched:

> The good of moral virtue consists chiefly in the order of reason, for 'the human good is to be in accordance with reason', as Dionysius says. Now reason's preeminent ordering consists in its ordering things to an end, and the good of reason consists chiefly in this ordering: for the good has the character of an end, and the end itself is the standard for those things that bear on the end. Now all pleasant things (*delectabilia*) that are used by human beings are ordered to some need of this life as to their end. And so the need of this life is the standard adopted by temperateness concerning those pleasant things of which it makes use; in other words, it makes use of them only to the extent that the need of this life requires.

In his reply to the second objection Aquinas again appeals to natural law considerations to clarify this standard. Human beings need not merely subsistence, but a graceful, fitting, well-disposed life. So the standard of temperateness does not imply that human beings may only eat and drink the bare minimum they need to survive, but that human beings may eat and drink whatever is necessary for health and well-being. Indeed, they may eat and drink even more than that, so long as they do not actually indulge themselves so much that they impair their own health or well-being or undermine harmonious relations within their community.

Natural law and justice

Having discussed the relationship between the theory of natural law and the affective virtues, we must return to natural law and show how it informs Aquinas's account of justice as well. Recall that the superordinate and inclusive good for human beings is the good of reason. And as Aquinas explicitly says in 1a2ae 94.2, reason orders us to a common, social good, which involves an individual's relationships with other people. As I have said before, reason does not supersede the lower goods; rather, it transforms them. So in human beings even the lower-level inclinations are transformed in light of this higher-level inclination 'to live in society'. Even though temperateness and fortitude are directed to the agent's own good, the domains in which temperateness and fortitude are exercised have implications for the common good. We see this clearly in the case of sexuality. Initially sexuality has to do with temperateness, but because sexuality has implications for the common good, there are precepts of justice that regulate our sex lives: fornication and adultery are violations not only of chastity but also of justice. Clearly fear and daring will have implications for the common good as well – think about soldiers. So there is a sense in which temperateness and fortitude are not completely specified and put into context until we have spelled out the demands of justice. What I want to draw your attention to is that neither natural law theory nor virtue theory stands alone here. Although the specific demands of justice are spelled out within virtue theory, it is natural law theory that exposes the need for justice to complete and transform the affective virtues.

This point about the relationship between justice and the affective virtues brings us back to my earlier point about how the goods are arranged inclusively. The goods of reason transform the lower-level goods: what it is for a human being to be good with respect to the lower-level goods is not the same as what it is for a cat to be good at the lower-level goods, precisely because we have reason and cats do not. For us to be good at the lower-level goods means not only for us to have our sensory desire aimed properly at our own attainment of human perfection, but to have both sensory desire and intellectual desire (will) aimed at the common good.

So justice, which modifies the intellectual desire, must trickle down into the sensory desire as well if we are to be aimed at the good according to reason.[3]

So far I have shown how the theory of natural law motivates Aquinas's doctrine of justice and its relation to the affective virtues. But as was also true for temperateness and fortitude, natural law theory does not merely motivate the doctrine of justice; it also supplies part of the content of the virtue. Aquinas derives many of the precepts of justice from his conception of the institutional or social necessities without which human beings cannot achieve the good of reason by living in a well-ordered community.

Consider, for example, the moral rules concerning murder and permissible homicide. Some homicide is morally justifiable, even praiseworthy. In *ST* 2a2ae 64, Aquinas offers two criteria by which to distinguish between permissible and impermissible (unjust) homicide. First, if a homicide is to be permissible, it must be done by someone acting at the behest of the community as a whole, not by any private person (2a2ae 64.3). Second, the person killed must have been lawfully convicted of some serious crime and shown to pose a threat to the community (64.2).

The arguments for both criteria come from Aquinas's conception of the common good. Human beings are parts of a whole; that whole is the community. And parts exist for the sake of the whole. Just as you should not impair the body's integrity for just any old reason (chop off your hand just because you feel like it), but you *should* amputate if that is the only way to save the body, so also you should excise dangerous people if that is necessary for the safeguarding of the community (64.2). People who have so deviated from the order of reason have fallen into the state of the beasts (64.2 ad 3). They have in effect put themselves outside the community of the truly human. They do not literally become animals, of course – that is why killing them is of greater significance than killing a stray animal and requires the judgement of the community (64.3 ad 2).

Natural law and practical wisdom

As I have said, the relation Aquinas envisions between the common good and the individual good means that justice, which directs us to the common good, sets the end for temperateness and fortitude. But what in turn

---

[3] See especially 2a2ae 58.5, 6.

sets the end for justice, and through justice for temperateness and fortitude as well? Aquinas argues that the end of the moral virtues is the
human good. And since the human good is simply to be in accordance
with reason, it follows that the end of the moral virtues must 'pre-exist
in reason' (*ST* 2a2ae 47.6). That is, the end of the moral virtues is established by certain self-evident, naturally known principles of practical reason. These are the precepts of the natural law, which are known through
synderesis.

There are three important points about the ends that are set for us by
synderesis. First, the self-evident principles are general. They are things
like 'Do no harm', not things like 'Return property entrusted to you
unless the person has become insane in the meantime.' We therefore need
something that will allow us to see how the principles are to be applied in
particular circumstances.

Second, they are capable of being realised in a variety of ways.
Synderesis tells us, for example, that we should live in accordance with
reason, but there are any number of ways to live in accordance with reason. We therefore need something that will allow us to specify and make
concrete the initially indeterminate goods set by *synderesis*.

Third, all of these goods can be realised in a properly human way only
in and through *action*. That is, *synderesis* tells us not merely what we
should be, but how it is good and reasonable for us to *act*. And action here
means rationally guided, conscious, deliberate action for an end, not just
instinctive acts (which according to Aquinas should not be called human
acts at all, but rather acts of a human being). We know this because of the
hierarchy among the principles set by *synderesis*. As I discussed earlier,
because the good of reason is the highest good, rational activity is in a
sense the specific end of human beings. So the human good is not simply
the actualising of distinctively human potentialities, full stop, as the bovine
good is simply the actualising of distinctively bovine potentialities. The
human good is the actualising of distinctively human potentialities *as the
individual human being's reason directs*.

The specifics of Aquinas's account of practical wisdom make complete
sense when understood against this background. Because the ends set by
synderesis are both non-specific and open-ended (points 1 and 2 above), we
need a kind of reasoning that takes us from the secure starting points set
by *synderesis* to the particular conclusions that can guide action (point 3).
That is what practical wisdom is.

The details of Aquinas's account of practical wisdom depend on his account of the cognitive processes involved in deliberate action. The latter account, in all its rich and intriguing detail, lies well beyond the scope of this introduction. But fortunately Aquinas himself offers us a sort of summary from which he then derives an overview of the aspects of practical wisdom (1a2ae 57.6). In deliberate action we apprehend the end; we take counsel about how that end can be realised and made concrete here and now; having taken counsel, we are then in a position to judge what is to be done; and finally, having judged that such-and-such is to be done, we command the external bodily members to do such-and-such. (The taking counsel part is optional. In order to determine what is to be done in order to act temperately when I am offered a third slice of cheesecake, I can immediately judge that the cheesecake is not to be taken, and I order my vocal apparatus to utter 'No thanks.')

Practical wisdom has no role to play at the level of apprehension, because that has to do with the end, which as we have seen is set by *synderesis*. But the other three acts of reason all require dispositions by which they are properly guided in matters pertaining to the end. So practical wisdom in the broadest sense is the intellectual virtue that ensures that we counsel well, judge well, and command well. The sub-virtue by which we counsel well is *euboulia*, excellence in deliberation. There are two virtues by which we judge well: in ordinary cases the practically wise person exercises *synesis* and in exceptional cases *gnome*. The sub-virtue by which we command well is practical wisdom itself, in the strict sense.

There are corresponding sub-vices for each of the three acts as well. Foolish haste or 'precipitation' is a failure in the act of taking counsel: you do not stop and think. Thoughtlessness is a failure in the act of judgement: you cannot be bothered to pay attention to the relevant considerations that count towards the right judgement. Inconstancy is a failure in the act of command: you judge what is to be done but you do not follow through with it.

What is interesting is that Aquinas thinks of all these defects as arising from *moral* defects. Anger, envy, and especially lust divert the reason from its proper role in governing action. They cause us to bypass rational consideration (counsel), ignore or misperceive relevant evidence (judgement), or veer away from what we have determined is to be done (command). What this shows, of course, is that practical wisdom is not possible without the moral virtues, just as the moral virtues were not possible without practical wisdom.

By now it may seem that natural law theory is very far away: the account Aquinas gives of practical wisdom takes its shape from his account of agency, not from his account of natural law. But that appearance is misleading. For one thing, since practical wisdom is inseparable from the moral virtues, and both the role and the content of the moral virtues can be explained only by reference to the natural law, natural law theory is not so far offstage after all. But there is an even closer connection between practical wisdom and natural law, a connection that brings us back to our starting point. Practical wisdom is, as we have seen, an account of excellence in practical reasoning. And practical reasoning, like theoretical reasoning, starts from principles and works towards conclusions. The principles of practical reasoning – the starting point from which the practically wise person sets out on a reasoned path to excellent action – are the precepts of the natural law.

I can draw out the significance of this point by pointing to another comparison between speculative and practical reasoning. In theoretical reasoning there is a purely formal science that sets the norms for proceeding properly from principles to conclusions. That science – called syllogistic or logic – can be expounded and practised perfectly well without any reference at all to the content of any (non-logical) principles. There can be no equivalent science of practical reasoning. Practical reasoning cannot be practised perfectly well without any reference at all to the content of any moral principles; good practical reasoning starts from a correct conception of the end. The account of practical reasoning therefore cannot stand without the account of the human end, and that account is given its general theoretical foundation in the theory of natural law and then fleshed out in a doctrine of virtue that is thoroughly dependent on the theory of natural law.

Natural and supernatural goods

I said earlier that the specifically human rational activity that constitutes our good is not theoretical but practical reasoning. The life of practical reasoning, which is the life of the activity of the moral virtues, is (as Aquinas likes to put it) 'proportionate to human beings'. To put it another way, the life of theoretical reason is in an important sense *superhuman*: 'the theoretical intelligence . . . is not found in human beings in the full way that it is in angels, but only through their participating in something else. That is why the life of contemplation is not, strictly speaking, human, but above what is human' (*DQCard* 1 rep.). But as a Christian Aquinas believes that God intends human beings for a life that surpasses their nature, a life that is not 'proportionate to human beings' and therefore cannot be attained merely by the cultivation of their natural capacities, even to that peak of perfection that constitutes complete moral virtue. This supernatural human life is a gift, not an accomplishment.

We must not, however, think of that supernatural life as something wholly unrelated to our natural life, merely tacked on afterwards but lacking any intelligible continuity with our natural desires, actions, and dispositions. In fact, the notion that our natural life is the life exclusively of this world, and our supernatural life exclusively the life of the world to come, is completely foreign to Aquinas. Heaven fulfils our nature, though in a way beyond nature's own power; and our supernatural life begins not with death but with baptism.

We can understand what is distinctive in Aquinas's view by looking at the intellectual context in which these disputed questions were raised. By about 1260, or roughly a decade before the *Disputed Questions on the Virtues* were argued, the faculty of arts at the University of Paris had become something like what we would think of as a philosophy department. The arts masters no longer thought of themselves chiefly as providing a preliminary grounding in the liberal arts for budding theologians, but as practitioners of a critical, philosophical discipline with its own independent dignity – a dignity that they were not shy of asserting both on their own behalf and on behalf of the discipline of philosophy itself. For the Aristotelian philosophy that it was their task to develop and teach offered a comprehensive view of the world that did not rely on any purported revelation. Some of the arts masters therefore made very strong claims about the preeminence of philosophy and of the life of speculative (as opposed to practical) reason, as we can see in some of the propositions later condemned by the Bishop of Paris in 1277:

> That there is no more excellent way of life than the philosophical way.
>
> That the highest good of which the human being is capable consists in the intellectual virtues.
>
> That the philosophers alone are the wise men of this world.

The arts masters' assertion of the autonomy and integrity of philosophy (and indeed of the whole natural order, which philosophy purports to explain) has come to be known as 'integral Aristotelianism', since it involved the use of Aristotle's work not merely as a conceptual apparatus for elucidating received theological wisdom but as a complete, free-standing philosophy in its own right.

Not surprisingly, some conservatives in the faculty of theology vigorously opposed this 'naturalistic' philosophy and were deeply suspicious of the influence of Aristotle. We can get a glimpse of their attitude by looking at the *Conferences on the Hexaëmeron*, a series of lectures given by Saint Bonaventure in April and May of 1273. Although by now his own faculty days were behind him, Bonaventure had supported theological opposition to what he saw as the over-exuberant Aristotelianism of many lecturers in the University of Paris. The tenor of that opposition can be seen in passages like these:

> Take note of Gideon, whom the Lord commanded to test the people by the waters. Those who lapped were chosen: that is, those who drink moderately from philosophy . . . The others who drank while lying down are those who give themselves entirely to philosophy and are not worthy to stand up in the battle-line, but are bent over in submission to infinite errors.
>
> One must not mingle so much of the water of philosophical science with the wine of Holy Scripture that the wine is transmuted into water . . . But in modern times the wine is changed into water and the bread into stone, just the reverse of the miracles of Christ.
>
> The professors – even if not openly, at any rate secretly – read, copy, and conceal the quartos of the philosophers as though they were idols, much as Rachel lied about concealing the stolen idols of her father.
>
> (*ConfHex* 3.7.13–15)

In short, those who do not rigorously subordinate Aristotelian philosophy to scriptural theology are deserters from Christ's army, reversers of his miracles, and indeed closet idolaters.

Aquinas aims at avoiding both the extreme naturalism of the integral Aristotelians and what we might call the 'rejectionism' of the conservative theologians. Far from rejecting philosophy in general or Aristotle in particular, Aquinas is thoroughly Aristotelian. As Ralph McInerny puts it,

When Thomas referred to Aristotle as the Philosopher, he was not merely adopting a *façon de parler* of the time. He adopted Aristotle's analysis of physical objects, his view of place, time and motion, his proof of the prime mover, his cosmology. He made his own Aristotle's account of sense perception and intellectual knowledge. His moral philosophy is closely based on what he learned from Aristotle and in his commentary on the *Metaphysics* he provides the most cogent and coherent account of what is going on in those difficult pages.[4]

But even as he adopted much of Aristotle's philosophy, he did not agree with the integral Aristotelians that philosophy by itself offers a comprehensive, autonomous account of everything there is. In addition to the natural order, which philosophy investigates, there is a supernatural order, which is beyond the competence of philosophy. Yet 'the highest does not stand without the lowest';[5] the supernatural order does not obliterate the natural. As Aquinas himself puts it, 'grace does not destroy nature, but brings it to fulfilment' (*ST* 1a 1.8 ad 2). This understanding of the relationship between the natural and the supernatural orders allows Aquinas to preserve the whole Aristotelian conceptual apparatus but put it to a wider use than Aristotle envisioned. Aquinas expects to find parallels between the natural and the supernatural orders. He therefore seeks 'the discovery of natural analogies to transcendent truths and the ordering of both natural and supernatural truths in a scientific way'.[6]

Within ethics, this approach allows Aquinas to affirm that there is indeed such a thing as natural happiness, and that it does not lose its importance for moral theory simply because, as Christians affirm, there is also such a thing as supernatural happiness. Jean Porter explains this particularly well:

> the natural end of human life, that is, the attainment of specific perfection as a human being, is not rendered otiose or irrelevant by the fact that we are actually directed toward a supernatural end. The specific natural ideal of humanity remains the proximate norm

---

[4] 'Saint Thomas Aquinas', *Stanford Encyclopedia of Philosophy*. http://plato.stanford.edu/archives/fall1999/entries/aquinas.

[5] Thomas à Kempis, *The Imitation of Christ*.

[6] C. H. Lohr, 'The Medieval Interpretation of Aristotle', in Norman Kretzmann, Anthony Kenny, and Jan Pinborg, eds., *The Cambridge History of Later Medieval Philosophy* (Cambridge: Cambridge University Press, 1982), pp. 80–98, at p. 93.

of morality. That is why Aquinas insists that while the theological virtues transform the cardinal virtues, they do so in such a way as to leave intact the rational structure of the latter, which is itself derived from their orientation toward the natural human good, that is, natural perfection in accordance with the specific kind of humanity.[7]

An application: the question on brotherly correction

The question on brotherly correction is especially useful for illustrating the ways in which this theoretical apparatus can be brought to bear so as to provide determinate moral guidance about highly concrete and specific situations. Brotherly correction involves rebuking or reproving a fellow-Christian – no doubt Aquinas is thinking in particular of one's brothers in a religious order, but the discussion is more broadly applicable. Aquinas's first question is whether 'there is a precept about brotherly correction' – that is, whether it is something we are required by a commandment to do.

He argues that it is. We are required by a commandment to love our neighbour, and to love someone is to will what is good for him: not just to want it in an idle way, but actually to take action to secure what is good for him. As Aquinas puts it, 'our wills are neither effective nor true if they are not proved in what we do' (*DQBrCorr* 1 rep.). There are three kinds of goods for human beings: external goods, such as money and other possessions; goods of the body, such as bodily health and integrity; and the good of the soul, which is virtue. This last sort of good is the most valuable, since it touches most closely on what is fundamental to and definitive of us as human beings: our capacity for the active exercise of reason in shaping our lives. Now wanting good for someone includes wanting the absence of what is bad. It would be an odd sort of love that worked only to bestow good things on the beloved, never to remove ills. Just as the greatest good is the good of virtue, the greatest ill is the evil of vice. So, as Aristotle says, 'someone ought to help a friend avoid sins more than loss of money' (*NE* 9.3.3, 1165b19).

But simply knowing that we are required by commandment to rebuke an errant brother does not tell us much. Unlike negative precepts

---

[7] *The Recovery of Virtue* (Louisville: Westminster/John Knox Press, 1990), p. 67. I have omitted parenthetical references.

(commandments that require us to refrain from doing certain things), positive precepts (commandments that require us to do certain things) are not to be acted upon all the time and in every possible way. For one thing, it would be impossible to do so. I cannot take every available opportunity for honouring my father and mother *and* for giving to the poor *and* for worshipping God *and* for the many other things I am obliged by positive precept to do. More important than this purely practical problem, however, is a difficulty that arises from the metaphysics of goodness sketched earlier. Goodness is perfection, completeness, full-being. So if an action is to be good, it must get everything right. It must be done by the right person, with the right aim, from the right state of character, and under the right circumstances. This is what Aquinas is getting at when, as he so often does, he quotes the dictum of pseudo-Dionysius that 'Goodness arises from an integral cause.'

So we are to act on the precept requiring brotherly correction only 'when the appropriate conditions are present regarding persons, places, reasons, and times' (*DQBrCorr* 1 rep.). Most important among these conditions is 'that the action corresponds to the end at which the virtue is aiming. When correcting an offender, charity aims at reforming him. The action would not be virtuous if the offender were corrected in such a way as to make him worse' (ad 1). Of course, this means that in order to act virtuously in performing the duty of brotherly correction, someone needs to be able to 'read' people well, to find the words and the tone of voice that will soften the offender's heart and inspire reform, not cause him to dig in his heels and add resentment to iniquity. And the other circumstances require astute discernment as well. 'It is not possible', Aquinas writes, 'to provide a discourse that defines these circumstances' – that is, some general rule or set of rules that could be applied mechanically and would invariably give the right answer about how to act in any given situation – 'because judging them must take place in individual cases. This is the job of practical wisdom, whether acquired by experience and over time, or, better still, infused' (rep.).

Natural and supernatural virtues

Notice that Aquinas here envisions two quite different ways in which one might acquire the practical wisdom that will enable one to judge correctly about how to act in particular situations. One might acquire it according to the natural means of which Aristotle speaks: 'by experience and over time'. But one might also acquire it in a supernatural way of which Aristotle knew nothing: it might be 'infused' – literally, 'poured in' – by God. Infused practical wisdom is even better than the acquired kind. This is not because it is *intellectually* superior to the acquired kind (say, because it is more comprehensive or more accurate), but because it is connected with our supernatural good. As Aquinas puts it,

> it is not necessary for [infused] practical wisdom that someone is good at taking counsel in every area, e.g. commerce or war, but only in those matters that are necessary for salvation. Those who are dwelling in grace do not lack that, however simple they are, in keeping with 1 John 2.27: 'Anointing will teach you about everything.'
>
> (*DQCard* 2 ad 3)

Aquinas holds that there are infused counterparts for all the cardinal virtues: not just infused practical wisdom, but also infused temperateness, courage, and justice. They differ, not in the actions they dispose us to perform, but in the end for the sake of which they dispose us to perform them. For example, the person with acquired temperateness, as we have seen, tempers his sensual desire for the sake of his own good as correctly discerned by reason. The person with infused temperateness does the same thing, but for God's sake.

In purely natural terms, the person with only the acquired virtues is in some ways better off than someone with only the infused virtues. Those who are in a state of grace possess the infused cardinal virtues, but 'they can still find it difficult to exercise the virtues which they have received as dispositions, because the tendencies resulting from their earlier sinful activity remain with them. This does not happen with virtues that are acquired through engaging in virtuous activity', because in the very process of acquiring those virtues one roots out the tendencies that oppose virtuous activity (ad 2).

Later theologians will question whether it is necessary, or even rational, to posit infused cardinal virtues.[8] Aquinas, however, is emphatic that there must be such virtues. His insistence on this point is another illustration

---

[8] Bonnie Kent writes that John Duns Scotus was 'the first Scholastic theologian to subject this class of virtues to intense critical scrutiny'; she sketches Scotus's arguments and their subsequent influence in 'Rethinking Moral Dispositions: Scotus on the Virtues' in *The Cambridge Companion to Duns Scotus*, ed. Thomas Williams (Cambridge: Cambridge University Press, 2003), pp. 352–76, especially in sections I and III.2.

of his distinctive way of negotiating a middle position between integral Aristotelianism and rejectionism. Although he upholds the integrity of the natural order, allowing that human beings have a natural end and a set of virtues that dispose them to achieve that end, he also acknowledges a distinct and superior supernatural order, with its corresponding set of virtues. Yet there is an intelligible continuity between the two. It is, in a sense, natural for there to be supernaturally infused virtues, and the supernatural has a parallel structure to the natural. Notice how all these points are made in his extended argument that there are some supernaturally infused virtues:

> Just as human beings acquire the *first* thing that completes them, i.e. the soul, from the action of God, so they also acquire the *last* thing that completes them, that is complete human happiness, directly from God, and they rest in him . . .
>
> It is appropriate, then, that just as the first thing that completes a human being, which is the rational soul, exceeds the abilities of the *material* body, so the last state of completeness that human beings can attain, which is the blessedness of eternal life, should exceed the abilities of human nature *as a whole*. Now, each thing is ordered to its end by what it does, and the things that contribute to the end ought to correspond in some way to that end. Consequently, it is necessary for there to be some sorts of completeness in us that exceed the abilities of the principles natural to us and that order us towards our supernatural end. This could only be the case if God infused in human beings certain *supernatural* principles of activity on top of the *natural* ones.
>
> (*DQVirtGen* 10 rep.)

So far I have been speaking only of the infused *cardinal* virtues, but there are other infused virtues. The infused cardinal virtues perfect our natural capacities so that we will deal with the concerns of our natural life in a way that is informed by our supernatural destiny. The other infused virtues perfect our natural capacities so that we can deal directly with concerns that transcend our natural life altogether. These virtues, in other words, are supernatural not only in the end to which they direct us but in the subject-matter they allow us to deal with. These are the three 'theological' virtues of faith, hope, and charity. 'By faith', Aquinas says, 'the intelligence may be enlightened concerning the knowledge of supernatural matters . . . By hope and charity the will acquires a certain tendency towards that supernatural good' (ibid.).

A summary of the argument

Early in this introduction I stated my conviction that Aquinas's moral theory is so systematically unified that no single discussion – whether of the human good, the natural law, the nature of responsible action, or the virtues – can claim pride of place. A full defence of this claim would require a whole book, but by now I have at least sketched enough of the connections to make the claim plausible. I want to conclude by summarising my line of argument. The doctrine of natural law identifies and characterises the ends that are presupposed by all genuinely human agency. As Aquinas explicitly says, 'the precepts of the natural law . . . are the first principles of human acts' (1a2ae 94.1 ad 3). Those precepts provide the necessary anchor for practical reasoning. That anchor is not explicitly identified when Aquinas comes to discuss the nature of responsible action, but it must be assumed if that discussion is to make sense. For while Aquinas's action theory clearly recognises that all action and all practical reasoning must rest on ends that are objects of both cognitive and appetitive powers, it does not offer us any account of what those ends are; nor does it explain how those ends come to be either known or desired. Without the theory of natural law, therefore, Aquinas's action theory is largely empty; it certainly does not contain all the materials needed to generate a normative ethical view.

But the theory of natural law cannot stand on its own either. Without the accounts of human agency, practical reasoning, and the virtues, natural law theory would offer us only a somewhat sketchy philosophical anthropology, not a fleshed-out ethics. The fleshing out happens only when Aquinas takes the general account of the human good provided by natural law theory and shows how it can be concretely realised by individual human beings through the use of practical reason to shape not only particular purposive actions but patterns of action and reaction. In order to do this, human beings must acquire dispositions – the virtues – that enable them to act readily, reliably, and with pleasure in ways that accord with their overall good. That good in turn is twofold. There is both a natural and a supernatural good, each with its own virtues. But even the supernatural good bears an intelligible relation to the natural, and the virtues by which we attain it have a structure parallel to that of the virtues by which we attain our natural good. Thus, even that aspect of Aquinas's ethics that one would expect to stand apart from the rest turns out to be thoroughly integrated with his whole system, as befits a thinker who holds that 'grace does not destroy nature, but brings it to fulfilment'. The theory of natural law, therefore, turns out to be a perfect springboard into a theory of supernatural virtue.

Chronology

This chronology is based on dating given by Jean-Pierre Torrell, OP, *St Thomas Aquinas*, volume 1 (Washington, DC: Catholic University of America Press, 1996). Simon Tugwell argues for some small differences in dating in *Albert and Thomas: Selected Writings* (trans., ed. and intro. by S. Tugwell, OP, New York and Mahwah, NJ: Paulist Press, 1988).

Further reading

Primary texts

The most widely used translation of the *Summa theologiae* is that of the English Dominican Fathers, available in a five-volume edition from Ave Maria Press (1981) and on the Web at http://ccel.org/ccel/Aquinas/summa.html. The livelier but freer Blackfriars translation, in sixty-one volumes, includes the Latin text on facing pages. Originally published by McGraw-Hill, it is now available from Cambridge University Press.

Most students will find it more practical to make use of translations of particular treatises from the *Summa*. The University of Notre Dame Press offers translations of *ST* 1a2ae 1–21 (*Treatise on Happiness*, trans. John A. Oesterle, Notre Dame, IN, 1983), qq. 55–70 (*Treatise on the Virtues*, trans. John A. Oesterle, Notre Dame, IN, 1984), and qq. 90–7 (*Treatise on Law*, trans. R. J. Henle, SJ, Notre Dame, IN, 1993), as well as 2a2ae 1–16 (*On Faith*, trans. Mark D. Jordan, Notre Dame, IN, 1990). *Saint Thomas Aquinas: Political Writings*, trans. and ed. R. W. Dyson (Cambridge University Press, 2002), includes extensive selections from the *Summa* and other texts of Aquinas on a variety of topics within moral and political philosophy, as does *Saint Thomas Aquinas: On Law, Morality, and Politics*, ed. and trans. William P. Baumgarth and Richard J. Regan, SJ (Indianapolis, IN: Hackett Publishing Company, 2nd edn, 2003). Hackett has also published Regan's translation of the *Treatise on Law* (2000).

John Patrick Reid's translation of *On the Virtues in General* (Providence, RI: Providence College Press, 1951) proved helpful to the translator of this volume. Ralph McInerny has translated the questions on the virtues in general and the cardinal virtues for Saint Augustine's Press (South Bend, IN, 1998). The disputed questions on evil have recently been published by Oxford University Press (2003) in a translation by Richard Regan, SJ, with an introduction and notes by Brian Davies, OP.

Studies

Readers who wish to start with a basic overview of Aquinas's thought might do well to consult Ralph McInerny's *A First Glance at Saint Thomas Aquinas: A Handbook for Peeping Thomists* (Notre Dame, IN: Notre Dame Press, 1990). Far more detailed, but still accessible, are *The Cambridge Companion to Aquinas*, edited by Eleonore Stump and Norman Kretzmann (Cambridge University Press, 1993), which focuses on Aquinas's philosophy, and *The Thought of Thomas Aquinas*, by Brian Davies, OP (Oxford University Press, 1993), which encompasses both theology and philosophy to present a picture of Aquinas's thought as a whole. On a larger scale is Eleonore Stump's *Aquinas* (London and New York: Routledge, 2003), which investigates a wide range of topics within Aquinas's theology and philosophy, juxtaposing Aquinas's thought with contemporary philosophical views in ways that illuminate both. Jean-Pierre Torrell's two-volume work, *Saint Thomas Aquinas* (Washington, DC: Catholic University of America Press, 1996), offers a detailed intellectual biography of Aquinas and a consideration of his entire body of work.

All these works devote at least some space to ethics. For works devoted specifically to ethics, a good starting point is Jean Porter's *The Recovery of Virtue: The Relevance of Aquinas for Christian Ethics* (Louisville, KY: Westminster/John Knox Press, 1990). (Attentive readers will notice the pervasive influence of Porter's work on the introduction to this volume.) Although Porter presents her interpretation of Aquinas in the context of contemporary debates within Christian theological ethics, readers with no particular interest in that context will still profit from her clear and helpful expositions of Aquinas's metaphysics of goodness, theory of natural law, and accounts of the virtues. Another useful general survey of Aquinas's ethics can be found in Ralph McInerny's *Ethica Thomistica: The Moral Philosophy of Thomas Aquinas* (Washington, DC: Catholic University of America Press, rev. edn, 1997). *The Ethics of Aquinas*, a collected of articles edited by Stephen J. Pope (Georgetown University Press, 2002), includes both overviews of general themes and specific discussions of each section of the second part of the *Summa theologiae*.

With a solid grounding in Aquinas's overall moral system, a student can proceed to works that explore more specialised topics. For Aquinas's conception of human action, see Ralph McInerny, *Aquinas on Human Action: A Theory of Practice* (Washington, DC: Catholic University of America Press, 1992), and Jean Porter, *Moral Action and Christian Ethics* (Cambridge University Press, 1999). Daniel Westberg's *Right Practical Reason: Aristotle, Action, and Prudence in Aquinas* (Oxford University Press, 1994), focuses particularly on the role of intellect in human action. Kevin L. Flannery, SJ, examines Aquinas's conception of practical reasoning and action in light of the logical structure of an Aristotelian science in *Acts Amid Precepts: The Aristotelian Logical Structure of Aquinas's Moral Theory* (Washington, DC: Catholic University of America Press, 2001). Aquinas's account of the ultimate end of human beings is the focus of Denis J. M. Bradley's *Aquinas on the Twofold Human Good: Reason and Human Happiness in Aquinas's Moral Science* (Washington, DC: Catholic University of America Press, 1997).

Translator's note on the text

The published text of *Quaestiones Disputatae de Virtutibus* (Rome: Marietti, 1953) has no critical apparatus and occasionally appears problematic or even clearly erroneous. Unfortunately the critical edition of the Leonine Commission is still in preparation, but I have been helped in this translation by the Commission's kindness in allowing me to consult their provisional text to assist with difficult passages. Where I have still been unable to make good sense of the printed text, I have sometimes resorted to speculative emendation of the text, but where I have done so I have marked this in the footnotes.

Because of the difficulties of rendering into English a very complex text that includes a high number of indefinite personal pronouns, it has sometimes been necessary for the sake of clarity to use non-inclusive language in the translation. Readers should be aware therefore that masculine forms of the third personal pronoun often refer inclusively to members of both sexes. The original Latin, unlike English, is usually neutral in this respect.

Abbreviations

Aquinas quotes a very large number of times from scripture and other authorities. He is not usually concerned to distinguish sharply between precise quotation, broadly accurate quotation, and paraphrase. Although the translation sometimes uses quotation marks and sometimes does not, readers should not assume that it thereby represents a sharp contrast between methods of citation in Aquinas's original. Where Aquinas's text gives an inaccurate reference, we have given the correct reference in the translation wherever we have traced this. It has not been possible in every case to identify the passage quoted. In such cases, where Aquinas himself gives a specific reference, we have retained it in the text. Otherwise, we have left whatever general reference Aquinas offers (e.g. 'as Averroes says').

Abbreviations of non-scriptural works are given in italics in the text and correspond to the works indicated in the list below. Abbreviations of books of the Bible are given in roman type in the text and can be found in the Index of scriptural citations.

We have used 'obj. x' to refer to objection x in a disputed question, 'rep.' to refer to the reply, and 'ad x' to refer to the reply to objection x.

83DQ	Augustine, *Eighty-Three Diverse Questions*
AA	Augustine, *Against Adimantus*
AdGr	Augustine, *On Admonition and Grace (De correptione et gratia)*
AF	Augustine, *Against Faustus*
AJ	Augustine, *Against Julian*

Ar	Boethius, *Arithmetic*
AverSoul	Averroes, *Commentary on Aristotle's On the Soul*
AvSoul	Avicenna, *On the Soul*
Cat	Aristotle, *Categories*
CG	Augustine, *The City of God*
CommEth	Thomas Aquinas, *Commentary on Aristotle's Ethics*
CommLuke	*Commentary on Luke*
CommMatt	*Commentary on Matthew*
CommMet	Thomas Aquinas, *Commentary on Aristotle's Metaphysics*
CommPhys	Thomas Aquinas, *Commentary on Aristotle's Physics*
CommSent	Thomas Aquinas, *Commentary on the Sentences of Peter Lombard*
CommSoul	Thomas Aquinas, *Commentary on Aristotle's On the Soul*
CommSS	Origen (trans. Rufinus), *Commentary on the Song of Songs*
Conf	Augustine, *Confessions*
ConfHex	Bonaventure, *Conferences on the Hexaëmeron*
Cons	Bernard of Clairvaux, *On Consideration*
ContLife	Prosper of Aquitaine, *On the Contemplative Life*
CT	Augustine, *On Christian Teaching (De doctrina christiana)*
DivNames	pseudo-Dionysius, *On Divine Names*
DQBrCorr	Thomas Aquinas, *Disputed Questions on the Virtues: On Brotherly Correction*
DQCard	Thomas Aquinas, *Disputed Questions on the Virtues: On the Cardinal Virtues*
DQChar	Thomas Aquinas, *Disputed Questions on the Virtues: On Charity*
DQEvil	Thomas Aquinas, *Disputed Questions on Evil*
DQHope	Thomas Aquinas, *Disputed Questions on the Virtues: On Hope*
DQTruth	Thomas Aquinas, *Disputed Questions on Truth*
DQVirtGen	Thomas Aquinas, *Disputed Questions on the Virtues: On the Virtues in General*
Dream	Macrobius, *Commentary on the Dream of Scipio*
FC	Augustine, *On Free Choice of the Will (De libero arbitrio)*
FirstPhil	Avicenna, *First Philosophy, or the Divine Science*
GA	Aristotle, *On the Generation of Animals*
GC	Aristotle, *On Generation and Corruption*
GMarr	Augustine, *On the Good of Marriage (De bono coniugali)*

GPers	Augustine, *On the Gift of Perseverance (De dono perseverantiae)*
GrFC	Augustine, *On Grace and Free Choice (De gratia et libero arbitrio)*
GS	Augustine, *On the Greatness of the Soul (De quantitate animae)*
Hand	Augustine, *Handbook (Enchiridion)*
HarmGosp	Augustine, *On the Harmony of the Gospels (De consensu evangelistarum)*
Heav	Aristotle, *On the Heavens*
HomEzek	Gregory, *Homilies on Ezekiel*
HomGosp	Gregory, *Homilies on the Gospels*
HomSS	Origen (trans. Jerome), *Homilies on the Song of Songs*
Int	Aristotle, *On Interpretation*
Inv	Cicero, *On Invention*
IS	Augustine, *On the Immortality of the Soul*
LA	Athanasius, *Life of Antony*
LCG	Augustine, *Literal Commentary on Genesis (De genesi ad litteram)*
Let	Augustine, *Letters*
LovGod	Bernard of Clairvaux, *On Loving God*
Ly	Augustine, *On Lying (De mendacio)*
Met	Aristotle, *Metaphysics*
MonInst	John Cassian, *Monastic Institutes (De institutis coenobiorum)*
MorCath	Augustine, *On the Morals of the Catholic Church*
MorJob	Gregory, *Moralia in Job*
NatGood	Augustine, *On the Nature of the Good*
NatGr	Augustine, *On Nature and Grace*
NE	Aristotle, *Nicomachean Ethics*
OrthF	John Damascene, *On Orthodox Faith*
PA	Aristotle, *On the Parts of Animals*
PHJ	Augustine, *On the Perfection of Human Justice (De perfectione iustitiae hominis)*
Phys	Aristotle, *Physics*
Pol	Aristotle, *Politics*
PostAn	Aristotle, *Posterior Analytics*
Pred	Augustine, *On the Predestination of the Saints*

Prin	Origen, *On First Principles*
Ps	Augustine, *Commentaries on the Psalms*
Quod	Thomas Aquinas, *Quodlibetal Questions*
Rev	Augustine, *Revisions (Retractationes)*
Rhet	Aristotle, *Rhetoric*
Rule	Augustine, *Rule of Augustine (Regula Augustini)*
SCG	Thomas Aquinas, *Summa contra gentiles*
Sent	Peter Lombard, *Sentences*
Sent(Is)	Isidore, *Sentences*
Serm	*Sermons*
SermMount	Augustine, *On the Lord's Sermon on the Mount*
SermSS	Bernard of Clairvaux, *Sermons on the Song of Songs*
Soul	Aristotle, *On the Soul (De anima)*
SL	Augustine, *On the Spirit and the Letter*
SR	Aristotle, *Sophistical Refutations*
SS	Alcher, *On the Spirit and the Soul*
ST	Thomas Aquinas, *Summa theologiae*
	1a First part
	1a2ae First part of the second part
	2a2ae Second part of the second part
TEpJn	Augustine, *Tractates on the [First] Epistle of John*
TGJn	Augustine, *Tractates on the Gospel of John*
Top	Aristotle, *Topics*
Trin	Augustine, *On the Trinity*
TrueRel	Augustine, *On True Religion*
TwoNat	Boethius, *On the Two Natures (Contra Eutychen)*
TwoSouls	Augustine, *On Two Souls (De duabus animabus)*
Virg	Cyprian, *On the Deportment of Virgins (De habitu virginum)*

Disputed Questions on the Virtues

On the Virtues in General

The first question is whether the virtues are dispositions.

The second is whether the definition of virtue given by Augustine is appropriate.

The third is whether a capacity of the soul can be a possessor of virtue.

The fourth is whether the aggressive or the sensual parts of the soul can be the possessors of virtue.

The fifth is whether the will is a possessor of virtue.

The sixth is whether virtue is found in the practical intelligence as its possessor.

The seventh is whether virtue is found in the theoretical intelligence.

The eighth is whether the virtues are in us by nature.

The ninth is whether we acquire the virtues by our actions.

The tenth is whether some virtues are infused into us.

The eleventh is whether infused virtue may be increased.

The twelfth is about the distinctions between the virtues.

The thirteenth is whether virtue is found in a mid-point.

Article 1: Whether the virtues are dispositions

Objections

It seems that they are not, but rather actions, because:

(1) Augustine says [*Rev* 1.9] that virtue is the good use of free judgement. But the use of free judgement is an action. Therefore virtue is an action.

3

(2) People are owed a reward only by reason of their actions. However, everyone who possesses virtue is owed a reward, because anyone who dies in a condition of charity will reach blessedness. Therefore virtue is something meritorious. But it is actions that are meritorious. Therefore virtue is an action.

(3) The more similar something in us is to God, the better it is. But we are most similar to God insofar as we are active, because God is pure activeness; therefore action is the best of the things that are in us. But virtues are the greatest goods in us, as Augustine says [FC 2.18, 19]. Therefore the virtues are actions.

(4) Whatever perfects us on our journey corresponds to whatever perfects us when we reach our homeland. But in our homeland we will be perfected by something active, that is to say, happiness, which, according to Aristotle [NE 1.7.15, 1098a16], consists in activity. Therefore whatever perfects us on our journey, that is to say virtue, is also an activity.

(5) Contraries are those things that are placed in the same class and are incompatible with one another. But a sinful act is incompatible with virtue precisely by being opposed to it. Therefore virtue comes under the class of action.

(6) Aristotle says [Heav 1.11, 281a15] that virtue is the upper limit of a capacity. But the upper limit of a capacity is an activity. Therefore virtue is an activity.

(7) The rational part of the soul is finer and more complete than the sensory part. But the sensory part functions without the mediation of any quality or disposition. Therefore one should not posit any dispositions in the intelligent part of the soul either, as intermediaries to complete the functioning of the intelligent part.

(8) Aristotle says [Phys 7.3, 246b2] that virtue is the tendency of something complete towards what is best. But what is best is an activity. Moreover, a tendency must belong to the same class as the thing towards which it makes something tend. Therefore virtue is activity.

(9) Augustine says [MorCath 15.25] that virtue is the ordering of love. Order, however, as he himself says elsewhere [CG 19.13], is the tendency of things equal or unequal that assigns each to its place. Therefore virtue is a tendency. Therefore it is not a disposition.

(10) A disposition is a quality that is difficult to change. However, virtue is easy to change, because it is lost by committing just one mortal sin. Therefore virtue is not a disposition.

(11) If we need certain dispositions, i.e. virtues, then we need them for doing things that are *either* (i) natural *or* (ii) meritorious and beyond what is natural. (i) But we do not need them for doing things that are natural; for any nature whatever, even one which lacks sensation, can fulfil its functions without any dispositions; this will be all the more true, then, of a nature that possesses reason. (ii) Again, we do not need virtues for doing things that are meritorious, because God achieves those in us, 'who works in us both wanting to do something and accomplishing it' etc. [Phil 2:13]. Therefore either way virtues are not dispositions.

(12) Everything which acts in accordance with its form always acts according to the demands of that form; e.g. something hot always acts by heating. Therefore if some form exists in the mind as a disposition, which we call 'virtue', then someone who possesses virtue will always have to function in accordance with virtue. This is false; for in that case anyone who had virtue would have it unshakeably. Therefore the virtues are not dispositions.

(13) Dispositions in our capacities are there to make them function more easily. But we do not need anything else to make us do virtuous actions more easily, or so it seems. For the latter depend principally upon our choice and our will. But nothing is easier to do than something that depends upon our will. Therefore virtues are not dispositions.

(14) An effect cannot be finer than its cause. But if virtue is a disposition, it will be the cause of an action, which is finer than a disposition. Therefore it does not seem appropriate for virtue to be a disposition.

(15) The mid-point and the extremes of something belong to the same class. But moral virtue is a mid-point among the emotions. The emotions, however, come under the class of active things. Therefore etc.

But on the other hand

(1) Virtue, according to Augustine [*FC* 2.19], is a good quality of mind. But this is not possible in any type of quality except the first, which consists of dispositions. Therefore virtue is a disposition.

(2) Aristotle says [*NE* 2.6.15, 1107a1] that virtue is a disposition that chooses, situated in a mid-point.

(3) The virtues exist in people who are asleep; for virtues are lost only through mortal sin. But virtuous actions are not performed by sleepers,

because they are not able to use free judgement. Therefore the virtues are not actions.

My reply

We must say that virtue, in accordance with the meaning of the word, refers to the fulfilment of a capacity. That is why it is also called a 'power', in that something is able to follow through its own impulse or movement because it possesses a potential that has been fulfilled. For virtue, in accordance with its name, refers to the perfecting of a capability; that is why Aristotle says [*Heav* 1.11, 281a15] that virtue is the upper limit of something with respect to its capacity. But because capacity is defined in relation to its actualisation, the fulfilment of a capacity will be found in its accomplishing fully what it does. The end of anything that does something is what it does, since everything, according to Aristotle [*Heav* 2.3, 286a8], is for the sake of what it does, as being its proximate end; for each thing is good insofar as it is fully ordered to its own end. That is why virtue makes its possessors good, and renders their works good, as Aristotle says [*NE* 2.6.2, 1106a17]; in this way it also becomes clear that it is the tendency of something complete to what is best, as he says elsewhere [*Phys* 7.3, 246b2].

All of this is true for the virtue of any kind of thing. For the virtue of a horse is what makes both it and its work good; similarly with the virtue of a stone, or of a human being or anything else.

However, because different things have different sorts of capacity, they are fulfilled in different ways. For (i) one sort of capacity only acts; (ii) a second is only acted upon or moved; (iii) a third both acts and is acted upon.

(i) The sort of capacity, then, that *only acts* does not need anything extra in order to be a principle of activity. That is why the virtue of this sort of capacity is nothing except the capacity itself. The capacity[1] of God is like this, as are the active intelligence[2] and the natural capacities. That is why the virtues of these capacities are not certain dispositions, but the capacities themselves, complete in themselves.

(ii) The capacities that are *only acted upon* are those that only act if they are moved by other things. It is not up to them whether they act

---

[1] In English we normally refer to God's *potentia* as 'power', because it is activated of itself and always.
[2] The active intelligence fits into (i) because it only acts: it actualises the capacity of the passive intelligence to acquire intellectual understanding. See further p. 46.

or not; they only act in accordance with an impulse from a 'virtue'[3] that moves them. Our powers of sense are like this considered in themselves. That is why Aristotle says [*NE* 6.2.2, 1139a19] that the senses are not principles of any actions. These capacities do indeed need something extra to complete them for their activities. However, this is not in them like some form that is immanent in its possessor, but rather only in the manner of a *passive experience*, like an image on the retina. That is why the 'virtues' of these sorts of capacities are not dispositions, but rather the *capacities* themselves, insofar as they are actively acted upon by their corresponding active powers.

(iii) The sort of capacity that *both acts and is acted upon* is moved by the powers that activate it in such a way that it is not determined by them to do one thing. It has the possibility of acting or not: for example, our powers that are in some way rational. These capacities are fulfilled for activity through the help of something extra; that, however, is in them in the manner not of passive experience, but of a *form* that rests and remains in its possessor; this happens, however, in such a way that the capacity is not forced necessarily by it to do one thing (for then the capacity would not be in control of its own actions). The virtues of this type of capacity are not the capacities themselves. Nor are they the passive experiences, as in our powers of sense. Neither are they qualities that act in a necessary way, such as the passive qualities of natural things. Rather, they are *dispositions*, such that someone is able to act with them when he wishes to, as Averroes says [*AverSoul* 3.18]. Augustine says [*GMarr* 21] that a disposition is the thing by which one acts, when it is time to do so.

In this way it is clear that the virtues are dispositions, and also how dispositions are distinguished from the second and third type of qualities. Moreover, it is obvious how they differ from the fourth: for a shape does not in itself imply being ordered to an action.[4]

From all this, it is clear that we need virtuous dispositions for three reasons:

(i') so that we might be *consistent* in what we do, for things that depend only on what we do change easily unless they are given stability by the weighting of some disposition;

---

[3] The argument here depends on taking the Latin *virtus* in the broad sense of 'power'.

[4] Aquinas follows Aristotle [*Cat* 8] in recognising four types of quality: (1) dispositions (which is what virtues are) and tendencies, (2) natural capacities and incapacities, (3) sensory qualities, and (4) shape.

(ii') so that we can *readily* do things in the proper way. For unless our rational capacity tends somehow towards one thing because of our disposition, then whenever it is necessary for us to do anything, we will have to begin by working out what to do. This is clear, for example, in the case of someone who wishes to think about something, but does not yet possess dispositional knowledge, or who wishes to act virtuously, but lacks a virtuous disposition. That is why Aristotle says [*NE* 3.8.15, 1117a22] that we act quickly whenever we act in keeping with our dispositions.

(iii') Thirdly, so that we might *take pleasure in* completing things in the proper way. This certainly happens because of our disposition; for since this works in the same way as a nature, it makes the doing of something our own, as if natural to us, so to speak, and therefore pleasurable. Indeed, we take pleasure in things because they are appropriate to us. That is why Aristotle [*NE* 2.3.1, 1104b5] makes it the mark of a disposition that doing something gives pleasure.

Replies to objections

(1) 'Virtue', like 'power', can be understood in two ways:

(i) first, in the sense of *matter*, as when we say that our capacity is the thing that we are capable of. It is in this sense that Augustine says that virtue is the good use of free judgement;

(ii) secondly, in the sense of *essence*. In this sense, neither virtue nor capacity is the same as action.

(2) 'To merit' can be understood in two ways:

(i) first, in a *strict* sense. In this sense, 'to merit' means nothing except to do some action for which one may receive a reward justly;

(ii) secondly, in a *loose* sense. In this sense any condition that in any way gives someone status is said to be meritorious. For example, we might say that Priam 'merited' to rule because of his appearance, because it was worthy of a ruler.

When, then, a reward is owed on merit, it is owed somehow because of a quality of disposition that renders someone suitable for the reward. That is the way in which it is owed to baptised babies. Again, it can be owed to actual merit; in this case, it is owed not to the virtue, but to virtuous actions. (However, it is also granted to babies in some sense on account of actual merit, insofar as the sacrament by which we are born again into life becomes effective through the merits of Christ.)

(3) Augustine says that the virtues are the greatest goods not absolutely, but of their class (just as fire, for instance, is said to be the lightest of physical things). Therefore it does not follow that there is nothing better in us than the virtues; but rather that numbered among the virtues are the greatest goods that exist in their class.

(4) Just as on our journey we can *both* be perfected in our disposition, i.e. have virtue, *and* be perfected in our activity, i.e. perform virtuous actions, so also in our homeland happiness is perfected activity that flows from a fulfilled disposition. That is why Aristotle says [*NE* 1.8.8, 1098b30; 1.8.14, 1099a25] that happiness is an activity in accordance with perfected virtue.

(5) A wicked action destroys a virtuous *action* directly, because they are contraries. However, it destroys a virtuous *disposition* only indirectly, by cutting it off from the source of infused virtue, that is, from God. That is why Isaiah says, 'Your sins have made a division between you and your God' [Is 59:2]. It is also why the acquired virtues are not destroyed by a single bad act.

(6) Aristotle's definition can be understood in two ways:

(i) with respect to the *matter* of virtue. Then, we would understand by virtue whatever virtue is capable of, i.e. the upper limit of whatever the capacity is capable of. For example, the virtue of someone who can lift a hundred pounds lies precisely in his being able to lift one hundred, not in his being able to lift sixty;

(ii) with respect to the *essence* of virtue. In this sense virtue is called the upper limit of a capacity because it signifies the fulfilment of that capacity. This is so whether or not the thing that enables the capacity to be fulfilled is the same as the capacity itself.

(7) We have already explained that the reasoning is different for senses and for our rational capacities.

(8) 'A tendency to x' refers to that by which something is changed so as to result in x. (i) Sometimes, indeed, change ends in a condition that is in the *same* class, as when a change in the sense of alteration concludes with a quality. That is why a tendency to this sort of end is always in the same class as the end. (ii) Sometimes, however, it has an end that belongs to a *different* class, as when generation[5] concludes with a substantial form. In this sense a tendency does not always come under the same class as

---

5 Reading *generationis* for *alterationis*.

the things towards which it is making something tend. For example, heat makes things tend towards the substantial form of fire.

(9) 'Tendency' can mean three things:

(i) the thing that makes matter tend to receive a form, as heat is what makes something tend towards the form of fire;

(ii) the thing that makes an agent tend to act, as speed is a tendency to run;

(iii) the actual ordering of things to each other.

It is in this third sense that Augustine uses the word. On the other hand, the sense of tendency that is contrasted with disposition is the first one;[6] virtue itself, though, is a tendency in the second sense.

(10) Nothing is so stable that it will not by itself disappear at once, if the cause that sustains it disappears. Therefore it is unsurprising if infused virtue disappears when the link with God disappears because of mortal sin. This fact does not conflict with its resistance to change, which can only be understood by assuming the persistence of its cause.

(11) We need a specific disposition for both types of activity: (i) for *natural* activities for the three reasons given above; (ii) for *meritorious* activities as something extra to lift our natural capacity to what is beyond nature, by means of a disposition infused in us. This need is not obviated by the fact that God works in us: for he acts in us in such a way that we too act. That is why we need a certain disposition, so that we are able to act adequately.

(12) Every form is received by its subject in a manner appropriate to the receiver. It is the distinctive feature of a rational capacity that it can go in opposite directions, and be in control of its actions. That is why a rational capacity is never forced to act in the same way because it has received a disposition as a form. Rather, it is able either to do something or not to do it.

(13) It is easy to do in some kind of way the things that depend on choice alone. However, it is not easy to do them as we ought, that is with speed, reliability and pleasure. It is for this that we need virtuous dispositions.

(14) Whenever a movement arises afresh in an animal or human being, it still comes from a mover that is moved, and it depends upon something active that already exists. In this way, the disposition does not evoke the action by itself, but only if it is aroused by some other agent.

---

[6] Here, as throughout, 'tendency' translates *dispositio*, while 'disposition' translates *habitus*.

(15) Virtue is a mid-point with respect to emotions, but not in the sense that it is itself some middling emotion. Rather it is something active that establishes a mid-point in the emotions.

Article 2: Whether the definition of virtue given by Augustine is appropriate, i.e. 'virtue is a good quality of mind by which we live rightly, which no one misuses, and which God works in us without our help'[7]

Objections

This does not seem to be appropriate, for the following reasons:

(1) Virtue is a sort of goodness. If then it is itself good, it is so either through its own, or through a different, goodness. If through a different goodness, we have an infinite regress; if through its own, then virtue must be the original goodness, because only the original goodness is good through itself.

(2) What is common to everything that exists should not be put into the definition of one thing. But 'being' is the class to which every being belongs. Therefore *good*, which is coextensive with this, ought not to be put in the definition of virtue.

(3) Goodness works in the same way in the moral domain as it does in the natural domain. Now in the natural domain, good and bad do not differentiate one type of thing from another. Therefore *good* should not be included in the definition of virtue, as if it were what distinguishes virtue from other types of quality of mind.

(4) The characterisation of a class does not include the distinguishing features of its types. But 'good', like 'being', is part of the characterisation of quality. Therefore *good* should not be added to the definition of virtue, in the words 'it is a good quality of mind', etc.

(5) Good and bad are opposites. But badness does not determine the type that something has, since it is in fact an absence.[8] Therefore neither does goodness; therefore *good* ought not to be put into the definition of virtue as if it were a constitutive distinguishing feature.

---

[7] This definition, attributed to Augustine at *Sent* 2.27.1.1, is actually pieced together from several passages: *Rev* 1.9.4 and 1.9.6, *FC* 2.19.50, *Ps* 118.26.1, *SL* 9.15.

[8] Only a positive feature of a thing can determine what type of thing it is. But badness, according to a common medieval view, is not a positive feature of a thing, but a mere absence of some feature needed to make the thing good.

(6) 'Good' is of wider extension than 'quality'. Therefore one quality does not differ from another by being good.[9] Therefore *good* should not be put into the definition of a virtue as if it were a distinguishing feature between qualities, i.e. of virtue.

(7) No one thing can come to be through two actualisations. But 'good' implies one actualisation and 'quality' another. Therefore it is a mistake to say that virtue is a *good quality*.

(8) Something that is qualified by an abstract predicate is not also qualified by a concrete one, e.g. redness is a colour, but it is not itself coloured.[10] But virtue is qualified by 'goodness' as an abstract predicate. Therefore it is not qualified by 'good' as a concrete one. Therefore it is a mistake to say that virtue is a *good* quality.

(9) A type does not have its distinguishing features predicated abstractly of it. That is why Avicenna says [*FirstPhil* 5.6] that a human being is not a rationality, but something rational. But a virtue is a goodness. Therefore goodness is not a distinguishing feature of virtue. Therefore it is a mistake to say, 'virtue is a *good* quality'.

(10) Badness of behaviour is the same thing as vice. Therefore goodness of behaviour is the same thing as virtue. Therefore *good* should not be put in the definition of virtue, because then one thing would be defining itself.

(11) The mind is a part of the intelligence. But virtue rather relates to feelings. Therefore it is a mistake to say that virtue is a good quality of *mind*.

(12) According to Augustine [*Trin* 12.1.3], 'mind' names the higher part of the soul. But some virtues are found in its lower capacities. Therefore it is a mistake to say that virtue is a good quality of *mind*.

(13) The possession of virtue should be attributed to a capacity rather than an essence. But 'mind' seems to identify an essential feature of the soul; for Augustine says [*Trin* 14.2.10] that intelligence, memory and will are in the mind. Therefore *mind* should not be put into the definition of virtue.

(14) Something that is distinctive of a type ought not to be put in the definition of a class.[11] But rightness belongs to justice. Therefore rightness

---

[9] See note 14.
[10] The Latin says 'white' rather than 'red'. However, in English 'white' is often contrasted with 'coloured'.
[11] See the Glossary for the technical sense of 'type' and 'class'.

should not be included in the definition of virtue, in the words, 'a good quality of mind, by which we live *rightly*'.

(15) For living things to live is to exist. But virtue does not come to completion in being but in doing. Therefore it is a mistake to say, 'by which we *live* rightly'.

(16) Someone who is proud of something misuses that thing. But sometimes people are proud of their virtues. Therefore sometimes people misuse virtues.

(17) Augustine says [*FC* 2.18] that it is only the greatest goods that no one misuses. But virtue is not one of the greatest goods; for the greatest goods are things that are sought on their own account. This does not fit the virtues, since they are sought on account of something else, i.e. happiness. Therefore it is a mistake to say 'which no one *misuses*'.

(18) The same agent is responsible for generating, nourishing, and increasing something. But virtue is nourished and increased by our actions, since reducing selfishness is increasing charity. Therefore virtue is generated by our actions. Therefore it is a mistake to say in the definition 'which God works in us without our help'.

(19) 'The removal of an obstacle' is held to be a source of change and a cause. But free judgement in a sense removes obstacles to virtue. Therefore it is a type of cause. Therefore it is a mistake to say that God works virtue *without our help*.

(20) Augustine says [*Serm* 169.11.13] that 'the one who created you without you will not justify you without you'. Therefore etc.

(21) This definition would be an appropriate one for grace, it seems. But virtue and grace are not one and the same. Therefore this is not a good definition of virtue.[12]

My reply

This definition includes in it the definition of virtue; moreover, if the last clause were omitted, it would also fit the whole of human virtue. For, as we said earlier, virtue perfects a capacity with reference to perfected action. But perfected action is the end of the capacity or of whatever acts. That is why virtue makes both the capacity and the person acting good, as was said above. For that reason something is included in the

---

[12] This article includes no *sed contra* ('but on the other hand').

definition of virtue that relates to the perfecting of the action, and something else that relates to the perfecting of the capacity or of whatever acts.

Two things are required to perfect an action. (i) The first is that the *action* itself is correct; (ii) the second is that the *disposition* cannot be the principle of a contrary action. For whatever is the principle of both good and bad actions alike cannot, of itself, be the perfect principle of a good action. This is because whatever perfects a capacity ought to be the principle of a good action in such a way that it could never be the principle of a bad one. That is why Aristotle says [*NE* 6.3.1, 1139b18] that opinion, which can be either true or false, is not a virtue; however, knowledge is, as this can only be based on truth. The first requirement is referred to in the words, 'by which we live rightly'; the second in the words, 'which no one misuses'.

Three points should be considered with reference to the claim that virtue makes its possessor good:

(i) the *possessor* itself: this is specified by the word 'mind'. For human virtue can only exist in something that belongs to a human being *qua* human;

(ii) the *perfecting* of this is specified by the word 'good', because good means in accordance with an ordering to an end;

(iii) the *way* in which it is possessed is specified by the word 'quality'; for virtue exists in someone in the manner not of an emotion but of a disposition, as was said above.

All these points, moreover, apply to moral as much as to intellectual, theological, or infused virtues. Augustine's additional phrase, 'which God works in us without our help,' applies only to infused virtues.

Replies to objections

(1) Accidents are not called beings in the sense that they have independent existence, but because something else is something *through* them. In this way, virtue is not said to be good because it is a good itself, but because other things are good through it. Hence there is no need for virtue to be good through a different goodness from its own, as if a different goodness gave it its form.

(2) This definition of virtue does not refer to the goodness that is coextensive with being, but rather to the goodness that is restricted to moral acts.

(3) What makes actions different is the form of the thing acting, for example, making something warm or cool. But with the will, good and bad are, so to speak, both its form and its object, because when it acts on or moves something else, it always prints its own form on that thing. That is why *moral* actions, which originate in the will, are of different types depending on whether they are good or evil. On the other hand, the origin of *natural* activities is not the end, but the form, of the thing that acts. That is why natural things are not different in type depending on whether they are good or bad; in moral matters, however, this is the case.

(4) *Moral* goodness is not already included in the understanding of quality. That is why the argument misses the point.

(5) What is bad does not determine something's type by reason of the absence of a positive quality, but by reason of the thing that underlies the lack of such a quality; this is because it does not allow the character of goodness to coexist with it. That is how it determines something's type.[13]

(6) The objection relies on natural rather than moral goodness; but the latter is meant in the definition of virtue.

(7) The goodness here does not imply any other goodness than virtue itself, as is clear from what has already been said. For virtue itself is in its essence a quality. That is why it is clear that 'good' and 'quality' do not refer to different actualisations, but only to one.

(8) This does happen in the case of the transcendentals,[14] which attach to every being. For an essence is a being; and a goodness is good; and a unity is one. However, a redness cannot said to be red in this sense. The reason is that whatever comes under our intelligence, must also be characterised as 'being', and therefore as both 'good' and 'one'. That is why an essence or a goodness cannot be understood without being understood as characterised as 'good' and 'one' and 'being'. It is because of this that a goodness can be said to be good and a unity one.[15]

---

[13] For example, if a cataract makes an eye blind, it does so not by giving the lens 'absence of sight', but by giving it an opaque texture that is incompatible with sight.

[14] Transcendentals are features that do not belong to just one of Aristotle's categories, but 'transcend' the categories. The list of transcendentals varies somewhat but generally includes at least the three mentioned here: 'being', 'good', and 'one'. Anything that falls under any of the categories will have being, goodness, and unity in some way.

[15] There are no replies to the remaining objections. Some editors add here, 'The solutions to the other objections are clear from what has been said.' Mandonnet's edition prints a continuation by Vincent de Castro Novo, OP, dated 1503.

Article 3: Whether a capacity of the soul can be a possessor of virtue

Objections

It seems not, because:

(1) According to Augustine [*FC* 2.19] virtue is something by which we live rightly. We live, however, not in accordance with a capacity of the soul, but in accordance with its essential nature. Therefore, virtue is not possessed by a capacity of the soul.

(2) Grace is higher on the scale of being than nature. But the being of nature exists through the essence of the soul, which is superior to its own capacities, in that it is their principle. Therefore the being of grace, which exists through the virtues, does not exist through the capacities of the soul. That is why virtue is not possessed by a capacity.

(3) An accident cannot be a possessor of attributes. But the capacities of the soul come under the class of accidents: in fact, both natural capacities and the lack of these belong to the second type of quality. Therefore virtue cannot be possessed by a capacity of the soul.

(4) If one capacity of the soul is the possessor of virtue, any one of them will be. This is because every capacity of the soul opposes the vices, and the virtues are directed against the vices. However, not every capacity of the soul can possess virtue, as will become clear later. Therefore virtue cannot be possessed by a capacity.

(5) The active principles in natural things, e.g. heat and cold, are not the possessors of other accidental qualities. But the capacities of the soul are a kind of active principle, since they are the principles of whatever the soul does. Therefore they cannot be the possessors of other accidental qualities.

(6) Capacities are possessed by the soul. Therefore, if a capacity is the possessor of another accidental quality, by parity of reasoning we will have one accident being the possessor of another one, and in this way we will have an infinite regress, which is inappropriate. Therefore virtue is not possessed by a capacity of the soul.

(7) Aristotle says [*PostAn* 1.22, 83a36] that there are no qualities of qualities. But a capacity of the soul is some quality of the second type of quality, while virtue is one of the first type of quality. Therefore virtue cannot be possessed by a capacity of the soul.

But on the other hand

(1) The principle of an action belongs to the doer of the action. But the actions of the virtues belong to the capacities of the soul. Therefore so do the virtues themselves.

(2) Aristotle says [*NE* 1.13.19, 1103a4] that the intellectual virtues are rational in their essential nature, whereas the moral virtues are rational by sharing in reason. But 'rational in their essential nature' and 'rational by sharing' describe certain capacities of the soul. Therefore the virtues are possessed by capacities of the soul.

My reply

A possessor of accidental qualities is related to them in three ways:

(i) as *sustaining* them: an accident cannot exist by itself, but is supported by its possessor;

(ii) as a *capacity* to its actualisation; for the possessor is qualified by the accidents in the way that a capacity is by its actualisation; in this way, an accident can be described as a form;

(iii) as a *cause* to its effect; for the principles of a possessor of accidents are through themselves principles of the accidents in question.

With reference to (i), one accident cannot be the possessor of another. For, since no accident has independent existence, it cannot sustain something else in existence; one might perhaps say, though, that insofar as it is sustained by its possessor, it can then sustain another accident.

With respect to (ii) and (iii), one accident is related to another as its possessor. For one accident has a capacity to be qualified by another, as 'transparent' is by 'light' or 'surface' by 'colour'. Again, one accident can be the cause of another, as wetness of flavour. In this way we can say that one accident can possess another. This is not because one accident can sustain another, but because its possessor receives the one accident through the mediation of the other.

In this way a capacity of the soul can be said to possess its accidents. Let me explain: {cf. (ii)} a disposition relates to a capacity of the soul as something that actualises it. The capacity is in itself not determined; its disposition determines it one way or the other. Furthermore, {cf. (iii)} acquired dispositions have as their cause the principles of the relevant capacities.

In this way, we conclude that the virtues are possessed by the capacities of the soul, because virtue exists in the soul, through the mediation of capacities.

Replies to objections

(1) In the definition of virtue, the reference to living refers to activity, as I have already said.

(2) Being spiritual comes through grace, not through the virtues. For grace is the origin of something's *being* filled with the spirit, while virtue is the principle of its *acting* in a spirit-filled way.

(3) A capacity is a possessor of attributes not in itself, but insofar as it is sustained by the soul.

(4) Now we are speaking about the human virtues. Therefore the capacities that cannot in any way be specifically human, in the sense that the command of reason cannot in any way reach them (e.g. those powers of life that are below the conscious level), cannot possess virtues. If any opposition arises as a result of these powers, it will be mediated through our sensory desire which can be affected by the command of reason (and can therefore be described as 'human', and a possessor of human virtue).

(5) The only capacities of the soul that are *active* are (i) the active intelligence and (ii) the pre-conscious powers of life; these do not possess any dispositions. Other capacities of the soul are *passive*. However, they can be principles of the soul's actions insofar as they are moved by what activates them.

(6) There should not be an infinite regress because one will reach an accident that is found in its capacity without reference to another accident.

(7) One quality is not said to be of another in the sense that one through itself possesses the other. That is not a part of our hypothesis, as I have explained above.

Article 4: Whether the aggressive or the sensual parts of the soul can be the possessors of virtue

Objections

It seems that they cannot, because:

(1) Contraries by their nature occur in the same sorts of things as each other. But mortal sin is contrary to virtue, and this cannot exist in the

sensory part of the soul (which consists of the aggressive and the sensual parts). Therefore virtue cannot be possessed by the aggressive and the sensual parts.

(2) Dispositions will be located in the same capacities as their related acts. But the principal act of virtue is choice, according to Aristotle [*NE* 6.2.2, 1139a23; 8.13.11, 1163a23]. This cannot be an act of the aggressive or sensual parts. Therefore nor can virtuous dispositions exist in the aggressive and sensual parts.

(3) Nothing perishable can possess something everlasting. That is how Augustine proves [*IS* 4.5] that the soul is everlasting, because it is the possessor of truth, which is everlasting. But the aggressive and sensual parts, just like the other sensory capacities, do not remain after the body has gone, or so some people think. However, the virtues do remain. For justice is everlasting and immortal, as Wisdom says [1:15]. The same reasoning holds for the other virtues. Therefore virtues cannot be possessed by the aggressive and sensual parts.

(4) The aggressive and sensual parts have their own bodily organs. Therefore if the virtues exist in the aggressive and sensual parts, they will be in those bodily organs. If so, they can be grasped by imagination;[16] hence, they are not graspable only by the mind. However, Augustine[17] says about justice that it is a correctness graspable only by the mind.

(5) *Rejoinder*: virtue can be possessed by the aggressive and sensual parts insofar as they share in some way in reason. *But on the other hand* the aggressive and sensual parts are said to share in reason insofar as they are ordered by reason. However, the ordering of reason cannot be what sustains virtue, since it does not itself exist independently. Therefore virtue cannot be possessed by the aggressive and sensual parts of the soul even insofar as they share in reason.

(6) Just as our aggressive and sensual parts, which are parts of the sensory desire, obey reason, so do our capacities for sense-perception. But virtue cannot be found in any of our capacities for sense-perception. Therefore it cannot be found in the aggressive and sensual parts.

(7) If the aggressive and sensual parts are able to share in the ordering by reason, then it will be possible to reduce the rebelliousness in regard to

---

[16] *phantasia*, the capacity that stores forms taken in by the senses and can combine them. Since I have seen both the colour gold and a mountain, I have images of both stored in my *phantasia*, which can combine the two images to make an image of a golden mountain.

[17] Actually Anselm, in *On Truth* 12.

reason of our sensual nature, which includes these two powers. Now that rebellion is not infinite, since our sensual nature is only a finite power, and a finite power cannot produce an infinite activity. Therefore it will be possible to quell this rebellion completely; for everything that is finite disappears if you take away bits of it sufficient times, as Aristotle makes clear [*Phys* 1.4, 187b26]. In this way, it would be possible to heal our sensual nature completely in this life. But that is impossible.

(8) *Rejoinder*: God, who infuses virtue in us, could totally quell the rebellion in question. It is from our side, however, that it cannot be completely quelled. *But on the other hand* human beings are human precisely insofar as they are rational; that is how they acquire their type. The more, then, that that which is in a human being is subject to reason, the more fully does it belong to human nature. The lower parts of the soul would then be supremely subject to reason if the rebellion in question were completely quelled. Therefore this would be supremely fitting for human nature. In this way there is no obstacle from our side to quelling the rebellion in question completely.

(9) Mere avoidance of sin is not sufficient to characterise virtue. For the fullness of justice consists in the condition to which Psalm 34:14 summons us with the words, 'Turn away from evil and do good.' It is the role of the aggressive part, however, to hate what is bad, as it says in the book *On the Spirit and the Soul* [*SS* 45]. Therefore, in the aggressive part at least virtue cannot exist.

(10) It says in the same book [*SS* 11, 45] that to seek the virtues lies in reason, but to hate the vices in the aggressive part. But the seeking of virtue and virtue itself are in the same part, since everything seeks what perfects it. Therefore all virtue is in reason and not in the aggressive and sensual parts.

(11) No capacity can have a disposition that is only acted upon and does not act: a disposition is something that enables you to act when you wish to, as Averroes says [*AverSoul* 3.18]. But the aggressive and sensual parts do not act; they are acted upon. Therefore, as Aristotle says [*NE* 6.2.2, 1139a19], the senses are not in control of any actions. Therefore a virtuous disposition cannot exist in the aggressive and sensual parts.

(12) Whatever is a distinctive feature belongs to a distinctive subject. Now virtue belongs to the reason, and not to the aggressive and sensual parts, which are shared with us by non-human animals; virtue, therefore,

only exists in human beings (as does reason). Therefore all virtues are found in the reason, and not in the aggressive and sensual parts.

(13) Romans says, according to the gloss [Rom 7], that the law is good, and, when it prohibits sensual desire, it prohibits all evil. Therefore all vices belong to the sensual part, where sensual desire is found. But virtues and vices are located in the same kinds of thing. Therefore the virtues are not in the aggressive part, but at most[18] in the sensual part.

But on the other hand

(1) Aristotle says [*NE* 3.10.1, 1117b24] that temperateness and courage belong to the non-rational parts of the soul. The non-rational parts, i.e. the sensory desire, consist of the aggressive and the sensual parts, as Aristotle also explains [*Soul* 3.9, 432b7]. Therefore the virtues can exist in the aggressive and sensual parts.

(2) Venial sin makes someone tend to mortal sin. But a tendency and its fulfilment are found in the same thing. Therefore since venial sin is found in the aggressive and sensual parts (for the first movement of sin is an act of the sensual faculty, as the gloss says [Rom 7]), it follows that there can be mortal sin there too. Therefore there can also be virtue, which is contrary to mortal sin.

(3) A mid-point and its extremes are found in the same thing. But virtue is a kind of mid-point between contrary emotions, just as courage is between fear and boldness, and temperateness between excessive and insufficient sensual desires. Therefore since this sort of emotion is found in the aggressive and sensual parts, it seems that virtue must be found there too.

My reply

On this question, in some respects there is general agreement, in others opinions conflict with each other.

Everyone agrees that there are some virtues in the aggressive and sensual parts, e.g. temperateness in the sensual and courage in the aggressive.

People differ over the following: some distinguish two sets of aggressive and sensual parts, (i) one in the higher and (ii) the other in the lower part

---

[18] The text reads *ad minus*, but 'at least' gives the wrong sense.

of the soul. (i) Thus they say that the aggressive and sensual parts that are in the *higher* part of the soul, since they belong to rational nature, can possess virtue. (ii) Those in the *lower* part, however, cannot; they belong to our sensitive and non-rational nature. This has been discussed in another question [*DQTruth* 25.3; *ST* 1a 82.5], i.e. whether two powers can be distinguished in the upper part of the soul, of which one is aggressive and the other sensual, speaking strictly. However, whatever is said about this, we ought still to put some virtues in the aggressive and sensual parts of the lower desire, as Aristotle says [*NE* 3.10.1, 1117b24], and as other people also agree.

The following makes this clear: virtue (as I said above) refers to the fulfilment of a capacity; a capacity is directed towards its actualisation. Therefore we ought to locate human virtue in the capacity that is the principle of human activity. An act is called human not just because it is done in any old way by or through a human being – for some things are shared with non-human animals, and even plants – but because it belongs *distinctively* to a human being. What is distinctive about human beings, compared to these other things, is that human beings are in control of their own actions. Actions are distinctively human, then, when human beings are in control of them, and not so when human beings are not in control of them, even when they happen in them (e.g. digesting or growing). Human virtue, then, can be located in whatever is the principle of an action of which a human being is in control.

We need to know that the principle of such an action can mean three things:

(i) the thing that first moves and commands it, in virtue of which human beings are in control of their actions. This is reason or will;

(ii) something that moves something else but is also moved, e.g. the sensory desire, which is moved by a higher desire insofar as it obeys reason, and which then in its turn moves the limbs of the body at its command;

(iii) something that is only moved, i.e. the limbs of the body.
Both of the latter two, i.e. the limbs of the body and the lower desires, are moved by the higher part of the soul; however, this happens in different ways. For the limbs of the body – unless something obstructs them – obey the higher power that commands them immediately and without any conflict, according to the order of nature, as is clear with a hand or foot. The lower desire, though, has an inclination of its own from its own nature, which means that it does not obey immediately the higher power

that commands it, but it sometimes resists it. That is why Aristotle says [*Pol* 1.3, 1253b19] that the soul controls the body as a master his slave, with a despotic rule (the slave, indeed, has no ability to resist any of his master's commands). Reason, however, controls the lower parts of the soul with a royal or political rule, i.e. as kings or princes of cities control free men, who have the right and the ability to resist with respect to some of the orders a king or prince may give. Therefore with the limbs of the body nothing is needed to complete a human action except their own natural tendency; this allows them to be moved, as is natural to them, by reason. In the lower desire, which can resist reason, it is necessary to have something extra that enables it to carry out without any conflict whatever reason commands it to do.

For if the immediate principle of what is done is incomplete, the action itself will be incomplete, no matter how complete the higher principle is. That is why unless the tendency of the lower appetite to carry out the commands of reason were complete, any action that had the lower desire as its proximate principle would not be completely good: the sensory desire would offer some resistance. As a result, the lower desire would suffer a kind of unease because it was being forced, so to speak, by the higher one. This happens to someone who has strong sensual desires, but does not follow them because reason forbids this.

When therefore someone has to deal with the objects of the sensory desire, he needs, in order to do this well, a kind of tendency or completeness in the sensory desire that will enable it to obey reason easily. That is what we call virtue.

Take, then, any virtue concerned with something that belongs distinctively to the aggressive power (as courage is concerned with fear and confidence, or greatness of spirit with difficult aspirations, or gentleness with anger). Such a virtue will be said to be possessed by the aggressive part. Now take any virtue concerned with something that belongs distinctively to the sensual part. Such a virtue will be said to be possessed by the sensual part (e.g. chastity, which relates to the pleasures of sex, or abstinence and soberness, which relate to the pleasures of food and drink).

Replies to objections

(1) Virtue and mortal sin can be thought of in two ways: (i) according to the action in question; and (ii) according to the disposition in question.

(i) If an *action* of the sensual or aggressive parts is examined in itself, it will not involve mortal sin. However, it can cooperate with an act that is mortally sinful when, under the influence of or with the consent of reason, it is directed against divine law. In a similar way the actions of these parts when considered in themselves cannot be virtuous acts; they can only be so when the parts cooperate to carry out the commands of reason. That is the way in which acts that are either mortally sinful or virtuous can belong to the aggressive and sensual parts.

(ii) That is why a virtuous or sinful *disposition* can also be found in the aggressive and sensual parts.

It is relevant here, though, that just as a virtuous act consists in the fact that the aggressive or sensual parts follow reason, so a sinful act consists in the fact that reason is drawn to follow the inclination of the aggressive and sensual parts. That is why sin is more often assigned to reason, as its proximate cause; and so, for the same reason, is virtue assigned to the aggressive and sensual parts.

(2) As I have already said, a virtuous act cannot belong to the aggressive or sensual parts independently, without reason. Indeed, the prior element in a virtuous act is something rational, that is, choice; for whenever A does something to B, the activity of A is prior to the passive experience of B. Reason, then, commands the aggressive and the sensual parts. Therefore when virtue is said to exist in these parts, this does not mean that they bring about either the whole of the virtuous act or the element prior to it; rather, the virtuous disposition makes the virtuous action as completely good as possible. It does so insofar as the aggressive and sensual parts follow the direction of reason without any struggle.

(3) Let us assume that the aggressive and sensual parts do not remain active in the separated soul. They do, however, remain in it as their root: for the essence of the soul is the root of its capacities. In the same way, the virtues that are assigned to the aggressive and sensual parts remain in reason as their root. For reason is the root of all the virtues, as will be shown later.

(4) There is a sort of scale of forms. Some forms and virtues are entirely reduced to the material, when all their activity and their accidental qualities are material. This is clear in the forms of the elements. The intelligence, though, is entirely free from matter; that is why its activity is not involved with physical things. The aggressive and sensual parts, however, have an intermediate position. The bodily changes that accompany their

actions show that they use bodily organs. But the fact that they are moved by commands and obey reason shows that that they are also in some sense raised above what is material. Virtue is found in them, then, just to the extent that they are raised above the material and obey reason.

(5) It is true that the ordering of reason in which the aggressive and sensual parts share does not exist independently, and cannot in itself possess accidents. However, it can be the reason why something else possesses accidents.

(6) The cognitive powers of the senses naturally precede reason, since reason receives data from them; the powers of desire, however, naturally follow the order of reason, as a lower desire naturally obeys a higher. Therefore the cases are not the same.

(7) The rebellion of the aggressive and sensual parts against reason cannot be quelled entirely by means of virtue; for since through their own nature those parts aim at what is good according to the senses, they sometimes conflict with reason. It could possibly happen, though, by means of divine power, which can even change something's nature. In any case, the rebellion is reduced through virtue, insofar as the powers in question become accustomed to obeying reason. Then they have what they need for virtue, from something outside, i.e. from the rule of reason over them. In themselves, however, they retain something of their own movements, which are sometimes contrary to reason.

(8) Although the principle in human beings is what is rational, the whole of human nature needs not only reason, but also the lower powers of the soul and indeed the body. That is why when human nature is in the state of being left to itself, the result is that something in the lower powers of the soul rebels against reason, as long as the lower powers of the soul move in their own way. It is different in the state of innocence, or of glory, when reason, by being joined to God, acquires the power to keep the lower powers entirely under itself.

(9) To detest what is bad, insofar as this is said to be the role of the aggressive part, implies not only a withdrawal from what is bad, but also a movement of the aggressive part to destroy what is bad: take, for example, someone angry who not only runs away from something bad, but also is stimulated to root out the evil by avenging it. This, though, is to do something good. Although it is the role of the aggressive part to hate what is bad, this is not the only activity in which it engages. For its role also includes lifting one to achieve a difficult good; this

requires not only the emotions of anger and of boldness, but also that of hope.

(10) These words should be taken in an extended sense, not strictly. Every capacity of the soul indeed seeks its own good; and so the aggressive part seeks victory just as the sensual part seeks pleasure. However, the sensual part is drawn towards things that are good for the whole animal simply or absolutely; that is why all seeking of the good is attributed to it.

(11) It is true that the aggressive and the sensual parts, considered in themselves, are acted upon but do not act. However, in human beings to the extent that these parts share in some way in reason, they also in some sense act; they are not entirely acted upon. That is another reason why Aristotle says [*Pol* 1.3, 1253b19; 1.5, 1254b4] that the rule of reason over these powers is 'political'; for such powers have some movement of their own, and so they do not obey reason entirely. The rule of the soul over the body, however, is not regal, but despotic, because the limbs of the body obey the soul immediately when they move.

(12) Although non-human animals do possess these powers, in them those powers do not share in reason at all. That is why non-human animals cannot have the moral virtues.

(13) (i) All bad things are related to sensual desire as being their primary root, not their proximate principle. For all emotions arise from the aggressive or the sensual parts, as we showed when we discussed the emotions in the soul [*ST* 1a2ae 22–3, esp. 22.2–3]. Indeed, the corruption of the reason and the will usually happens as a result of emotions.

(ii) Alternatively, one can say that by 'sensual desire' the gloss means not only what is distinctive to the power of sensual desire, but also what is shared by all the powers of desire. Sensual desire for something can be found in each part of this, and sin is connected with sensual desire: for no one can sin except by some sort of desire for something.

Article 5: Whether the will is a possessor of virtue

Objections

It seems so, because:

(1) Something that commands needs to be more complete in order to command in the right way than does something that carries out the command in order to carry it out in the right way. This is because the

latter depends upon the former. But in a virtuous action, the will is in the position of giving commands, while the aggressive and sensual parts are in the position of obeying them and carrying them out. Since, then, virtue is in the aggressive and sensual parts, in the sense that they possess it, it seems that *a fortiori* it should be in the will.

(2) *Rejoinder*: the natural inclination of the will towards good that is its end is enough for it to do things in the right way, since we naturally seek an end. That is why we do not need any extra virtuous disposition to make us do so in the right way. *But on the other hand* the will responds not only to the ultimate end, but also to other ends. The will may be in the right condition or not with respect to the desire for other ends; after all, good men set themselves good goals, but bad men bad goals, as Aristotle says [*NE* 3.5.17, 1114b1]: 'How the end appears to people reflects the sort of people they are.' Therefore for the will to be in the right condition, it needs to have a virtuous disposition to complete it.

(3) The soul's cognitive capacity possesses a certain natural knowledge, that is, of first principles. However, we do possess a kind of intellectual virtue with respect to this knowledge, that is our intelligence, which is the disposition relevant to principles. There ought, then, to be a virtue in our will too that relates to whatever it naturally inclines towards.

(4) Just as there are moral sorts of virtue relevant to emotions, such as temperateness and courage, so there are virtues relevant to activities, such as justice. Activity that is independent of emotions is the province of the will, just as activity that depends upon emotions is the province of the aggressive or sensual parts. Therefore just as there are moral virtues in the aggressive and sensual parts, so there must be also in the will.

(5) Aristotle says [*NE* 8.5.5, 1157b30] that love or affection stems from emotions. However, friendship stems from choice. Choice,[19] which is independent of emotion is, however, an activity of the will. Therefore since friendship is either actually a virtue or inseparable from virtue, as Aristotle says [*NE* 8.5.4, 1157b28], it seems that virtue is found, in the sense of possessed by, the will.

(6) Charity is the strongest of the virtues, as St Paul says [1 Cor 13:13]. However, it can only be the will that possesses charity: it cannot be

---

[19] Reading *electio* for *dilectio*; this seems to be the only way of making sense of the argument. Cf. also *ST* 1a2ae 26.1, 3; 2a2ae 24.1.

possessed by the lower, sensual, part of the soul, for this covers only goods perceived by the senses. Therefore virtue is possessed by the will.

(7) According to Augustine we are joined to God through the will in a more immediate way. But it is virtue that joins us to God. Therefore it seems that virtue is found in, in the sense of possessed by, the will.

(8) Happiness, according to Hugh of St Victor, lies in the will. However, the virtues are a kind of tendency to happiness. Since therefore a tendency to something and its fulfilment must both be found in the same place, it seems that the will has, i.e. possesses, virtue.

(9) According to Augustine [*Rev* 1.9.4], it is the will that enables us either to sin or to live rightly. Living in the right way, however, is the job of virtue, which is why Augustine says elsewhere [*FC* 2.19] that virtue is a good quality of mind by which we live rightly. Therefore virtue lies in the will.

(10) Contrary qualities occur by their nature in the same sorts of thing. Sin, however, is contrary to virtue. Therefore since all sin is found in the will, as Augustine says [*TwoSouls* 9.12], it seems that virtue should be found there too.

(11) Human virtue ought to lie in that part of the soul that is distinctive of human beings. But the will, like reason, is distinctive of human beings; indeed, it is closer to reason than are the aggressive and sensual parts. Therefore since virtue is possessed by the aggressive and sensual parts, *a fortiori* it seems to be possessed by the will.

But on the other hand

(1) It is clear from Aristotle [*NE* 1.13.19, 1103a4] that all virtue is either (i) intellectual or (ii) moral. (i) *Moral* virtue, however, is possessed by something that is rational not in its essence but by sharing in something else's reason. (ii) *Intellectual* virtue, by contrast, is possessed by something that is rational in its essence. Therefore, since the will cannot be counted as either of these, as neither is it a cognitive capacity (which would be rational in its essence) nor does it belong to the irrational part of the soul (which would be rational by sharing in reason), it seems that the will cannot in any way possess virtue.

(2) Several different virtues ought not to be directed to the same action. However, that would follow if the will possessed virtue. This is because (as I have shown) there are virtues in the aggressive and sensual parts.

Since the will is in some way related to actions characterised by those virtues, there would need to be virtues in the will that related to those actions. Therefore we should not say that the will possesses virtue.

My reply

When a capacity possesses a virtuous disposition, it is that disposition that enables it to act in a complete way. That is why it does not need a virtuous disposition insofar as it achieves something just by being the capacity that it is. Virtue directs our various capacities towards the good: it both makes its possessor a good person and renders his work good. But the will, just by being the capacity that it is, already has what virtue accomplishes for the other capacities. This is because it aims at the good; therefore inclining to the good is related to the will in the way that inclining to pleasure is related to the sensual part, or attending to sound is related to the hearing. That is why the will does not need any virtuous disposition to make it incline towards the good; not, at any rate, towards the good that is on its own level, because it aims at this just by being the capacity that it is.

However, it does need a virtuous disposition to aim at a good that surpasses the level of its own capacity. Now a thing's desire aims at its own distinctive good. We can, then, say that a good can exceed the level of the will in two ways: (i) in terms of the *species*; (ii) in terms of the *individual*.

(i) The first happens when the will is raised to aim at a good that exceeds the boundaries of human good, where by 'human' I mean something that human nature can achieve by its own powers. The good that is higher than human is divine good, and it is charity that raises the human will towards this, and similarly hope.

(ii) The second happens when someone seeks a good that belongs to someone else, but without the will's being drawn beyond the boundaries of human good. In this case, justice is needed to complete the will, along with all the virtues that are directed at other people, for example liberality. For justice is another's good, as Aristotle says [*NE* 5.1.17, 1130a4].

There are therefore two virtues that the will possesses, namely charity and justice. Evidence for this is that although those virtues belong to a faculty of desire, unlike temperateness and courage they do not deal with the emotions. That is why it is clear that they are found not in the sensory desire, where the emotions are found, but rather in the rational desire, that is the will, where there are no emotions. (For all the emotions are located in the sensory part of the soul, as Aristotle proves [*Phys* 7.3, 248a6].)

By the same reasoning, the virtues that relate to the emotions, for example courage to fear and boldness or temperateness to sensual desires, ought to be located in the sensory desire. The will does not in fact need a virtue to deal with those emotions; this is because what is good in the area of those emotions is simply what accords with reason. The will naturally aims at that good just by virtue of its own capacities, for that is the good that belongs distinctively to the will.

Replies to objections

(1) The judgement of reason is enough for the will to command, since the will naturally desires whatever is good according to reason, just as the sensual part desires whatever is pleasurable according to the senses.

(2) The will naturally inclines not only towards the ultimate end, but also to any good that reason presents to it. For the will aims at whatever is understood to be good, and it is naturally directed towards this. It does this in the same way that every capacity is directed towards its own object, so long as that is its own distinctive good (as we said above). However, someone can go wrong in respect of this when emotions get in the way of the judgement made by reason.

(3) Knowledge takes place through concepts. The capacity of the intelligence is only sufficient by itself for knowledge if it can receive the concept from the objects of the senses. That is why, even in the case of things that we know naturally, we need a disposition that also takes its principle in a way from the senses, as Aristotle says [*PostAn* 2.19, 100a10]. However, the will does not need any such concept for willing; therefore the cases are different.

(4) The virtues that relate to emotions are in the lower desire. For the reasons already given, no other virtue is needed, for matters of this sort, in the higher desire.

(5) Friendship is not a virtue strictly speaking, but a result of virtue: it follows from the fact that someone is virtuous that he loves others who are like him. The case is different with charity, which is a kind of friendship with God, and which raises human beings to a level above their natural measure. That is why charity is in the will, as we have said.

(6) and (7) The same point makes it clear how to reply to the sixth and seventh objections; for the virtue that joins the will to God is charity.

(8) (i) When it comes to happiness, some things, like tendencies, are *prerequisites*, such as the activity of the moral virtues. This allows us to remove obstacles to happiness, specifically those emotions or external disturbances that unsettle the mind.

(ii) There is second sort of virtuous activity that, at its fullest, is in its essence happiness *itself*; this is the activity of reason or intelligence. For the happiness of contemplation consists precisely in the fullest contemplation of the highest truth; while the happiness of action consists in the activity of that practical wisdom that human beings exercise in organising themselves and other people.

(iii) A third element is found in happiness as something that *completes* it. This is pleasure, which makes happiness complete, as beauty does youth, to quote Aristotle [*NE* 10.4.8, 1174b32]. This does indeed belong to the will. Charity completes the will by directing it towards this, if we are talking about the happiness of heaven, which is promised to the saints.

However, if we are discussing the happiness of contemplation with which the philosophers have dealt, then the will is directed to enjoyment of this sort by its own natural longing.

From all this, it is clear that not all the virtues are to be found in the will.

(9) We live rightly, or else sin, through our will, in that it *commands* all virtuous or wicked actions. However, it does not *draw them out*. That is why the immediate possessor of a virtue need not be the will.

(10) All sin lies in the will as its *cause*, in that all sin comes about with the will's consent. All sin, however, need not lie in the will as its *possessor*: for example, gluttony and lust are in the sensual part, while anger and pride are in the aggressive part.

(11) Since the will is so near to reason, it happens that the will agrees with reason, just by being the capacity that it is. Therefore it does not need to acquire a virtuous disposition in addition, unlike the lower capacities, i.e. the aggressive and sensual parts.

In response to the points under 'But on the other hand'

(1) Charity and hope, which exist in the will, are not included under Aristotle's categorisation, because they are in another class of virtues, called the *theological* virtues. Justice, however, is included in the *moral*

virtues. For the will, like the other desires, shares in reason insofar as it is directed by reason. For although the will, like reason, belongs to the intelligent part of the soul, it does not belong to the capacity of reason itself.

(2) There is no need to have virtue in the will for the reasons for which it is found in the aggressive and sensual parts, for the reasons now given.

Article 6: Whether virtue is found in practical intelligence as its possessor

Objections

It seems that it is not, because:

(1) Aristotle says [*NE* 2.2.1, 1103b27] that knowledge gives little or no support to virtue. He is speaking there about practical knowledge. That is evident from the fact that he goes on to say that many people do not put into practice such knowledge as they possess; for the knowledge that is ordered towards action belongs to the practical intelligence. Therefore practical intelligence cannot possess virtue.

(2) Without virtue, no one can act as he should. But someone can act as he should without having a perfected practical intelligence, because he can be instructed by someone else about what to do. Therefore practical intelligence is not perfected by a virtue.

(3) The more one abandons virtue, the more one sins. But abandoning perfected practical intelligence reduces sin, since ignorance excuses sin either partly or wholly. Therefore practical intelligence is not perfected by a virtue.

(4) According to Cicero [*Inv* 2.53] virtue acts in the same way as nature. But the way that nature acts is opposed to the way that reason, or practical intelligence, acts. This is clear from Aristotle [*Phys* 2.1, 193a32], where he makes a division between agents that act by nature and those that act according to purpose. Therefore virtue does not seem to exist in the practical intelligence.

(5) Good and true are formally different insofar as each has its own distinctive character. However, dispositions differ from one another when there is a difference of form in their objects. Therefore since virtue has as its object what is good, while it is truth that perfects the practical intelligence, albeit truth directed towards action, it seems that practical intelligence is not perfected by a virtue.

(6) According to Aristotle [*NE* 2.6.15, 1107a1] a virtue is a voluntary disposition. However, the dispositions of practical intelligence differ from those that belong to the will or to the desiring part of the soul. Therefore the dispositions which are in the practical intelligence are not virtues. That is why the practical intelligence cannot possess virtue.

But on the other hand

(1) Practical wisdom is given as one of the four principal virtues, yet it is possessed by practical intelligence. Therefore practical intelligence can possess virtue.

(2) Human virtue is possessed by human capacities. But practical intelligence is a human capacity to a greater extent than the aggressive and sensual parts: for something that is x in its essence is more x than something that is x only by participation. Therefore practical intelligence can possess human virtue.

(3) When A is x because of B, B is also more x than A. But the virtues in the feeling parts of the soul are there because of reason; for virtue is placed in the power of feeling precisely so that the latter will obey reason. Therefore virtue ought to be found more strongly in the practical intelligence.

My reply

We must say that:

(i) the difference between *natural* and *rational* virtues is that natural virtues aim at *one* thing, but rational virtues are related to *many* things;

(ii) both *rational* and *animal* desires ought to incline towards whatever each finds desirable, through a pre-existing recognition of it, while it is the mark of *natural* desires to incline towards their goal *without* any pre-existing understanding, in the way that a heavy object inclines towards the centre of the earth.

Since, then, both rational and animal desires should aim at something that they recognise as good, in cases where that good is also unchanging, the inclination of the desire can also be natural, as can the judgement made by thinking; this is what happens in animals without speech. For they engage in a limited number of activities, because of the weakness of their active principle, which can only cope with a small number of things.

As a result, all the members of a single species have the same good. That is why their desire gives them a natural inclination towards it, and their powers of thought a natural judgement concerning their own particular good, which is the same for all. And because of this natural judgement and natural desire, every swallow alike makes a nest and every spider alike makes a web. One can ponder the same phenomenon in all animals that lack speech.

Human beings, however, engage in many diverse activities. This is because of the excellence of their active principle, i.e. their soul, which has the power to embrace, to some degree, an infinite number of things. That is why neither a natural desire for the good nor natural judgement would on its own be enough for a human being to act rightly. These need to be given a more precise determination, and brought to completion.

Human beings do indeed incline towards seeking their own distinctive good through their natural desires. However, this good comes in many varieties, and what is good for human beings comprises many different things. Therefore there could not be a natural desire in human beings for a determinate good that suited all the conditions needed for something to be good for them. For this good comes in so many varieties, depending on the different situations of individuals and time and place and so on.

The same reasoning applies to natural judgement, which is uniform, and is therefore not adequate for seeking the sort of good under consideration.

All this explains why human beings need *reason*, which is capable of comparing different things, to discover and discern their own distinctive good, determined in the light of all relevant circumstances, as it should be sought at this time and in this place. Reason is capable of doing this even without acquiring a disposition to complete it in this respect; similarly in theoretical matters reason can, without having acquired knowledge as a disposition, make a judgement about a conclusion from some branch of knowledge.

This, however, can be done only incompletely and with difficulty. Consequently, just as *theoretical* reason ought to be made complete by acquiring the disposition of knowledge, for the purpose of making correct judgements about the knowable elements of a branch of knowledge, similarly, *practical* reason ought to be made complete by a certain disposition that enables it to make correct judgements about the human good in particular contexts of action.

This virtue is known as *practical wisdom*, and it is possessed by the practical reason. It brings to completion all the moral virtues, which are found in the desiring part. Each of these virtues makes the relevant desire incline towards a specific class of human good. For example, justice makes it incline towards the good that is equality in things that are part of our shared life, while temperateness makes it incline towards the good of restraining oneself from the objects of sensual desire, and so on with each virtue.

Each of these things can be done in many ways, and are not done in the same way in all circumstances. That is why one needs practical wisdom in one's judgement to determine the correct way. That is how correctness and full goodness in all the other virtues depend upon practical wisdom. Hence Aristotle says [*NE* 2.6.15, 1107a1] that the mid-point in moral virtue is determined by reference to right reason. Now since all the dispositions of the desire acquire the character of virtue from this correctness and full goodness, it follows that practical wisdom is the cause of all the virtues of the desiring part, which are called 'moral' insofar as they are practically wise. Therefore Gregory says [*MorJob* 22.1.2] that the other virtues do not deserve the name of virtue unless they lead to wise action regarding the particular goods that each one seeks.

Replies to objections

(1) Aristotle is speaking there about practical *knowledge*. But practical wisdom means more than practical knowledge. Practical knowledge comprises general judgement of what should be done, for example that fornication is bad, that theft should be avoided, and so on. Even if this exists, it can happen that the judgement of reason about a particular act is blocked, so that one does not judge rightly. Therefore practical knowledge is said to give little support to virtue because even where it exists, someone might sin against virtue.

It is the job of practical *wisdom*, on the other hand, to judge correctly about particular things that are to be done, at the moment when they need to be done. This judgement is spoiled by any sort of sin. Therefore while practical wisdom is present, a person does not sin; that is why it contributes not a little, but greatly, to virtue. Indeed, it actually causes virtue, as I have said.

(2) One person can receive from another advice in general about what to do. However, only the correctness provided by practical wisdom can

enable one to stick to one's judgements in the right way, for a particular action, in the face of all the emotions. That is why this cannot happen without virtue.

(3) (i) The ignorance that is contrasted with practical *wisdom* is ignorance in choice: every bad person is ignorant in this respect. This stems from the fact that the judgement of reason is blocked by the inclination of one's desire. This does not excuse a sin; rather it constitutes one. (ii) The ignorance that is contrasted with practical *knowledge*, however, excuses or reduces the degree of sin.

(4) Cicero's words should be taken to refer to the inclination of a desire that is drawn towards some general good, for example, acting bravely, and so on. But if this is not controlled by the judgement of reason, an inclination of this sort would often lead us to our downfall, and the more forceful the inclination, the truer that would be. That is why Aristotle gave us [*NE* 6.13.1, 1144b11] the example of a blind man who, the faster he runs, the more he hurts himself when he bangs into a wall.

(5) Two parts of the soul have as their object what is good and true, i.e. the desiring and the intelligent parts. These two are so disposed that each of them is active in respect of the other's action: the will wants the intelligence to understand something and the intelligence understands that the will wants something.

In this way these two, what is good and what is true, are included in each other. (i) The good is something true, insofar as it is grasped by the intelligence: that is, insofar as the intelligence understands that the will wants the good, or even insofar as it understands that something is good. (ii) Similarly, the true itself is also a kind of good for the intellect, and it also falls under the will, insofar as human beings want to understand what is true.

Now the good of the practical intelligence is no less something true just because it is an end of activity. For good does not move the desire unless it is recognised as such. Therefore nothing prevents there being virtue in the practical intelligence.

(6) Aristotle is defining *moral* virtue in *Ethics 2.* He describes *intellectual* virtue in *Ethics* 6 [1–7, 1138b19–1141b23]. For the virtue that exists in the practical intelligence is not moral, but intellectual: Aristotle includes practical wisdom in the intellectual virtues, as is clear from *Ethics* 6 [6.5.6, 1140b20].

Article 7: Whether virtue is found in the theoretical intelligence

Objections

It seems that it is not, because:

(1) All virtue is ordered towards action; for it is virtue that renders the things that we do good [*NE* 1.7.15, 1098a16]. The theoretical intelligence, however, is not ordered towards action; for it has nothing to say about imitating or avoiding things, as is clear from Aristotle [*Soul* 3.7, 431b10]. Therefore virtue cannot exist in the theoretical intelligence.

(2) It is virtue that makes its possessor good, as Aristotle says [*NE* 2.6.2, 1106a17]. But the disposition of one's theoretical intelligence does not make one good: someone is not called good just because he possesses knowledge. Therefore such dispositions as the theoretical intelligence possesses are not virtues.

(3) The theoretical intelligence is completed chiefly by having the disposition of knowledge. However, knowledge is not a virtue: that is clear from the fact that it is divided off from the virtues; for the first type of quality is said to include disposition and tendency, and disposition is said to include knowledge and virtue [*Cat* 8, 8b29]. Therefore virtue is not found in the theoretical intelligence.

(4) All virtue is ordered towards something, because it is ordered towards happiness, which is the end of virtue. However, the theoretical intelligence is not ordered towards anything: for theoretical branches of knowledge are not sought for their usefulness, but for themselves, as Aristotle says [*Met* 1.2, 982a14]. Therefore virtue cannot exist in the theoretical intelligence.

(5) The activity of virtue is meritorious. However, understanding something is not enough to be meritorious. Indeed, James 4:17 says, 'Someone who knows what is good and does not do it sins.' Therefore virtue does not exist in the theoretical intelligence.

But on the other hand

(1) Faith is found in the theoretical intelligence, since its object is the first truth. However, faith is a virtue; therefore the theoretical intelligence can possess virtue.

(2) What is true and what is good are equally excellent. Indeed, they overlap: for truth is something good and goodness is something true, while both of them are shared by everything that exists. Therefore if there can be virtue in the will, which has as its object what is good, there can also be virtue in the theoretical intelligence, which has as its object what is true.

My reply

We must say that virtue is identified in each thing by reference to its good. This is because each thing's virtue, as Aristotle says [*NE* 2.6.2, 1106a17], is what makes it good and what makes whatever it does good. For example, the virtue of a horse makes it a good horse, that moves well and carries its rider well: for these things are what a horse does. Consequently, a disposition will possess the character of a virtue insofar as it is ordered towards good.

This can happen in two ways, either (i) in respect of *form*, or (ii) in respect of *matter*. (i) It happens in respect of form when a disposition is ordered towards something good *qua* good. (ii) It happens in respect of matter when it is ordered towards something that is good, but not towards it *qua* good.

Only the *desiring* part of the soul aims at what is good *qua* good, since the good is what all things desire. Therefore the dispositions that exist in, or depend upon, the desiring part, are directed in respect of form towards whatever is good {cf. (i)}. Therefore they possess the character of virtue in its fullest sense. The dispositions that are not found in, nor dependent upon, the desiring part, can be ordered in respect of matter towards something that is good, but not in respect of form, i.e. towards it *qua* good {cf. (ii)}. For this reason, they can be called virtues in one sense, but not strictly speaking, as can the first sort of dispositions.

We need to know also that the *intelligence*, both theoretical and practical, can be brought to completion through a disposition in two ways:

(i') absolutely and in itself, in that it *precedes* the will, as something that moves the will;

(ii') in that it *follows* the will, as drawing out its own activity at the will's command.

Therefore, as I have said, these two capacities, i.e, the intelligence and the will, are mutually dependent.

Those dispositions, then, that are in the practical or theoretical intelligence in the first way {cf. (i')} can be called virtues in some sense, although not here in its fullest sense. In this way, knowledge and wisdom exist in the theoretical intelligence, and skill in the practical intelligence. Someone is called intelligent or knowledgeable, then, because his intelligence is perfected for knowing the truth; indeed, that is the good of the intelligence.

It is true that truth may *also* be something that is wanted, in that someone can want to understand what is true; however, it is not in this respect that the dispositions in question have been perfected. For just because someone is knowledgeable, it does not mean that he automatically *wants* to think about what is true, but only that he *can*. Therefore in itself consideration of the truth does not depend on the knowledge's being something *willing*, but on its focusing directly on its object. The same is true of skill with respect to the practical intelligence: skill does not make someone perfect in the sense of making him *want* to do good work in accordance with his skill, but only in the sense of making him know how to and be able to.

By contrast, those dispositions that are in the theoretical or practical intelligence insofar as the intelligence *follows* the will {cf. (ii')} possess the character of virtue more truly. I mean that through them someone becomes not only capable of and knowledgeable about acting rightly, but also willing so to act. This is the case with both faith and practical wisdom, but in different ways.

Faith completes the *theoretical* intelligence in the sense that the latter receives commands from the will. This is clear in the case of action: for someone only assents with the intelligence to things that are above human reason if he is willing to do so; as Augustine says [*TGJn* 26.2], someone can only believe if he is willing to. Thus faith will exist in the theoretical intelligence, by being subject to the command of the will, in a way parallel to that in which temperateness exists in the sensual part of the soul, by being subject to the command of reason. Consequently, when it comes to believing, the will commands the intelligence not only in respect of carrying out an action, but also in respect of deciding about its object. For the intelligence assents at the command of the will to a decision on what to believe. Similarly, the sensual part, through temperateness, is drawn towards a moderate limit that is decided by reason.

Practical wisdom, however, is found in the *practical* intelligence or reason, as I have said. This is not because the will determines the object of practical wisdom; it determines only its end. Practical wisdom itself searches for the object: it assumes as the end a good given by the will, and then looks for ways to achieve and preserve that good.

It is clear in this way that the dispositions that exist in the intelligence relate in different ways to the will:

(i") Some of them do not depend at all upon the will, except for being used. That is something accidental to them, since the use of this sort of disposition depends in one way on the will and in another way on the disposition in question. This is the case, for example, with knowledge, wisdom and skill. For these dispositions in themselves do not complete their possessors to be the sort of people who *want* to make good use of them. They only make them capable of doing so.

(ii") Some of these intellectual dispositions depend on the will to receive their principle: for the end of action is a principle. This is the case with practical wisdom.

(iii") Some of these dispositions are such that the will decides what their object is, and they receive this from the will. This is the case with faith.

All these can be called virtues in some sense. However, the last two possess the character of virtue more strictly and more completely. From this, though, it does not follow that they are more excellent or more complete as dispositions.

Replies to objections

(1) A disposition of the *theoretical* intelligence is ordered towards its own distinctive activity, which it makes complete; and this is reflection upon the truth. However, they are not ordered towards some external action as their end, but they have their end in their own distinctive activity.

The *practical* intelligence is ordered towards a further, external, activity as its end. For reflection on what should be done or made is the job of the practical intelligence only for the purpose of actually doing or making something.

In this way, the dispositions of the theoretical intelligence make their actions good in a more excellent way than do those of the practical intelligence. This is because the former do them as their end, the latter for another end. However, the dispositions of the practical intelligence, because they are ordered to goodness *qua* goodness, in that they presuppose the will, possess the character of virtue in a stricter sense.

(2) No one is called good *without qualification* for being partly good, but for being wholly good. This depends upon possessing a good will, since the command of the will actualises all the capacities we have as human beings. This arises from the fact that every actualisation is what is good for the relevant capacity. Therefore someone is only called a good person without qualification if he has a will that is good.

On the other hand, someone who is good in respect of some other capacity, without having a good will, is called good *in a relative sense*; if he has good eyesight or hearing, he is described as someone who sees or hears well. In this way, it is clear that a man who has knowledge is not for that reason called good, simply speaking, but good in respect of his intelligence, or someone who 'understands well'. The same is true for skill and other dispositions of this sort.

(3) (i) Knowledge is divided off from *moral* virtue, yet it is itself an *intellectual* virtue. Alternatively, (ii) it is divided off from virtue in the very strictest sense, for in that sense it is not itself a virtue, as I have explained.

(4) The theoretical intelligence is not ordered to something outside itself. Rather, it is ordered towards its own distinctive activity as its end. Nevertheless, our ultimate happiness, which will be contemplation, consists in the activity of the theoretical intelligence. That is why its present activities are nearer to our ultimate happiness, in the sense of being comparable to them, than are the dispositions of the practical intelligence. The latter, however, are perhaps closer to it in the sense that they prepare for it or merit it.

(5) Someone can gain merit through the activities of knowledge, or other similar dispositions, insofar as they are commanded by the will; for nothing that is not commanded by the will merits anything. However, knowledge does not complete the intelligence in this respect, as I have said. For having knowledge is not enough to make someone good at *wanting* to reflect on it, but only good at being capable of this. That is why an evil will is not incompatible with knowledge or skill, as it is with practical wisdom or faith or temperateness. For this reason Aristotle says [*NE* 6.5.7, 1140b24] that someone who errs in what he does because he wants to has little practical wisdom. In the case of knowledge or skill, the opposite is true: a schoolteacher who makes a grammatical mistake without meaning to seems through this to be less knowledgeable about grammar.

Article 8: Whether the virtues are in us by nature

Objections

It seems so, because:

(1) John Damascene says [*OrthF* 3.14], 'The virtues are natural, and they are in us naturally and equally.'

(2) The gloss comments on Matthew 4:23, 'Jesus went about teaching', that 'He teaches natural sorts of justice, i.e. chastity, justice, and humility, which human beings possess naturally.'

(3) Romans 2:14 says that those who do not have the law do by nature the things that the law says. But the law stipulates acts of virtue. Therefore human beings naturally do virtuous acts; it seems, then, that virtue comes from nature.

(4) Antony says [*LA*, paragraph 21 of Greek *Life*], 'If the will changes nature, that is corruption. If its condition is preserved, that is virtue.' In the same sermon he says that natural adornment is enough for human beings. This would not be true if the virtues were not natural. Therefore the virtues are natural.

(5) Cicero says [*Inv* 2.53] that by nature we possess a loftiness of mind. This seems to refer to greatness of spirit. Therefore greatness of spirit is in us by nature; and by the same reasoning so are the other virtues.

(6) In order to carry out virtuous activity we need only (i) to be capable of good, (ii) to want it, and (iii) to recognise it. (iii) To *recognise* what is good is in us by nature, as Augustine says [*FC* 2.6]. (ii) To *want* what is good is also in us by nature, as Augustine also says. (i) To be *capable* of what is good is also in us by nature, since our will governs our actions. Therefore nature is adequate to carry out the activities of virtue. Virtue therefore is natural to a human being, at least in respect of its predispositions.

(7) *Rejoinder*: someone might say that virtue is natural to human beings only in the sense that *predispositions* to virtue are; complete virtue does not come from nature. *But on the other hand* John Damascene says [*OrthF* 3.14], 'Abiding by what is according to nature, we remain in virtue. But if we fall away from what is according to nature, we descend from virtue to what is contrary to nature and we find ourselves in wickedness.' This makes it clear that according to nature we have in us the ability to turn away from wickedness. But this belongs to complete virtue; therefore complete virtue comes from nature.

(8) Since virtue is a form, it is simple and lacks parts. Therefore if it comes from nature in one respect, it seems that it must come entirely from nature.

(9) Human beings are more valuable and perfect {i.e. elevated} than other, non-rational, creatures. However, other creatures receive from nature enough to perfect {i.e. complete} them in their own way. Therefore since the virtues are a kind of perfection of a human being, it seems that they are in us by nature.

(10) *Rejoinder*: someone might say that this cannot be so, since human beings are perfected in many different ways. However, nature is ordered towards only one. *But on the other hand* virtue inclines us towards one thing, just as nature does. For Cicero says [*Inv* 2.53] that a virtue is a disposition that acts in the manner of nature, which also agrees with reason. Therefore nothing prevents virtues from being in human beings by nature.

(11) Virtue consists in a mid-point. But a mid-point is one, determinate, point. Therefore nothing prevents nature from inclining towards what is virtuous.

(12) Sin is the absence of measure, type, and order {cf. Wisd 11:15–20}. But sin is the absence of virtue. Therefore virtue consists in measure, type, and order. These, however, are natural to human beings. Therefore virtue is also natural to us.

(13) The desiring part of the soul follows the cognitive part. But there is a natural disposition in the cognitive part, namely the understanding of principles. Therefore there is some natural disposition also in the desiring or feeling part, which can possess virtue. Therefore it seems that some virtue is natural.

(14) A is natural to B if the principle of A is in B, e.g. it is natural for fire to rise, because the principle of this movement is within the thing that moves. But the principles of virtue are in human beings. Therefore virtue is natural to human beings.

(15) If the seed of something is natural, that thing is also natural. But the seed of virtue is natural; for one of the glosses says on Hebrews 1 that God was willing to implant in every soul the beginnings of wisdom and understanding. Therefore it seems that the virtues are natural.

(16) Contraries belong to the same class. But wickedness is opposed to virtue. However, wickedness is natural, for Wisdom 12:10 says, 'His

wickedness was natural,' and Ephesians 2:3 says, 'We were the children of wrath by nature.' Therefore it seems that virtue is natural.

(17) It is natural for the lower powers to submit to reason; for Aristotle says [*Soul* 3.11, 434a14; {cf. *NE* 1.13.16, 1102b22}] that the higher desire, which belongs to reason, moves the lower, which belongs to the sensory part of the soul, just as the higher spheres move the lower.[20] But moral virtue consists in the lower powers submitting to reason. Therefore these virtues are natural.

(18) For some change to be natural, it is enough that something has a natural aptitude in an interior and passive principle. That is why the generation of simple bodies can be called natural, and also the movements of the heavenly bodies, even though the *active* principle of the heavenly bodies is not nature, but intelligence, while the principle of generation of the simple bodies is *external*. Now human beings do have in them a natural suitability for virtue. For Aristotle says [*NE* 2.1.2, 1103a25], 'We are apt by nature to receive from nature, but we are perfected from practice.' Therefore it seems that virtue is natural.

(19) Something is natural if it is in someone from birth. According to Aristotle [*NE* 6.13.1, 1144b4], some people, as soon as they are born, seem to be brave or temperate, or disposed towards other virtues. Also, Job 31:18 says, 'Since I was a baby my compassion has grown with me, and it left my mother's womb with me.' Therefore the virtues are natural to us.

(20) Nature does not fail in what is necessary. But virtues are needed by human beings for the end towards which they are naturally ordered, i.e. for happiness, which is the activity of perfected virtue. Therefore human beings possess the virtues by nature.

But on the other hand

(1) What is natural is not lost through sin. That is why Dionysius says [*DivNames* 4.23] that natural gifts remain even in the demons. However, virtues are lost through sin. Therefore they are not natural.

(2) We do not acquire or lose through habit whatever is in us naturally, or things that come from nature. However, we can acquire or lose through habit the properties of a virtue. Therefore virtues are not natural.

---

[20] In Aristotelian cosmology, the motion of the higher (or more outward) spheres causes the motion of the lower spheres (those nearer the centre of the universe, the earth).

(3) Whatever is in us naturally is in everyone alike. However, virtues are not found in everyone alike, since in some people there are vices, which are opposed to the virtues.

(4) We neither gain nor lose merit because of natural properties, because they are not up to us. However, we do gain merit through our virtues, and lose it through our vices. Therefore the virtues and vices are not natural.

My reply

Opinions differ about the acquisition of knowledge and of virtue in the same way that they differ about the production of natural forms:

(i) Some people used to believe that forms pre-existed in matter in actuality, but in a hidden way, and that they were led from being unseen to being obvious by means of a natural agent. Anaxagoras thought this; he held that everything is in everything, so that everything can be generated from everything [Aristotle, *Phys* 1.4, 187b22].

(ii) However, others said that the forms came completely from outside, i.e. by sharing in the ideas, as Plato held [*Met* 1.9, 991b2], or through an active intelligence[21], as Avicenna held [*AvSoul* 5.5]. They also said that natural agents do no more than prepare the material for the form.

(iii) Aristotle took a middle way [*GA* 2.3, 736b14]. He held that the forms pre-exist in the capacity of the material, but are brought to actual existence through an external natural agent.

Opinions vary in a similar way about knowledge and virtue:

(i) Some hold that knowledge and virtue exist in us by nature, and that study only needs to remove whatever is blocking knowledge or virtue. Plato seems to have thought this. He held that knowledge and virtue come to exist in us through our participating in separated forms. However, the soul is hindered in making use of these because of its union with the body. Studying branches of knowledge or exercising the virtues is needed to counteract this hindrance.

(ii) Others have said that knowledge and virtue exist in us because of the influence of the active intelligence. On this view, the study and effort prepare someone to receive this influence.

---

[21] Whereas Aquinas holds that individual human beings have within themselves an active intelligence that provides forms for their understanding, Avicenna held that the active intelligence is a separate entity, providing such forms from the outside.

(iii) Thirdly, the middle way: we possess by nature a suitability for knowledge and the virtues. However, they are not made complete in us by nature. This is the best opinion, because just as with respect to natural forms it takes nothing away from the power of the natural agents, so with respect to acquiring knowledge and virtue it preserves the effectiveness of the study and exercise.

We ought also to know that the suitability for being perfected and becoming a form can exist in something in two ways: by (a) a *passive capacity* only, e.g. the matter of air is suited to receive the form of fire; and by (a, b) *both a passive and an active capacity* at the same time, e.g. a body that can be healed is suited to health, and also has in itself an active principle of health. The latter is the way in which human beings are naturally suited to virtue; they are like this partly through possessing the nature of their *species*, in that all human beings share a suitability for virtue, and partly through each possessing their own *individual* nature, which fit some better than others for virtue.

In order to show this, we need to know that:

(1) With reference to the *species*, there are three faculties in human beings capable of possessing virtue, as is clear from our previous discussion. These are: (i') intelligence, (ii') will, and (iii') the lower desire, which is divided into the sensual and the aggressive parts. We should consider for each one of these that there exist in some sense both (a) receptivity to virtue and (b) an active principle of virtue.

It is clear, then, that in the *intelligent part*, there exists the potential intelligence (i'a) which has the capacity to receive any intelligible thing; and intellectual virtue consists in knowing things of that sort. Then there is the active intelligence (i'b); it is by the light of this that such things actually become intelligible. Some of these things, indeed, are naturally known to human beings straight away, without study or inquiry. The first principles are of this sort, both in theoretical matters (for example, 'Every whole is greater than a part of it,' and so on) and in practical matters (for example, 'Everything bad should be avoided,' and so on). These are known naturally, and are the principles on which subsequent knowledge, such as is acquired by study, depends, whether it is practical or theoretical.

Similarly, with the *will* it is clear that there is a natural active principle (ii'b); for the will naturally inclines towards the ultimate end, while in a practical context this end has the character of a natural principle.

Therefore the inclination of the will functions as a certain active principle in relation to whatever tendency the affective part acquires through exercise. It is clear, though, that the will itself, being a capacity that can go in different directions with respect to the things that contribute to the end, is receptive (ii'a) to acquiring a dispositional inclination in one particular direction.

The *aggressive and sensual parts* are naturally capable of listening to reason. Therefore they are naturally receptive (iii'a) to virtue, which is perfected in them insofar as they are disposed to follow the good proposed by reason.

All of these predispositions to virtue follow from the nature of the human species, and therefore they are shared by everyone.

(2) With reference to one's *individual nature*, there are also certain pre-dispositions to virtue which follow from this, and which make one incline towards acts appropriate to a particular virtue, whether by natural temperament or by the influence of the heavenly bodies.[22] This inclination is a sort of predisposition to the virtue. It is not yet, however, complete virtue, since that requires the moderation of reason. That is why the definition of virtue includes the idea that it chooses the mid-point according to right reason [*NE* 2.6.15, 1107a1]. Anyone who followed an inclination of this sort without rational discernment would frequently sin.

In the same way that this predisposition to virtue without the activity of reason does not have the character of a complete virtue, neither do a few premises; for it is through rational inquiry that we reach specific conclusions from universal principles. It is also the job of reason to lead someone from his desire for the ultimate end to whatever is conducive to that end. Again, reason, by governing the aggressive and sensual parts, subjects them to itself. Hence it is clear that the activity of reason is needed for full-blown virtue, whether virtue is in the intelligence or in the will or in the aggressive and sensual parts.

Full-blown virtue involves the predisposition to virtue that is in the higher part being ordered to the virtue of the lower part. Thus, someone is suited for the virtues of the will by the predispositions found both in the will and in the intelligence; and for the virtues of the aggressive and sensual parts by the predispositions to virtue found both in them and in

---

[22] Although he of course rejects astrological determinism, Aquinas does allow that the heavenly bodies can have some indirect causal influence over human actions. See *ST* 1a2ae 9.5.

47

the higher parts. The converse is not true. From this it is also clear that reason, which is higher, is active in fulfilling all of virtue.

We also need to divide *reason* from *nature* as active principles, as is clear from Aristotle [*Phys* 2.8, 199a10]. The power of reason can be ordered towards *opposite* things, but nature to only *one*. Therefore it is clear that virtue is completed not by nature, but by reason.

Replies to objections

(1) The virtues are called natural with respect to the natural predispositions that exist in us, not with respect to their being completed.

The same response will deal with objections (2) to (5).

(6) (i) We are naturally able to do what is good, simply speaking, because we have a natural capacity for this. Again, (ii) wanting and (iii) knowing are in us by nature in some sense, i.e. with respect to a predisposition in a general sense. This, however, is not enough for virtue: acting well, which is the effect of virtue, also requires us to achieve what is good in a ready and faultless way, for the most part. No one can do that without possessing virtue as a disposition. In the same way, it is clear that someone can know in a general sense how to do some thing that a skill achieves, e.g. giving proofs or carving, but to do this readily and without making mistakes requires that they actually possess the skill. The same is true for virtue.

(7) To some degree we naturally avoid evil; but to do so readily and reliably requires possessing virtue as a disposition.

(8) Virtue is not said to come partly from nature in the sense that one part of it is from nature and another not, but because it comes from nature incomplete in respect of what it is, that is, it comes merely as capacity and suitability.

(9) God is in himself perfect in goodness, which is why God needs nothing else to achieve goodness. The higher beings and those nearest to him need only a few things to acquire perfect goodness from him. Human beings, who are further from him, need more to acquire complete goodness, since they are capable of blessedness. Those lower creatures that are not capable of blessedness need fewer things than human beings. That is why human beings have greater worth than they, even though being in need of more things. Similarly, someone who could achieve perfect health by doing a great deal of exercise is in a better condition than someone

who could achieve only a moderate degree of health, but would need only moderate exercise for this.

(10) There can be a natural inclination to do what is characteristic of *one* virtue. However, there cannot be such an inclination to do what is characteristic of *all* the virtues. The reason is that a natural tendency that inclines towards one virtue will incline to conflict with another. For example, someone who is naturally disposed to be courageous, which is shown in pursuing difficult things, will be less disposed towards gentleness, which consists in restraining the emotions of the aggressive faculty. That is why we see that animals which naturally incline to do what one virtue does also incline towards the vice that is the opposite of a different virtue; for example, a lion, which is naturally daring, is also naturally cruel.

This natural inclination to one or other virtue is enough for *other* animals, which cannot achieve complete goodness in respect of virtue, but follow a good of a determinate sort. *Human beings*, however, are apt by nature to reach goodness that is complete with respect to virtue: for that reason, they need to possess an inclination to all kinds of virtuous activity. This could not happen by nature. Therefore it needs to happen in accordance with reason; the seeds of all the virtues exist in that.

(11) The mid-point of virtue is not determined in accordance with nature, as is the middle of the world, towards which heavy things move. Rather, the mid-point of virtue needs to be determined according to right reason, as Aristotle says [*NE* 2.6.15, 1107a1]. For what is in the middle for one person is too little or too much for someone else.

(12) Every sort of good is constituted by measure, type, and order, as Augustine says [*NatGood* 3]. Therefore the measure, type, and order that make up the good of our nature exist in us naturally, and cannot be removed by sin. However, sin is said to be an absence of measure, type, and order in the sense that the good of virtue also consists in these.

(13) The will, unlike the potential intelligence, does not need to be informed by concepts in order to carry out its activity. That is why there is no need for a natural disposition in the will to produce a natural longing. This is especially true since the will is moved by a natural disposition of the intelligence, in that the will aims at something that it understands as good.

(14) Although the principle of virtue, i.e. reason, is inside someone, this principle does not act in the manner of nature; that is why whatever is derived from it is not described as natural.

This response is appropriate for (15).

(16) The wickedness of such people was natural to the extent that it had become habitual; for a habit is something 'second nature' to us. We were 'children of wrath', however, through original sin, which is a flaw in our nature.

(17) It is natural for the lower powers to be liable to be subject to the higher, but not natural for them to be subject to them *through a disposition*.

(18) A change is called natural because of A's natural suitability for it, when B moves A to an end in a way determined in the manner of nature. For example, B might be whatever generates in the case of the elements, or whatever moves the heavenly bodies. However, this is not the case for what we are discussing, therefore the reasoning does not apply.

(19) The natural inclination to virtue, which makes some people brave or temperate almost as soon as they are born, is not enough for complete virtue, as I have argued.

(20) Nature does not leave us lacking in necessities; however, it does not give us everything that is necessary, but gives us enough to be able to acquire all that we need, i.e. reason and whatever is subject to that.

Article 9: Whether we acquire the virtues by our actions

Objections

It seems not, because:

(1) Augustine says[23] that virtue is a good quality of mind by which we live rightly, which no one can misuse, and which God works in us without our help. But if something comes about through our actions, then God does not work this in us. Therefore virtue is not brought into being through our actions.

(2) Augustine says, commenting on Romans 4:23, 'Everything that is not from faith is sin',[24] 'The life of all those without faith is sin, and nothing is good without the highest good; wherever knowledge of the truth is lacking, then any virtue is false even if one's behaviour is excellent.' From this it follows that there can be no virtue without faith. However,

---

[23] See note 7.
[24] Augustine, according to the gloss; in fact, the quotation is from Prosper of Aquitaine, *Sentences Drawn from Saint Augustine* 106.

faith does not come from anything we do, but from grace, as Ephesians 2:8 makes clear: 'You are saved by faith, and not through yourselves; nor should anyone boast, for it is a gift of God.' Therefore virtue cannot be brought into being through our actions.

(3) Bernard says [*SermSS* 22.5.11] that all those who do not realise that it is from the Lord that they should hope to obtain virtue are labouring in vain for it. Anything that we hope for as needing to be obtained from God is not brought into being through our actions. Therefore virtue is not brought into being through our actions.

(4) Self-control is something less than virtue, as Aristotle makes clear [*NE* 7.1.5, 1145b1]. However, self-control exists in us only by God's gift, since Wisdom 8:21 says, 'I know that I cannot be self-controlled unless God grants this.' Therefore we cannot acquire the virtues either through our own actions, but only by God's gift.

(5) Augustine says[25] that no one can avoid sin without grace. However, virtue enables us to avoid sin; for no one can be vicious and virtuous at the same time. Therefore virtue cannot exist without grace. Therefore it cannot be acquired through actions.

(6) We reach happiness by means of virtue, since happiness is the reward of virtue, as Aristotle says [*NE* 1.9.3, 1099b16]. Therefore if we could acquire virtues through our own actions without grace, we would seem to be able to reach eternal life, which is the ultimate happiness for human beings, without grace. That contradicts the words of St Paul [Rom 6:23], 'The grace of God is eternal life.'

(7) Virtue is counted among the greatest goods according to Augustine [*FC* 2.18], because no one misuses it. But the greatest goods are from God, according to James 1:17, 'Every excellent gift and every perfect gift comes from above, coming down from the Father of lights.' Therefore it seems that there is virtue in us only by the gift of God.

(8) Augustine says [*FC* 2.7] that nothing is able to give itself form. But virtue is a kind of form of the soul. Therefore we cannot cause virtue in ourselves by our own actions.

(9) Just as the intelligence from the outset has in its essence the capacity for knowledge, so the same is true for the power of feeling with respect to virtue. But the intelligence, although it has in its essence this capacity for knowledge, also needs an external trigger to bring it to actual knowledge,

---

[25] In many places. See, for example, *PHJ* and *NatGr*.

i.e. a teacher, so that it actually acquires the knowledge. In a similar way, someone needs an external agent in order to acquire virtue; our own acts, then, are not enough for this.

(10) We acquire things by receiving them. But we do not act by receiving; rather the action is discharged by or goes out from the agent. Therefore we do not acquire virtue by performing some action.

(11) If we acquire virtue in us through our actions, we acquire it either (i) from one action, or (ii) from many. (i) Not from *one*, because no one acquires a worthy character by doing something once, as Aristotle says {cf. *NE* 2.1.8, 1103b22}. (ii) Nor again, from *many* actions, because when many actions occur at different times, they cannot produce an effect at the same time. Therefore it seems that there is no way for virtue to be brought into being through our actions.

(12) Avicenna says that virtue is a capacity attributed essentially to things, for them to carry out their activities. But what is attributed to a thing essentially is not brought into being through its own activity. Therefore virtue is not brought into being through the activity of someone who already possesses virtue.

(13) If virtue is brought into being through our actions, this is achieved through either (i) virtuous or (ii) vicious actions. (ii) Not through *vicious* ones, because they rather destroy virtue; again, (i) not through *virtuous* ones, because they presuppose virtue. Therefore there is no way that virtue can be brought into being in us through our own actions.

(14) *Rejoinder*: virtue may be brought into being through actions that are virtuous in an incomplete way. *On the other hand* nothing acts in a way that is beyond its type. Therefore if the actions that precede the virtues are incomplete, it seems that they cannot bring into being complete virtue.

(15) Virtue is the upper limit of a capacity, as Aristotle says [*Heav* 1.11, 281a15]. But a capacity is natural. Therefore virtue is natural and is not acquired through actions.

(16) As Aristotle says [*NE* 2.6.2, 1106a17], virtue makes its possessor good. But human beings are good because of their nature. Therefore the virtue of human beings is in them by nature, not acquired through their acts.

(17) No one acquires new dispositions from repeatedly doing an action that is natural.

(18) Everything has its being from its form. But the form of the virtues is grace; for without grace, the virtues are formless. Therefore virtues arise because of grace not because of our actions.

(19) According to St Paul [2 Cor 12:9], 'Virtue[26] is made perfect in weakness.' However, weakness is something we experience rather than something we do. Therefore virtue comes more from what we experience than from what we do.

(20) Since virtue is a quality, a change in respect of virtue seems to be an 'alteration', for an alteration is a change of quality {cf. *Cat* 14, 15b11}. But an alteration is something that is experienced, and only in the sensory part of the soul, as is clear from Aristotle [*Phys* 7.2, 244b10]. Therefore if we acquire virtue by our actions through experiencing something and being altered, it will follow that virtue is found in the sensory part. That contradicts Augustine, who says that it is a good quality of *mind*.

(21) Virtue enables someone to make the right choice about an end, as Aristotle says [*NE* 6.13.7, 1145a5]. But we do not seem to have the power to choose rightly about the end: as Aristotle says [*NE* 3.5.17, 1114b1], the end will appear to each person in a way that corresponds to what he is like. This happens to us because of our natural temperament or through the influence of the heavenly bodies. Therefore it is not in our power to acquire the virtues. Therefore they are not brought into being through our own actions.

(22) We neither acquire nor lose natural things through habit. But some people possess natural inclinations to certain vices, as to certain virtues. Therefore inclinations of this sort cannot be removed through acting habitually in a certain way. If they remain in us, we cannot also possess the virtues. Therefore we cannot acquire virtue for ourselves by our actions.

But on the other hand

(1) Dionysius says [*DivNames* 4.3] that what is good is more powerful than what is bad. But vicious dispositions are caused in us through bad actions. Therefore virtuous dispositions are caused in us through good actions.

(2) According to Aristotle [*NE* 2.1.4, 1103a32; {cf. 1.8.12, 1099a17}] it is what we do that causes us to become a worthy person. This, though,

[26] *Virtus* here translates the Greek *dunamis*, meaning 'power' or 'strength'.

happens through virtue. Therefore virtue is caused in us through our actions.

(3) Generation and destruction must be the consequences of contrary things. But virtue is destroyed through bad actions. Therefore it is generated through good actions.

My reply

Virtue is the upper limit of a capacity, and the upper limit towards which every capacity reaches is to carry out its activity in a complete way, which is what it is for such activity to be good. Consequently, it is clear that a thing's virtue is what enables it to do well what it does. For everything exists for the sake of its own activity; but each thing is good to the extent that it is properly related to its own end. It should be the case, then, that each thing is good, and does what it does well, through its own distinctive virtue.

However, the distinctive good of one thing is different from that of another. After all, if the things capable of perfection are diverse, what perfects them will also be diverse: the good of a human being is different from that of a horse or of a stone. Moreover, what is good for human beings comes in different sorts depending on what aspect of them is under consideration. For example, (i) someone's good *qua* human being is different from (ii) his good *qua* citizen. (i) The good of a human being *qua* human being is to have reason perfected for knowing the truth and the lower appetites governed by the rule of reason. For a human being is human precisely by being rational. (ii) The good of a human being *qua* citizen, however, is to be ordered to everyone else in a way appropriate to the city. That is why Aristotle says [*Pol* 3.2, 1276b34; {cf. *NE* 5.2.11, 1130b28}] that the virtue of a human being *qua* good person is different from that of a human being *qua* good citizen.

Furthermore, a human being is not only a citizen of the *earthly city*, but is also a member of the *heavenly city* of Jerusalem, which is governed by the Lord and has as its citizens the angels and all the saints, whether they are already reigning in glory and at rest in their homeland, or still pilgrims on earth, as St Paul says in Ephesians 2:19, 'You are fellow-citizens of the saints and members of the household of God', and so on. But for us to become members of this heavenly city, our own nature is not enough; we need to be lifted up to this by the grace of God. For it is clear that the virtues of a human being *qua* member of this city cannot be acquired just

54

virtues of the heavenly city

through what is natural to him. These virtues, therefore, are not caused through our actions, but infused in us by God's gift.

On the other hand, the virtues of a human being *qua* human being or *qua* citizen of the earthly city do not exceed the capacities of human nature. That is why we can acquire them through what is natural to us, by our own actions, as is clear from the following.

Our natural potential for being perfected in some way depends upon either:

(i') only a *passive* principle. In this case, we are perfected not by what we do ourselves, but rather by what some other, external, natural agent does. This is like the way in which air receives light from the sun; or

(ii') *active and passive* principles together. In this case, we are perfected by what we do ourselves. This is like the way in which a sick person's body is naturally suited to getting better. Because people are naturally able to become healthy through the natural active power that is in them of getting better, it sometimes happens that sick people are cured without any external agent doing anything.

We showed in the previous question that we have a natural potential for virtue that depends upon both active and passive principles {cf. (ii')}. This is clear from the way our capacities are ordered. For the *intelligent part* possesses a passive principle, so to speak, in the potential intelligence, which is perfected by means of the active intelligence. Next, the intelligence, when it is actualised, moves the *will*, since something understood as good is the end which moves the desire. Then, when the will is moved by reason, it naturally moves the *sensory desire*, i.e. the aggressive and sensual parts, which are apt by nature to obey reason. From this it is clear that any virtue, in making us do things well, has an active principle in us; and this can, by its own actions, bring the virtue into active existence, whether in the intelligence, the will, or the aggressive and sensual parts.

However, the virtues in the intelligent part and those in the desiring part are brought into active existence in different ways:

(i") The activity of the *intelligence* – or of any cognitive power – is what assimilates it somehow to something that is knowable. That is why intellectual virtue is in the intelligent part insofar as the active intelligence enables intelligible concepts to develop here, whether actively or as dispositions.

(ii") The activity of the virtues of the *desire*, however, consists in a certain inclination towards something desirable. That is why, in order for the desiring part to have virtues in it, it needs to be furnished with an inclination towards something determinate.

We need to know also that the inclination of a *natural* thing follows from its form. That is why it is directed towards one thing, in keeping with the demands of its form. As long as the form remains, the inclination cannot be removed, nor the opposite inclination brought into play. Because of this, natural things neither acquire nor lose anything through habit. For however often a stone is thrown upwards, it will never get into the habit of this, but will still always incline to fall downwards.

By contrast, things that can go in either direction do not possess the kind of form that makes them incline in one determinate direction. Rather, it is their own motivating force that directs them in one determinate direction. But the very fact that they are directed towards this, in some way also *disposes* them towards this. Then, when they repeatedly incline and are directed in the same direction by their own motivating force, then their inclination in that direction becomes determinate and reinforced. In this way, they acquire a tendency towards it, like a sort of form, similar to a natural one, which tends in a single direction. Because of this, we speak of habit as 'second nature'.

Now because the power of desire is one that goes in any direction, it tends in one direction only where reason determines it to do so. And so when reason makes the desiring power incline repeatedly in one direction, then a reinforced tendency develops in the power of desire, which makes it incline in the one direction that has become habitual. Now a virtuous disposition is just a tendency that is reinforced in this way. That is why, if we think about it properly, the virtue of the desiring part is simply a kind of tendency or form that is sealed and stamped by reason on the power of desire. It follows that however strong a tendency in one direction there is in the power of desire, this will not have the character of virtue unless it possesses what is rational. That is why reason is included in the definition of virtue: for Aristotle says [*NE* 2.6.15, 1107a1] that virtue is a disposition that chooses, consisting in a mid-point determined by reason in the way that a wise man would decide.

Replies to objections

(1) Augustine is speaking here of those virtues through which we are ordered to eternal blessedness.

The same reply should be given to objections (2) to (4).

(5) Acquired virtue does not make us avoid sin always, but only for the most part; for it is also true of natural occurrences that they happen for the most part. It does not follow from this that someone is both virtuous and vicious, because a single action is not enough in a capacity to remove the disposition of a vice or of an acquired virtue. Also, one cannot avoid all sin through an acquired virtue; for acquired virtues do not save us from the sin of lack of faith, or from the other sins that are opposed to the infused virtues.

(6) We do not reach heavenly happiness through acquired virtues, but only the kind of happiness that we can naturally acquire in this life by our own natural qualities, through the actualisation of perfected virtue, as Aristotle discusses [*Met* 9.8, 1050b1].

(7) Acquired virtues do not constitute the greatest good in an absolute sense, but the greatest in the class of human goods. Infused virtues constitute the greatest good in an absolute sense, in that they order us towards the supreme good, which is God.

(8) One and the same thing cannot, as such, give itself form. Sometimes, though, one thing possesses both an active and a passive principle, and then it can form itself because it has parts: that is, one part does the forming and another is formed. An example would be when something moves itself in such a way that one part does the moving and another part is moved, as Aristotle says [*Phys* 8.4, 254b30; {cf. 8.4, 255a14; 8.5, 257b2}]. This is the case in the generating of virtue, as I have shown.

(9) In the intelligence, knowledge can be acquired both by finding out for oneself and through being taught, that is, by someone else. Similarly, in acquiring virtues, a person is helped by being corrected and trained, that is, by someone else. The more that people are disposed in themselves to virtue, the less they need this. Similarly, the clearer someone's own intellect, the less he needs teaching by someone else.

(10) The active and the passive powers work together within a person's activity. It is true that the powers reach out and do not receive anything, insofar as they are active; however, the passive powers, insofar as they are passive, quite appropriately acquire things by receiving them. That is why a capacity that is only active, such as the active intelligence, does not acquire a disposition through activity.

(11) The more effective an agent's activity, the more quickly it brings into being a form. Thus, we see in intelligible matters that one proof is

effective, as it is enough to give us knowledge. However, in dialectic one syllogism is not enough to make us have an opinion, even though that is less than knowledge.[27] Several of them are needed, because they are not very strong on their own.

In practical matters too, what the soul does is not effective in the way that a proof is. This is because practical things are contingent and no more than plausible, and therefore one action is not enough to create virtue; several are needed. Even if they do not all occur at once, they can still bring into being the disposition of virtue. This is because the first action creates a tendency; the second, finding its matter disposed in that way, so disposes it even more; and the third still more. In this way, the final action, acting on the strength of all the previous ones, completes the process of generating virtue; it works in the way that many raindrops can hollow out a stone.

(12) Avicenna intended to define *natural* virtue, which follows something's form, which is the principle of its essence. For this reason the definition is irrelevant to the argument.

(13) Virtue is generated by actions which are virtuous in one sense and not in another. The actions that occur before virtue exists are virtuous from the point of view of *what* is done, e.g. the person is doing just or brave things. They are not virtuous from the point of view of *how* it is done; for before someone has acquired the disposition of a virtue, he does not do the things that virtue does in the way that a virtuous person does them, that is, readily, without any hesitation, with pleasure, and without difficulty.

(14) Reason is more excellent than the virtue that is generated in the desiring part, since this sort of virtue only exists because it participates in reason. Therefore the activities that precede virtue are able to cause virtue to the extent that they are rational. For reason is what gives it whatever perfection it has. The lack of perfection here is found in the desiring capacity, where this still lacks the disposition that enables it to carry out promptly and with pleasure whatever reason commands.

(15) Virtue is called the upper limit of a capacity not because it exists always, as part of the essence of the capacity, but because it inclines towards the point that the capacity is able to reach at its upper limit.

---

[27] A genuine proof offers certainty about its conclusion, so only one is required in order for someone to gain knowledge in a full-blown sense. Dialectical arguments, by contrast, merely offer 'good points' in favour of their conclusions; for that reason, it may take several dialectical arguments to establish that the weight of evidence supports their conclusion, rather than its denial.

(16) Human beings are good in their own nature in some sense, but not absolutely. In order for something to be good absolutely, it needs to be complete in all respects. Similarly, in order for something to be beautiful absolutely, it cannot have any part that is misshapen or ugly. A person is called good absolutely and in every respect if he has a good will, because it is through the will that human beings exercise all their other capacities. For that reason, it is a good will that makes someone good in an absolute sense. Consequently, the virtue of the desiring part, which is what makes the will good, is the thing that makes its possessor good in an absolute sense.

(17) The actions that precede the arrival of virtue can be called natural in that they derive from natural reason, if you contrast 'natural' with 'acquired'. However, they cannot be called natural in the sense that 'natural' is contrasted with 'rational'. In this sense we say that we do not through habit lose or acquire natural things, i.e. in the sense of 'natural' that is contrasted with 'rational'.

(18) Grace is said to be the form of an infused virtue. This is not so, however, in the sense that it gives the virtue its *type*, but rather insofar as the *activity* of that virtue is somehow informed by grace. That is why it is not appropriate for civic virtue to come about through the infusion of grace.

(19) (i) Virtue is made perfect in weakness not because weakness causes virtue, but because it gives *opportunities* for a specific virtue, i.e. humility.

(ii) It is also the *matter* of another virtue, i.e. endurance, and also of charity, when someone comes to the help of a neighbour who is in a state of weakness.

(iii) Weakness is also naturally a *sign* of virtue, because the weaker someone's body when he attempts an act of virtue, the more virtuous the soul is shown to be.

(20) Strictly speaking, something is not said to 'alter' insofar as it achieves its own distinctive fulfilment. That is why, since virtue is the fulfilment distinctive of human beings, human beings are not said to 'alter' when they acquire virtue. This might, though, occur *per accidens*, insofar as changes in the sensitive part of the soul, where the emotions of the mind are found, are a part of virtue.

(21) Someone's character can be described as 'like' something:

(i) according to what his *intelligent* part is like. In this sense, someone is not so described on account of the body's natural temperament, or the influence of the heavenly bodies, since the intelligent part is independent of any body; or

(ii) according to the tendency of his *sensory* part. In this sense, one can be so described according to the natural temperament of one's body, or the influence of one of the heavenly bodies. However, because this part naturally obeys reason, the tendency that is in this part is also subject to human reasoning, and it is therefore capable of being diminished or completely removed through habitual activity.

From this the reply to objection (22) is clear. For on account of the tendency that is in their sensitive part, some people are said to possess a natural inclination to some vice or some virtue.

Article 10: Whether some virtues are infused into us

Objections

It seems not, because:

(1) Aristotle says [*Phys* 7.3, 246a14], 'Each thing is complete when it attains its own distinctive virtue.' The distinctive virtue of something, though, is what naturally completes it. Therefore our natural virtue is enough to complete us as human beings, and natural principles are enough to bring this into being. Therefore infused virtues are not needed to complete us as human beings.

(2) *Rejoinder*: human beings need virtue in order to be complete in the way that they are ordered not only towards their natural end, but also towards their supernatural end. That is the blessedness of eternal life, and it is through the infused virtues that we are ordered towards this. *But on the other hand* nature does not lack what is necessary. If we need something to achieve our ultimate end, then that is necessary to us. Therefore we can achieve this through natural principles; therefore we do not need infused virtues for this.

(3) A seed acts by the power of the organism that produced it. Otherwise, just by its own action, the seed of an animal, since it is undeveloped, could not grow into a developed instance of its species. The seeds of the virtues, though, were put into us by God. For the gloss says on Hebrews 1:5, 'Since he is the splendour of glory', 'God sowed in every soul the seeds of intelligence and wisdom.' Since, then, an acquired virtue is brought into being from seeds of this sort, it seems that acquired virtue is able to lead us to the enjoyment of God, which is what constitutes the blessedness of eternal life.

(4) Virtue orders human beings towards the blessedness of eternal life insofar as it consists of meritorious activity. But the activity of acquired virtues can merit eternal life if it is informed by grace. Therefore we do not need to possess the infused virtues to achieve the blessedness of eternal life.

(5) Charity is the root of merit. Therefore if we needed to possess infused virtues to deserve eternal life, it seems that charity alone would be enough. For this reason we do not need to possess any other infused virtues.

(6) Moral virtues are necessary for the lower powers to be subordinated to reason. This is achieved adequately by the *acquired* virtues. Therefore no *infused moral* virtues are needed. To order reason towards an end proper to us, it is enough for human reason that it is directed towards its supernatural end. That, though, is adequately achieved through *faith*. Therefore we do not need the *other* infused virtues.[28]

(7) Something that happens by divine power does not differ in type from something that happens through the activity of nature. For example, health that is miraculously restored is of the same type as health that is brought about naturally. If, then, there were some, infused, virtues which were in us from God, and other virtues that we acquired through our own activity, the two would not for this reason differ in type: take, for example, acquired temperateness and infused temperateness. But two forms of a single type cannot exist at the same time in the same subject. Therefore the same person cannot possibly possess *both* acquired *and* infused temperateness.

(8) (i) We recognise the type of a capacity or of a virtue from its activities.

(ii) But acquired and infused temperateness carry out activities of the same type.

(iii) Therefore they themselves are of the same type. To prove the minor premise (i.e. (ii)): when two things agree in both matter and form, they are of the same type. But the activities of acquired and infused temperateness agree in their matter, for they both deal with things that are pleasurable to touch. They also agree in form, because they both consist in a mid-point. Therefore the activities of infused and of acquired temperateness are of the same type.

---

[28] The text is problematic. The translation modifies it slightly to make better sense of the argument.

(9) *Rejoinder*: they differ in type because they are ordered towards different ends; for in moral matters the type depends upon the end. *But on the other hand* things can indeed differ in type according to whatever their type depends upon. Now in moral matters the type depends upon not the ultimate, but the *proximate* end. Otherwise, all the virtues would be of a single type, for they are all ordered towards blessedness as the ultimate end. Therefore we cannot say that in moral matters things are of the same or of different types because of the way they are ordered with respect to the ultimate end. That is why infused temperateness does not differ in type from acquired merely because it orders human beings towards a higher form of blessedness.

(10) No moral disposition acquires its type from being affected by some other disposition. For it can happen that one moral disposition is affected or governed by dispositions that differ in type. For example, a disposition of intemperateness is affected by a disposition of avarice in the case where someone fornicates in order to be able to steal; or by a disposition of cruelty in the case where someone fornicates in order to kill. Conversely, dispositions that differ in type can be governed by one and the same disposition. For example, one person may fornicate, and another may kill, both in order to steal. Now temperateness and courage, like the rest of the moral virtues, do not have their own actions ordered towards the blessedness of eternal life, except insofar as they are governed by charity, which does have the ultimate end as its object. Therefore they do not take their type from that end. Thus infused moral virtue does not differ in type from acquired virtue merely on the grounds that it is ordered towards eternal life as its end.

(11) Infused virtue exists as something possessed by the mind: for Augustine says that virtue is 'a good quality of mind, which God works in us without our help'. But the moral virtues are not possessed by the mind: temperateness and courage belong to the non-rational parts, as Aristotle says [*NE* 3.10.8, 1118a25]. Therefore the moral virtues are not infused.

(12) Contraries share a single character. But vice, which is contrary to virtue, is never infused, but is brought about only through our actions. Therefore virtues cannot be infused either, but are all brought about through our actions.

(13) Before someone acquires any virtue, he possesses a capacity for the virtues. However, a capacity and its actualisation belong to the same

class: for every class is divided into capacity and actualisation, as Aristotle makes clear [*Phys* 3.1, 201a10; {cf. *Met* 10.1, 1045b34}]. Since, therefore, the *capacity* for virtue does not come from being infused, it seems that neither can virtue itself come from this.

(14) If the virtues are infused, they should all be infused at the same time as grace. Grace, though, is infused into someone who is in a state of sin by an act of repentance; the dispositions of the moral virtues are not, however, infused in him at that same time. For even after repenting, we are still troubled by the emotions; this is the experience of someone who is self-controlled, but not of someone who is virtuous. For the self-controlled person differs from the temperate one in that the former experiences inappropriate emotions but is not led astray by them, while the temperate person does not even experience them, as Aristotle explains [*NE* 7.9.6, 1152a1]. Therefore it seems that the virtues are not infused in us by grace.

(15) Aristotle says [*NE* 2.3.1, 1104b5] that when someone begins to take pleasure in what he does, we should take this as a sign that he has acquired the relevant disposition. However, we do not immediately after repenting begin to take pleasure in behaving in a way appropriate to the moral virtues. Therefore we do not yet possess the dispositions of those virtues. Therefore the *moral* virtues are not brought into being in us through the infusion of grace.

(16) Take those who have acquired some vicious disposition from performing a number of bad actions. It is clear that their sins are forgiven and grace infused in them through a single act of repentance. However, an acquired disposition cannot be wiped out by a single action, just as it cannot be generated by a single action. Since, then, the moral virtues are infused along with grace, it would follow that a morally virtuous disposition would coexist with the disposition that is its opposing vice; but that is impossible.

(17) Virtue is generated and destroyed by the same thing, as Aristotle says [*NE* 2.1.6, 1103b8]. If, then, virtue is not brought into being in us through our actions, it seems to follow that it is not destroyed through our actions either. From this, it follows that someone who commits mortal sin does not lose virtue; but that is wrong.

(18) Mores {Latin: *mos*} and habits seem to be the same thing. Therefore moral virtue and habitual virtue are the same thing. But habitual virtue gets its name from habit, because it is brought about through repeatedly

doing something well. Therefore all *moral* virtue is brought about through actions, and therefore not by the infusion of grace.

(19) If some virtues are infused, the activity that depends upon them must be more effective than the activity of someone without virtue. But the activity of someone without virtue is what brings about a virtuous disposition in him. Therefore the activity of the infused virtues, if they exist, will have the same effect. But Aristotle says [*NE* 2.1.1, 1103a16; 2.1.4, 1103b1; 2.1.7, 1103b20; 2.2.1, 1103b30; 2.4.5, 1105b10] that dispositions lead to activity that is of the same kind; again, activity causes dispositions that are of the same kind. Therefore dispositions that are brought about through the activities of an infused virtue must be of the same type as that infused virtue. It follows that two forms of the same type will exist in the same subject at the same time. But that is impossible. Therefore it seems impossible for there to be any infused virtues in us.

But on the other hand

(1) Luke 24:49 says, 'Remain here in the city until you are clothed with virtue from on high.'

(2) Wisdom 8:7 says of divine Wisdom that it 'teaches soberness and justice', and so on. The spirit of Wisdom, though, teaches virtue by bringing it into being. Therefore it seems that the moral virtues are infused in us by God.

(3) The activities of any virtues at all ought to be meritorious in such a way that we are led by them to blessedness. But there can be no merit except through grace. Therefore it seems that the virtues are brought about in us through the infusion of grace.

My reply

As well as the virtues that we acquire by our actions, which I have already discussed, we need to posit other virtues that are infused in us by God. We can accept as the reason for this the fact that virtue, as Aristotle says [*NE* 2.6.2, 1106a17], is something that makes its possessor good, and makes whatever he does good. Therefore since human beings have different sorts of good, they also need different sorts of virtues. For example, it is clear that a human being has one good *qua* human being and another *qua* citizen. It is clear that some activities can be appropriate for a human being *qua* human being, but not *qua* citizen. That is why Aristotle says [*Pol* 3.4, 1276b34] that the virtue that makes someone a good person is different from the virtue that makes him a good citizen.

We must note that the human good is twofold: (i) what *corresponds* with our own nature; (ii) what *exceeds* the abilities of our own nature. The reason for this is that something that is acted upon is made complete by the agent in question in different ways that correspond with the different powers of the agent. That is why we see that when a natural agent acts on something, it completes it and gives it form in a way that does not exceed its natural abilities. For a natural active power corresponds to a natural passive capacity {cf. (i)}. However, a supernatural agent, whose power is infinite, that is to say, God, completes something and gives it form in a way that does exceed the abilities of its nature {cf. (ii)}. That is why the rational soul, which is brought into being directly by God, exceeds the limits of its matter, that is to say, the material body cannot wholly contain and enclose it: there remains a certain power and activity in it that the material body does not share. This is not true for any of the other forms, which are brought about through natural agents.

Just as human beings acquire the *first* thing that completes them, i.e. the soul, from the action of God, so they also acquire the *last* thing that completes them, that is complete human happiness, directly from God, and they rest in him. This is clear from the fact that the natural longing of a human being cannot rest in anything else except in God alone. For human beings have an innate longing that moves them from the things that have been brought into being to seeking their cause. Therefore this longing will not rest until it reaches the first cause, which is God.

It is appropriate, then, that just as the first thing that completes a human being, which is the rational soul, exceeds the abilities of the *material* body, so the last state of completeness that human beings can attain, which is the blessedness of eternal life, should exceed the abilities of human nature *as a whole*. Now, each thing is ordered to its end by what it does, and the things that contribute to the end ought to correspond in some way to that end. Consequently, it is necessary for there to be some sorts of completeness in us that exceed the abilities of the principles natural to us and that order us towards our supernatural end. This could only be the case if God infused in human beings certain *supernatural* principles of activity on top of the *natural* ones.

Now our *natural* principles of activity are the essence of the soul and its capacities, i.e. the intelligence and will, which are the principles of human activities *qua* human. They could not be this unless the intelligence also possessed an awareness of the principles through which it is directed in natural activities, and unless the will also possessed a natural inclination to the good that corresponded to its own nature, as I discussed in a previous question.

On the other hand, to enable us to carry out activities that are ordered towards the end of eternal life, the following are *divinely* infused in us: first (i') *grace*, through which the soul acquires a certain spiritual way of being; then (ii') faith, hope and charity. Thus by *faith*, the *intelligence* may be enlightened concerning the knowledge of supernatural matters, which function at that level just as naturally known principles do at the level of our natural activities. By *hope* and *charity*, the *will* acquires a certain inclination towards that supernatural good; the human will just by its own natural inclination is not sufficiently ordered towards this.

In sum: we need not only the natural principles, but also the dispositions of the virtues, in order to be completed as human beings in the way that is natural to us, as I said above. Similarly, then, we have poured into us by God not only the supernatural *principles* just mentioned, but also certain infused *virtues*, through which we can be completed for doing whatever is ordered to the goal of eternal life.

Replies to objections

(1) Human beings are completed in respect of the first thing that completes them {i.e. their soul} in two ways: (ia) in being nourished and having sense-perception. To be complete in these areas does not exceed the abilities of the natural body; (ib) in being intelligent. To be complete in this does go beyond their natural and bodily parts. Through (ia) we are completed in a relative sense, through (ib) in an absolute sense. Similarly, we may be completed in two ways with respect to the completeness of our end: (iia) according to the abilities of our own nature, and (iib) according to a supernatural completeness. Through (iia) we become complete in a relative sense; through (iib) in an absolute sense. That is why human beings can possess two types of virtue: one (iiia) relates to the first kind of completeness, and this is not complete virtue; the second (iiib) relates to the second kind of completeness, and this is true and complete human virtue.

(2) Where nature provides what is necessary for us, it does so in accordance with its own power. That is why in respect of those things that do not exceed the abilities of our nature, we receive from nature not only receptive principles, but also active ones. In respect of those things that exceed the abilities of nature, we receive from our nature the fact that we are suited for receiving them.

(3) The seed of a human being is active with all the power possible for a human being. However, the seeds of virtue that are naturally placed in the human soul do not act with all the power possible for God. That is why it does not follow that they are able to cause anything that God is able to cause.

(4) Since we can merit nothing without charity, the actions of an acquired virtue cannot have merit without charity. However, the other virtues are infused in us together with charity; that is how the actions of an acquired virtue can be meritorious only by means of an infused virtue. For a virtue that is ordered towards a lower end can only bring about actions that are ordered to a higher end if this is done by means of a higher virtue. For example, the courage that is a virtue of a human being *qua* human being does not order its actions to the civic good except by means of that courage that is the virtue of a human being *qua* citizen.

(5) When an action is produced by several different agents that are ordered towards each other, it is possible that something that hampers one of these agents will spoil the perfection and goodness of the action as a whole, even if another of the agents is perfect. For however perfect a craftsman, he will not do his work perfectly if his tools are flawed.

In the case of those human activities that need to be given their goodness by virtue, we need to consider that what is done by a higher capacity does not depend on a lower capacity, but vice versa. That is why perfecting the actions of the lower, i.e. the aggressive and sensual, powers, needs the intelligence, through faith, and the will, through charity, both to be ordered to the ultimate end; it also needs the lower, i.e. the aggressive and sensual, powers to carry out their own activities in such a way that their actions are good and can be ordered to the ultimate end.

From this the answer to objection (6) is also clear.

(7) Wherever nature produces a form, God is able to produce one of the same type by himself, without nature's doing anything. Thus, when God miraculously makes someone better, the resulting health is of the same type as the health that nature produces. It does not follow from this

that nature can produce every form that God can produce. That is why infused virtue, which comes directly from God, does not need to be of the same type as acquired virtue.

(8) Infused and acquired temperateness agree in their *matter*, for they both deal with things that are pleasurable to touch. They do not, however, agree in the *form* of their effects or actions. For although they both seek the mid-point, each, however, looks for that mid-point by different reasoning. *Infused* temperateness looks for the mid-point that accords with the reasons of God's law, which we take as ordered towards the final end. *Acquired* temperateness, however, takes a mid-point according to lesser reasons, ordered towards the good of this present life.

(9) The ultimate end does not determine the type in moral matters except insofar as the proximate end corresponds duly to the ultimate end. For whatever contributes to an end ought also to correspond to it. Good counsel also requires someone to achieve the end by a means that is suitable, as Aristotle says [*Top* 6.9, 147a15; *NE* 3.3.11, 1112b16].

(10) The actions of any disposition, *qua* being governed by another disposition, receive their moral type, formally speaking, from the disposition itself. Thus when someone fornicates in order to steal, although this action belongs as regards material to intemperateness, as regards form it belongs to avarice. But although the intemperate *action* takes its type {i.e. is avaricious} from being governed by avarice, this does not mean that intemperateness *itself* should take its type from the fact that its action has been governed by avarice. Therefore when the actions of temperateness or of courage are governed by charity, which orders them to their final end, the *actions* take their type, as regards form, from that; for formally speaking they are actions of charity. It would not follow from this, however, that temperateness or courage *themselves* should take their type from that.

Consequently, infused temperateness and courage do not differ in type from acquired temperateness and courage just in the fact that their actions are governed by charity. The difference, rather, is that reason determines the mid-point for their actions in a way that can order them towards the ultimate end, which is the object of charity.

(11) Infused temperateness is found in the sensual part, just as infused courage is found in the aggressive part. However, the aggressive and sensual parts are called 'rational' insofar as they share in reason in some way, by obeying it. Similarly, they are called 'mental' insofar as they obey

the mind. That is the sense in which Augustine's words are true, that infused virtue is a good quality of mind.

(12) Human vices drag us down to lower things; human virtue raises us up to higher things. That is why virtue alone, and not vice, can exist by infusion.

(13) Something that is acted upon is apt by nature to be developed in different ways when different agents affect it. Then, the differences within and the ordering of the passive capacities in that thing will correspond to the differences within and the ordering of the active capacities in the agents; for the active capacity responds to the passive one. For example, it is clear that water and earth have one natural capacity to be changed by fire, and another to be changed by the heavenly bodies, and a third to be changed by God. For something can be made out of water or earth by the power of the heavenly bodies in a way that cannot happen by the power of fire. Similarly, something can be made out of them by the power of God in a way that cannot happen by the power of any natural agent. For this reason we say that the whole of creation has some capacity to obey, insofar as every creature obeys God, to the extent of receiving in itself whatever God wills.

Consequently, there exist within the soul: (i) capacities which are apt by nature to be actualised by another natural agent. This is how the capacities for the *acquired* virtues exist in the soul; (ii) capacities which are apt by nature to be actualised only through divine power. This is how the capacities for the *infused* virtues exist in the soul.

(14) Those emotions that incline us towards evil are not completely removed either through acquired or through infused virtue, except, maybe, by a miracle. For the struggle of the flesh against the spirit always remains, even when we possess moral virtue. St Paul says about this in Galatians 5:17, 'The flesh lusts against the spirit, and the spirit against the flesh.' But emotions of this sort are modified both by acquired and by infused virtues, so that we are not stirred by them in an unrestrained way.

However, (i) acquired virtue achieves this in one way and (ii) infused virtue in another. (i) For *acquired* virtue is effective to the extent that the struggle is felt less. This comes about from its own particular cause: when someone becomes accustomed to virtue through repeated actions, they then become unaccustomed to obey those emotions, and accustomed to resist them. The consequence of this is that they feel less troubled by them. (ii) *Infused* virtue, by contrast, is effective to the extent that even if emotions of this sort are felt, they do not take control. For infused virtue means that we refrain totally from obeying sinful desires, and as long as it remains in us, we do so unfailingly. (Acquired virtue can fail in this way, but rarely, in the way that all natural inclinations occasionally let us down.) That is why St Paul says in Romans 7:5–6, 'When we were in the flesh, the sinful emotions which arose through the Law acted in our limbs to produce fruit for death. Now, however, we are freed from the law of death that held us, so that we may serve in the new life of the spirit, and not in the old life of the letter.'

(15) Since infused virtue does not always remove the experience of the emotions straight away in the way that acquired virtue does, it does not in the same way give pleasure straight away. However, this is not inconsistent with the character of virtue, because sometimes it is enough for virtue that it does what it does without regret, and unnecessary for it to take pleasure in doing what it does, when this feels burdensome. Similarly, Aristotle says [*NE* 3.9.4, 1117a32; 2.3.1, 1104b8] that it is enough for bravery if someone acts without regret.

(16) It is true that a single, simple, action is not enough to destroy an acquired disposition. However, an act of repentance is, by virtue of grace, able to destroy a vicious disposition that has been generated. That is why, if someone has the disposition of intemperateness, when he repents it no longer remains there alongside the infused virtue of temperateness in the character of a *disposition*. Rather, it is already in the process of being destroyed, and has become instead a sort of *tendency*. However, a tendency is not the contrary of a full-blown disposition.

(17) Although infused virtue is not brought about through our actions, our actions can still dispose us to it. That is why it is not inappropriate for it to be destroyed by our actions. This is because form is removed when the matter is inappropriately disposed, just as the soul separates from the body when the body is inappropriately disposed.

(18) 'Moral' virtue gets its name from 'mores' as referring not to habit, but to the inclination of the power of desire. In this sense, the infused virtues too might be called 'moral', although they are not caused by habit.

(19) The activities of infused virtues do not bring about any disposition, but strengthen a pre-existing disposition. Indeed not even the actions of an acquired virtue actually generate a further disposition; otherwise, our dispositions would be multiplied indefinitely.

Article 11: Whether infused virtue may be increased

Objections

It seems not, because:

(1) Things only increase in respect of quantity. But virtue is not a quantity, but a quality. Therefore it is not increased.

(2) Virtue is an accidental form. A form is something that consists in an utterly simple and unchanging essence. Therefore virtue does not vary in respect of its own essence. Therefore it is not increased in its essence.

(3) Anything that is increased changes. Anything, then, that is increased in its essence, changes in its essence. But anything that changes in its essence is either destroyed or generated. Generation and destruction are both changes in a thing's substance. Therefore charity cannot be increased in its essence, except by being destroyed or generated.

(4) What belongs to something's essence can be neither increased nor decreased. But it is clear that the essence of virtue belongs to its essence. Therefore virtue cannot be increased in its essence.

(5) Contraries occur in respect of the same thing. Increase and decrease are contraries. Therefore they occur in respect of the same thing. However, infused virtue is not decreased, because it cannot be decreased either (i) through virtuous action, which instead *strengthens* it; or (ii) through a venially sinful action, because then a number of venially sinful actions would completely remove charity and the other infused virtues, and this is impossible; for then a number of venial sins would be of equal gravity to one mortal sin; or (iii) through mortal sin. For mortal sin *removes* charity and the other infused virtues. Therefore infused virtue cannot be increased.

(6) Like things are increased by like, as Aristotle says [*Soul* 2.4, 415a28]. Therefore if infused virtue is increased, it ought to be increased by the addition of virtue. But this cannot happen, because virtue is something simple. One simple thing added to another does not make it bigger; for example, if you add a point to a point, it does not make the line longer. Therefore infused virtue cannot be increased.

(7) Aristotle says [*GC* 1.5, 320b30] that an increase is an addition to a pre-existing magnitude. Therefore for virtue to be increased, it needs something to be added to it. But then it will become more composite, and move further from likeness to God, and therefore be less good. That

71

must be wrong. Therefore the only possibility left is that virtue is not increased.

(8) Everything that is increased changes. Everything that changes is physical. Virtue is not something physical. Therefore it does not change.

(9) If something has a cause that does not vary, it does not vary itself. But the cause of infused virtue is God, who does not vary. Therefore infused virtue does not vary. Therefore it does not admit of less or more. Therefore it does not increase.

(10) Virtue, like knowledge, comes under the class of disposition. Therefore if virtue can be increased, it ought to be increased in the way that knowledge is. But knowledge is increased by multiplying its objects, that is, by extending itself over more things. Virtue does not increase in this way, as is clear in the case of charity: for the smallest amount of charity extends itself to loving everything that ought to be loved through charity. Therefore there is no way for virtue to be increased.

(11) If virtue is increased, its increase must count as some type of change in it. But it can only count as 'alteration', which is a change in quality [*Cat* 14, 15b11]. However, according to Aristotle [*Phys* 7.3, 245b2], 'alteration' can occur in the soul only in the sensory part. Charity is not found there, nor most of the other infused virtues. Therefore not every type of infused virtue can be increased.

(12) If infused virtue can be increased, it must be increased by God, who is its cause. However, if God increases it, this must happen through a fresh inpouring by him. But there cannot be a fresh inpouring unless there is a new infused virtue. Therefore infused virtue can only be increased by the addition of new virtue. But it cannot be increased in this way, as has been shown above. Therefore there is no way for infused virtue to be increased.

(13) Dispositions are greatly increased by actions. Therefore since virtue is a disposition, if it is increased, it will be increased greatly by its own actions. But this cannot happen, so it seems, as an action is something that comes from a disposition. For things are only increased when something goes into them, not when something comes out of them. Therefore there is no way that virtue can be increased.

(14) All the activities of a single virtue share a single character. If, then, a given virtue is increased by its own actions, it ought to be increased by any such action. Experience seems to prove this false. For we do not find through experience that virtue grows with any such action.

(15) Something that is in its character the best of its kind cannot be increased: for nothing can be better than the best, nor whiter than pure whiteness. However, the character of virtue just is that it is the best of its kind, for virtue is the upper limit of a capacity. Therefore virtue cannot be increased.

(16) Something that is in its character indivisible cannot be made more or less intensive: for example, the form of a substance, or a number, or a figure.[29] But virtue is by definition something indivisible, for it consists in the mid-point. Therefore virtue cannot be made more or less intensive.

(17) Nothing infinite can be increased, because nothing is larger than something infinite. But infused virtue is infinite, because through it a person can merit infinite good, i.e. God. Therefore infused virtue cannot be increased.

(18) Nothing advances beyond its own completeness because that is a thing's finishing-point. However, virtue is what completes whatever has it; for Aristotle says [*Phys* 7.3, 246b2] that virtue is the tendency of something complete towards what is best. Therefore virtue does not increase.

But on the other hand

(1) 1 Peter 2:2 says, 'As newborn babies, reasonable and without guile, desire milk, so that you may grow into salvation.' However, no one grows into salvation except by increasing virtue, which is what orders a person towards salvation. Therefore virtue can increase.

(2) Augustine says [*TGJn* 74.2] that charity will increase in such a way that when it is increased it will also merit being completed.

My reply

(i) Many make mistakes about *forms* by treating them as if they were substances. This seems to happen because forms are described by using nouns, just as substances are, albeit abstract nouns, such as whiteness or virtue, and so on. That is why some are led by this way of speaking to treat them as if they were substances. From this two errors arise: (a) some

---

[29] Thus, being a dog (substance), being three (number), and being a triangle (figure) do not come in degrees of more and less. Either a thing is, or it is not, a dog, three, or a triangle.

people posit a *hidden existence* for forms; (b) others hold that forms exist by being *created*. For they reckon that whatever is true of a substance ought to be true of a form, and so, when they fail to find a source from which forms can be generated, they hold either that they are created {cf. (b)}, or that they pre-exist in matter {cf. (a)}.

They do not notice that just as *being* belongs not to a form but to a subject by means of the form, so too the process of *coming into being* (which concludes with there being a form) does not belong to the form, but to the subject. A form x is called a 'being' not because *it itself is*, if we speak strictly, but because *something is it*. In the same way, a form is said to 'come into being' not because it itself comes into being, but because something comes to be it: namely when its subject is brought from capacity to actualisation.

(ii) Similarly, on the question of increase in *qualities*, some people speak of this as if qualities as well as forms were substances. Now a substance is said to increase insofar as it is the subject of a change from a smaller quantity to a greater quantity. This change is what is called 'increasing'. Since the increase of a substance happens by adding one quantifiable substance to another, these people think that charity and the other infused virtues are increased in the same way, by adding charity to charity or virtue to virtue.[30]

But this cannot stand. The reason is this: we can only understand the idea of adding one thing to another if we have first understood them as two. But we can only grasp that there are two different things of a single type if they belong to distinct subjects. For the forms of a single type can only be numerically distinguished if they inhere in different subjects. For one quality to be added to another, then, one of two conditions is needed: (a) one subject is added to another; so, for example, one white thing is added to another white thing; or (b) in a subject that is becoming whiter, something becomes white which was not previously white, as some people believe happens with *physical* qualities. Aristotle, however, disproves this possibility [*Phys* 8.8, 264b6]. For when something becomes more curved, it is not that some new thing is curved that was not curved before, but that the whole thing becomes more curved. In the case of qualities that are *spiritual*, which have either the soul or part of the soul as their subject, we cannot even imagine such a possibility.

---

[30] The text adds 'or whiteness to whiteness'.

(iii) That is why yet others say that charity and the other infused virtues are *not* increased *in their essence*, but are said to be increased, either because they become more firmly rooted in their subject, or because they are exercised more fervently and more intensively. Now this claim would be reasonable if (a) charity were a substance which existed in itself separately from any other substance. That is why Peter Lombard, who holds [*Sent* 1.17.1.2] that charity is a *substance*, i.e. the Holy Spirit itself, does not seem unreasonable in holding that it can be increased in this way. Others, however, who consider that (b) charity is some *quality*, are basically unreasonable in holding the same view.

The reason is that a quality's being increased is nothing other than its subject's sharing to an increasing degree in that quality: indeed, a quality does not exist except insofar as it inheres in a subject. Precisely from the fact that a subject shares more in such a quality, it is more strongly active. This is because each thing acts insofar as it is actualised; that is why the more it is brought to actualisation, the more completely it acts. Therefore to hold that some quality is *not* increased in its essence, but *is* increased in its degree of rootedness in its subject, or in the degree of intensity of its actualisation, is to hold contradictory beliefs at the same time.

(iv) Finally, therefore, we need to consider (a) *how* certain qualities and forms are described as being increased, and (b) *which* are the ones that can be increased.

(a) Now we need to know that since names are the signs for concepts, as Aristotle says [*Int* 1, 16a3], in the same way that we learn things that are less well known from things that are better known, we also name things that are less known from things that are better known. That is why, since change of place is the best known of all types of change, the phrase 'at a distance', meaning 'not in the same place', is applied to all contrasts in things that change, as Aristotle tells us [*Met* 10.1, 1052a27; *Phys* 7.7, 260a27]. In a similar way, since we perceive more easily when something changes its size than when it changes in the sense of altering in quality, it comes about that words suitable for change of size are used also in the context of altering in quality. Now a body that changes its size until it is complete is said to increase, and the final, complete, size is called 'big' by comparison with the incomplete. Similarly, then, for the reasons I have explained, something that changes in its quality from incomplete to complete is said to 'increase' in quality, and the complete quality is described as 'big' by comparison with the incomplete. Moreover, since the completeness of a thing is its goodness, Augustine says [*Trin* 6.2.8] that even in things that are not big in terms of size, we still take 'more' to mean better.

When something changes from having an incomplete to having a complete form, all that happens is that the subject is more fully actualised, since a form is an actualisation. That is why, for the subject to participate in the form more means simply that the subject is actualised more fully in respect of that form. Just as something can be brought by another agent from being in a state of pure capacity to having the form actualised, in the same way it can be brought by another agent's activity from being less than completely to being completely actualised.

(b) This, however, does not happen with every type of form. There are two exceptions, for the following reasons:

(α) because of the *character* of the form, for example when the character of the form is completed by something that cannot be divided, such as a number. For every time you add one to a number, you change its type: you cannot talk about more or less twoness or threeness. That is why you will also fail to find more or less in those quantities that can be labelled by numbers, such as a double cubit or a triple cubit, or in figures such as triangles or squares, or in ratios, such as double or triple;

(β) because of the *relation* between a form and a subject, when the form exists in the subject in an indivisible way. That is why a substantial form cannot be made more or less intensive, because it gives the thing its being as a substance, which happens only in one way. For where the substance has a different being, there is a different thing. That is why Aristotle likens definitions to numbers [*Met* 8.3, 1044a9]. It is also why any x that is predicated as a substance of some y, even if x actually belongs to the category of accidents, cannot be predicated of y more or less. For example, whiteness is not said to be more or less a colour. For the same reason, abstract qualities too, since they are described in the same manner as are substances, do not become more or less intensive. Something is not said to be more or less *whiteness*, only more or less *white*.

Now neither of these reasons applies to charity and the other infused virtues to prevent them from existing more or less intensively. They are not in their character indivisible in the way that a number is {cf. (α)}. Nor do they give their subject its being as a substance, as the substantial forms do {cf. (β)}. Therefore they *do* exist in a more or less intensive way, to the extent that the subject is brought to actualise them more fully, through the activity of the agent that causes them. That is why just as the acquired virtues are increased by the actions that cause them, so the infused virtues can be increased by the action of God, who is their cause.

Our own actions, too, can be related to the increase of charity and the infused virtues as *tendencies*, in the same way that they make us tend towards receiving charity in the first place. For we can do what is in our own power to prepare ourselves to receive charity from God. Our further actions can be meritorious to the degree that charity increases, because they presuppose charity, which is the basis for meriting anything. But no one can have any merit at all from having received charity in the first place, for without charity we can merit nothing.

In sum, we say that charity can be increased by *becoming more intensive*.

Replies to objections

(1) Just as we talk about 'increase' in charity and the other virtues by analogy, so we talk of 'quantity', as is clear from my reply.

(2) The form does not vary because it is not a subject that varies. However, it can be said to vary in the sense that the subject varies in respect of it, by sharing in it more or less fully.

(3) Changes in something in respect of its essence can be understood in two ways:

(i) with reference to what is distinctive of the thing, that is, what it essentially is or is not. Changes in essence of this sort are simply changes in and out of being, that is, cases of generation and destruction;

(ii) as a change in something that adheres in the essence. For example, we say that a body has in its essence changed its place, because the subject has moved from one place to another. Similarly, we can say that some quality changes in its own way with respect to essence when it varies in degrees of completeness, or rather, when the subject does so in respect of it. This is clear from what I said in my response.

(4) Something that is predicated essentially of charity cannot be predicated of it to a greater or lesser degree: we do not say that it is 'more' or 'less' a virtue. But 'more' charity can be *called* 'more' virtue, because of our way of talking, since we talk about it as if it were a substance. Now since charity is not predicated essentially of its subject, the latter may admit of it to a greater or lesser degree. This is how the subject is said

to 'have more or less' charity. What, then, has more charity, is also more virtuous.

(5) Charity is not decreased, because there is no cause that can decrease it, as Ambrose proves.[31] However, it has a cause that can increase it, i.e. God.

(6) Increase by addition is an increase in a substance characterised by quantity. Charity is not increased in this way, as I said in my reply.

From this, the answer to objection (7) is also clear.

(8) Charity is said to increase or change not because it is *in itself* the subject that changes, but because its subject changes and increases *in respect of it*.

(9) Although God does not vary, things can vary without God's varying. For it is not necessary that everything that changes something else is changed itself, as Aristotle proves [*Phys* 8.5, 256b19]. This is true in particular of God, who acts not by necessity of nature, but by will.

(10) There is one sense in which the idea of size, as I have explained, applies to all qualities and forms alike, that is, with reference to their degree of completeness in their subject. Size or quantity in this sense applies to them *per se*. However, size or quantity in a different sense can also apply to some qualities *per accidens*. This happens in two ways:

(i) by reason of the *subject*. So, for example, whiteness is quantified *per accidens*, because its subject is something of a certain size: if the subject gets bigger, then whiteness is increased *per accidens*. However, this increase only allows us to say that there is more white*ness* there, but not that the thing is whiter. Then we can talk of 'more' white, because we attribute this increase to whiteness in the same way that we attribute it to the subject that is the reason for the whiteness being said, *per accidens*, to increase. This type of quantity and increase, however, does not apply to the qualities of the soul, i.e. to knowledge or virtue;

(ii) quantity and increase can be attributed to a quality *per accidens*, with reference to the *object* on which it acts. This is the sense in which we talk about a 'quantity' of virtue; it is said to be more because of the quantity of its object either (a) understood as *continuous*. For example, someone who is very strong can carry a large weight, or do something great in whatever way (whether that thing is great in the sense of size or degree of completeness); or (b) understood as *discrete*, in the sense that

[31] Cf. *ST* 2a2ae 24.10.

someone who is very strong can do many different things. In this way, quantity can be attributed *per accidens* to the qualities of the soul, i.e. to knowledge and the virtues.

However, there is this difference between knowledge and virtue: since it is not part of the character of knowledge that it *actually* embraces all objects, there is no need for someone knowledgeable to know everything that can be known. However, it is part of the character of virtue that it acts virtuously in every respect. That is why knowledge can be increased or decreased both with respect to the number of its objects {cf. (b)} and with respect to how intensively the subject possesses it {cf. (a)}. However, virtue can be increased only in the second of these ways.

We ought to notice that it is the same character that means that a quality (i') is able to achieve something large; and (ii') is large itself, as is clear from the preceding argument. That is why a large degree of completeness can be described as a large degree of virtue.

(11) A change in charity in the sense of an increase cannot count as an alteration between contrary states, which would only occur in sensible things or in the sensitive part of the soul, but only as an alteration, or passive experience, in the sense that it involves receiving something and being completed. Similarly, feeling and understanding are both passive experiences or alterations. Aristotle distinguishes senses of alteration or passive experience in this way [*Soul* 2.5, 417b5].

(12) God increases charity but not by pouring in fresh charity, rather by making more complete that which is already there.

(13) An act that comes from an agent can cause acquired virtue by impressing active virtue on something that receives it passively, as I argued above. It can increase it in the same way.

(14) Charity and the other infused virtues, as I have argued, are increased by actions as being dispositions and as being meritorious, rather than as being *active*. Moreover, a certain degree of virtue does not have to include completed action that corresponds to it, for it is not necessary for someone who possesses charity always to act in accordance with the full potential of charity. For our use of our dispositions is subject to our will.

(15) (i) The character of virtue does not consist in being the best of its kind in itself, but with reference to its object. For it is through virtue that someone is ordered towards the upper limit of his capacity, that is towards doing things well. That is why Aristotle says [*Phys* 7.3, 246b2] that virtue is the tendency of something complete towards what is best.

However, someone can be more disposed or less disposed towards what is best; accordingly, he has virtue to a greater or lesser degree.

(ii) Or perhaps we should say that 'upper limit' is not meant absolutely, but as 'upper limit of its kind'. For example, within their types, fire is the lightest, i.e. of physical bodies, and human beings are the finest, i.e. of creatures. However, one human being is finer than another.

(16) The character of virtue is not indivisible in itself, but by reason of its object, insofar as it is aiming at the mid-point. People can be disposed to aim at this in different ways, either better or worse. Moreover, the mid-point itself is not altogether indivisible, for it has a certain breadth: it is enough for virtue that it comes near to the mid-point, as Aristotle says [*NE* 2.6.13, 1106b28]. That is why one action can be called more virtuous than another.

(17) The virtue of charity is infinite from the side of God, that is, of its end. However, charity disposes us in a finite way for that which is infinite. That is why there can be more or less of it.

(18) Not everything that is complete in some sense is as complete as possible, but only what is actualised to its upper limit. Therefore nothing prevents something from being complete with respect to virtue, and then being completed still further.[32]

Article 12: Whether the virtues are properly distinguished from one another

Objections

It seems not, because:

(1) Moral activities take their type from their end. Therefore if the virtues are distinguished in type, this should depend on their ends. But this could not depend on their *proximate* end, because the result would be an infinite number of types of virtue. Therefore it must depend on their *ultimate* end. But all the virtues share one ultimate end, that is, God or happiness. Therefore there is only one virtue.

(2) One kind of activity leads to one kind of end. But one kind of activity must depend on one form. Therefore human beings are ordered towards one end by means of one form. But human beings have only a single end,

---

[32] This argument depends on the range of meaning of *perfectus*: see Glossary.

that is, happiness. Therefore there is only one virtue, because it is the form through which human beings are ordered towards happiness.

(3) Forms and accidents are numerically distinct because of their matter or subject. But the subject of a virtue is the soul, or one of its capacities. Therefore it seems that there is only one virtue, because we have only one soul; or at least, the number of virtues should not exceed the number of capacities in the soul.

(4) Dispositions, like capacities, are distinguished by their object. Since, then, the virtues are dispositions, it seems that we ought to characterise differences among the virtues and the capacities of the soul in the same way. Consequently, the number of virtues should not exceed that of the capacities of the soul.

(5) *Rejoinder*: dispositions are distinguished not by the capacities to which they belong, but by their actions. *But on the other hand* whatever is based on a principle is distinguished according to that principle and not vice versa; for the unity of a thing has the same source as its being what it is. But dispositions are the principles of actions. Therefore actions should be distinguished according to dispositions rather than vice versa.

(6) Virtue is necessary for someone to incline in a natural manner to virtuous behaviour. For virtue, as Cicero says [*Inv* 2.53], is a disposition agreeing with reason in a natural manner. Therefore we do not need virtue to achieve whatever our own capacities naturally incline towards. But human will naturally inclines towards its ultimate end. Therefore we do not need any virtuous dispositions with respect to our ultimate end. That is why the philosophers did not posit virtues that had happiness as their object. Therefore neither ought we to posit any theological virtues, because they have as their object God, who is the ultimate end.

(7) Virtue is a tendency of something complete towards what is best [*Phys* 7.3, 246b2]. However, faith and hope imply something that is not complete, for faith is about what is not yet seen, and hope about what is not yet grasped. That is why 'When what is complete comes, what is in part will pass away', as 1 Corinthians 13:10 puts it. Therefore faith and hope ought not to be posited as virtues.

(8) No one can be ordered towards God except through his intelligence and his feelings. But faith is enough to order the human intelligence towards God, and charity the feelings. Therefore hope is not needed as a theological virtue on top of faith and charity.

(9) If something is shared generally by all the virtues, it should not be posited as a special virtue. But charity seems to be shared by all the virtues: Augustine says [*MorCath* 15.25] that virtue is nothing but the order of love; also, charity is said to be the form of all the virtues. Therefore it should not be posited as one particular kind of theological virtue.

(10) In God we need to consider more than just the truth to which faith relates, the exaltedness to which hope relates, and the goodness to which charity relates. God also has many other attributes, for example, wisdom, power, and so on. Since all these attributes are one in God, it seems that there should be only one theological virtue. Or else, there should be as many theological virtues as there are attributes of God.

(11) A theological virtue is one the activity of which is ordered directly towards God. But there are several other virtues of which this is true: for example, wisdom, which contemplates God, and fear, which gives him reverence, and piety which worships him. Therefore there are more than three theological virtues.

(12) The end provides the reason for things that contribute to the end. Therefore once you possess the theological virtues, which enable someone to be rightly ordered towards God, it seems superfluous to posit any other virtues.

(13) Virtue is ordered towards what is good. For virtue is what makes both its possessor and what he does something good [*NE* 2.6.2, 1106a17]. But only the will and the desiring part concern what is good. Consequently, it seems as if there are no other, i.e. no intellectual, virtues.

(14) Practical wisdom is a kind of intellectual virtue. However, it is classed among the moral virtues. Therefore it seems that the moral virtues are not to be distinguished from the intellectual.

(15) Moral knowledge has to do only with moral matters. However, moral knowledge has to do with the intellectual virtues. Therefore the intellectual virtues are moral.

(16) If A is included in the definition of B, then A is not distinguished from B. But practical wisdom is included in the definition of moral virtue; for moral virtue is a disposition connected with choice, consisting in a midpoint that is determined in accordance with right reason, as Aristotle says [*NE* 2.6.15 1107a1]; for right reason about what is to be done is practical wisdom, as Aristotle also says [*NE* 6.5.6, 1140b21]. Therefore the moral virtues are not distinguished from practical wisdom.

(17) Just as practical wisdom is a part of practical knowledge, so also is skill. But in addition to skill there are in the desiring part no further dispositions that are ordered towards skilful activities. Therefore by parallel reasoning, in addition to practical wisdom there are no further virtuous dispositions in the desire that are ordered towards practical activities. Consequently, it seems that there are no other moral virtues that are distinct from practical wisdom.

(18) *Rejoinder*: the reason that there is no virtue in the desire that corresponds to skill is that desire aims at one specific object, whereas skill aims at universals. *But on the other hand* Aristotle says [*Rhet* 2.4, 1382a4] that anger is always about something specific, but hate is also of universals: for we hate every class of robber. But hate is a part of desire. Therefore desire can function in respect of universals.

(19) Each capacity naturally aims at its own object. The object of the desire, however, is the good that is apprehended: desire naturally inclines towards the good because it has apprehended it. But practical wisdom is adequate to complete us for apprehending what is good. Therefore we do not need any other moral virtues in our desire apart from practical wisdom, since our natural inclination is adequate for all this.

(20) Awareness and activity are adequate for virtue. But we have both of these through practical wisdom. Therefore we should not posit any other moral virtues apart from practical wisdom.

(21) Just as dispositions of our desire are distinguished by their objects, so are dispositions of our cognitive powers. But in moral matters there is only one such cognitive disposition, or kind of moral knowledge, for all moral questions (and also practical wisdom).[33] Therefore there is only one moral virtue in the desire.

(22) Things that agree in form and differ only in matter are of the same type. But all the moral virtues agree in their formal element, because they all have a mid-point that is given by right reason. Therefore they differ only in their matter. Therefore they do not differ in type, but only numerically.

(23) Things that are different in type are not described in terms of one other. However, the moral virtues are described in terms of one other. For, as Augustine says [*Trin* 6.1.4], justice ought to be brave and temperate,

---

[33] The text is puzzling here: 'and also practical wisdom' looks like an afterthought or interpolation.

and temperateness ought to be just and brave, and so on for the rest. Therefore the virtues are not distinguished from each other.

(24) The theological and the intellectual virtues are more fundamental than the moral virtues. But neither the intellectual virtues nor the theological are called 'cardinal'. Therefore neither ought any of the moral virtues to be called 'cardinal', as if they are fundamental virtues.

(25) There are held to be three parts of the soul, the rational, the aggressive, and the sensual. Therefore if there are more fundamental virtues than one, it seems that there should be only three.

(26) Other virtues seem to be more fundamental than {the so-called 'cardinal' ones}, for example greatness of spirit, which achieves great things in all the virtues, as Aristotle says [*NE* 4.3.14, 1123b30]; or humility, which is the guardian of the virtues; gentleness, too, seems to be more fundamental than courage, since it concerns anger, which gives its name to the aggressive part. Again, liberality and magnificence, which give of what belongs to them, seem to be more fundamental than justice, which restores to others what is owed to them. Therefore it seems that other virtues than those usually so described are in fact cardinal.

(27) A part is not distinct from its whole. But Cicero [*Inv* 2.53–4] classes the other virtues as parts of these four, i.e. practical wisdom, justice, courage, and temperateness. Therefore the other moral virtues, at least, are not distinguished from these. Therefore it seems that it is not appropriate to distinguish the virtues in the usual way.

But on the other hand

1 Corinthians 13:13 says, 'Now, however, there remain faith, hope, and charity, these three', and according to Wisdom 8:7, 'It teaches soberness and practical wisdom, and justice and courage.'

My reply

Things are classed by type according to their *formal* element. But the formal element in something is what completes its definition, since it is its ultimate distinguishing feature that constitutes its type; hence it is through that that the defined item differs in type from other things. Now if that distinguishing feature can itself in respect of its form be divided according to its diverse characteristics, then the defined item

84

will be divided into diverse types that correspond to the diversity of the distinguishing feature.

The element that completes the definition of virtue and is its ultimate formal element is *goodness*. For virtue understood in the general sense is defined as follows: virtue is what makes its possessor good and what he does good, as Aristotle says [*NE* 2.6.2, 1106a17]. That is why human virtue, of which we are speaking, ought to be split into diverse types to correspond to the diverse characters of goodness that it possesses. Now since human beings are human insofar as they are rational, what counts as a human good must be the good of something that is in some way rational. But the rational, or intelligent, part includes both (i) the cognitive and (ii) the desiring parts. Again, two sorts of desire come under reason: (a) the will, which is naturally found in the rational part and follows the perceptions of reason; and (b) the desire that is found in our sensory part and is divided into the aggressive and the sensual. For in a human being this second desire too follows the perception of reason insofar as it obeys the commands of reason; in this way it is said to participate, in some sense, in reason. Therefore human goods are goods of both the cognitive part and the desiring parts.

However, a good is not attributed to each part under the same characterisation. It is attributed to the desiring part in a *formal* sense, in that the good itself is the object at which this part aims {cf. (ii)}. However, it is attributed to the intelligent part not in a formal but only in a *material* sense, since knowing the truth is a sort of good for the cognitive part {cf. (i)}; *qua* good, though, it is related to the desiring rather than to the cognitive part, since knowing the truth is itself something desirable.

Therefore the *virtues* that complete the cognitive part for knowing the truth and those that complete the desiring part for seeking the good must have different characters. That is why Aristotle distinguishes [*NE* 1.13.19, 1103a5] the intellectual from the moral virtues. The *intellectual* are described as completing the intelligent part to know the truth and the *moral* as completing the desiring part to seek the good.

It is because goodness is more closely connected with the desiring than with the intelligent part that the name of virtue is more generally and more strictly used of the virtues of the desiring part than those of the intelligent part. However, as kinds of completeness, the intellectual virtues are more excellent than the moral virtues, as Aristotle proves [*NE* 6.7.3, 1141a20].

To sub-divide further: (1) *knowledge of the truth* does not have the same character in respect of everything. For example, (i) *necessary* and (ii) *contingent* practical truths are known under a different characterisation. Again, the same is true of (ia) necessary truths *known in themselves*, in the way that the first principles are known by *intelligence*, and (ib) necessary truths *known from something else*, like the conclusions known by *knowledge*, or *wisdom* about the highest truths. In such cases the character of knowing is different, precisely because we are led to know different things by these different faculties of knowing.

(ii) In the same way, in *contingent* practical matters the character of knowing how to do things is different (iia) for things that are *in us* and (iib) for things that are *outside us*. (iia) In the first case, i.e. where we act and the activity is ours, we can often make mistakes due to our emotions. *Practical wisdom* deals with these. (iib) In the second case, i.e. where we make things and *skill* is responsible, the soul's emotions do not corrupt our good judgement.

Because of all this, Aristotle [*NE* 6.3.1, 1139b17] posits intellectual virtues, i.e. wisdom, knowledge, intelligence, practical wisdom, and skill.

(2) Again, the good of the *desiring* part does not have the same character in all human matters. Its good is sought in these three domains: (i) in the emotions of the *aggressive* part; (ii) in the emotions of the *sensual* part; and (iii) in those activities of ours that deal with *external* things that we happen to use, activities such as buying and selling, renting and letting, and so on.

Human good is found in the emotions, where we are so disposed that the force of our emotions does not divert us from the judgement of reason. Therefore if there are some emotions that are apt by nature to hinder the good of reason by arousing us to action or to the pursuit of some goal, then in this the good of virtue will particularly consist in restraining us and holding us back {cf. (ii)}. This clearly happens with *temperateness*, which restrains and curbs the sensual desires. On the other hand, if an emotion is apt by nature to hinder the good of reason by pulling it back, as fear does, then the good of reason in relation to this emotion will consist in supporting reason {cf. (i)}. This is what *courage* does. In respect of external matters, the good of reason consists in accepting a fair share in whatever is part of a shared human life {cf. (iii)}. That is why it is given the name of *justice*, because its job is to give guidance and discover what is fair in this area.

86

(3) We need to consider too that the good of the intelligent part is double, just like the good of the desiring part. There is the good that is the ultimate end and the good that contributes to the end. The character of each is different. That is why we need other virtues besides those we have discussed, which will enable us to pursue the goods that contribute to the end. The additional virtues make us relate well to our ultimate end, which is God. That is why they are called the *theological* virtues, because they have God not only as their final end but also as the *object* at which they are aiming.

Now in order to be moved as we should towards our end we need both (i) to *know* and (ii) to *long for* the end. Longing for the end requires two things: (a) *trust* that we will obtain it, since no wise person is moved to pursue something that he cannot achieve; and (b) *love* of the end, because you only long for things that you love. Consequently there are three theological virtues, i.e. *faith*, by which we know God; *hope*, by which we hope that we will attain him; and *charity*, by which we love him.

From all this, then, it is clear that there are three classes of virtue – theological, intellectual, and moral – and that each class contains within it several types.

Replies to objections

(1) Moral activities take their type from their proximate ends. However, these are not infinite if you look only at the distinguishing features of their forms. For the proximate ends of the virtues are the goods which they each achieve, which differ in their characters in the way I have explained.

(2) This reasoning holds good where things act by natural necessity, because they achieve their end with a single form by performing a single kind of action. Human beings, however, possess reason because they need to reach their own end through many different things; that is why they need several different virtues.

(3) Within a single thing, accidents or forms are not multiplied numerically, but only according to their type. That is why we ought not to work out whether there are one or more virtues from the subject, which is the soul or its capacities; that is, except insofar as the different characterisations of good follow the diversity of the capacities. At any rate, it is those characterisations that provide the criteria for distinguishing the virtues, as I have said.

(4) Something is an object of a capacity and of a disposition under different characterisations. For a capacity enables us simply to do something, e.g. be angry or trust. A disposition enables us to do something *well or badly*, as Aristotle says [*NE* 2.5.2, 1105b27]. Therefore, a difference in something's characterisation as a good will make it a different object from the point of view of the disposition, though not from the point of view of the capacity. That is why one capacity turns out to possess several dispositions.

(5) Just because A is the final cause of B, it does not mean that B cannot be the efficient cause of A. Medicine, for example, is the efficient cause of health, while health is the final cause of medicine, as Aristotle says [*NE* 1.7.1, 1097a20]. Dispositions, then, are the efficient causes of acts; but acts are the final causes of dispositions. That is how dispositions are distinguished in a formal sense by their acts.

(6) With respect to the end that corresponds to human nature, our natural inclinations are enough to put us in the right condition. That is why the philosophers do not posit any virtues which have happiness as their object, or discuss these themselves. We, however, hope for blessedness in an end that exceeds the abilities of our nature, that is, in God. That is why, on top of our natural inclinations, we also need virtues that allow us to be raised to our ultimate end.

(7) To reach God in any way at all, even incompletely, belongs to a higher state of completeness than does obtaining things other than God in a complete way. That is why Aristotle can say [*PA* 1.5, 644b33] that the little that we see of the higher beings is more valuable than the lot that we know of other things. Therefore nothing prevents faith and hope from being virtues, even though we reach God only incompletely through them.

(8) Our feelings are ordered towards God through hope insofar as we *trust* in God and through charity insofar as we *love* him.

(9) Love is the principle and root of all the feelings. For we only rejoice when we encounter something good insofar as we love it. The same is obvious for all other feelings. Therefore every virtue that orders any emotion also orders love. But it does not follow from this that charity, which is love, is not a particular virtue. It ought, though, to be the principle of all the other virtues in this sense, in that it moves them all towards its own end.

(10) We do not need to have theological virtues that correspond to all the divine attributes, but only to those which move our *desire* as their end. That is why there are three theological virtues, as I have explained.

(11) *Piety* has God for its end; however, its object, rather than God, is whatever is offered in worshipping him. That is why it is not a theological virtue. Similarly, *wisdom*, which allows us now to contemplate God, does not look directly at God himself; rather, at the present time, we contemplate him through what he brings about. *Fear* looks at something other than God as its object, for example, punishment, or our own insignificance; by thinking on such things, we are able to submit ourselves with reverence to God.

(12) Just as in theoretical matters there are principles and conclusions, so in practical matters there are ends and things that contribute to the end. In order to acquire a complete awareness that is readily accessible, it is not enough just to relate properly, through the virtue of *intelligence*, to the principles of knowledge; one also needs the virtue of *knowledge* with respect to the conclusions. Similarly, in practical matters we need not only the theological virtues, which make us properly disposed to the ultimate end, but also other virtues, which order us properly towards whatever contributes to the end.

(13) Although the good *qua* good is the object of the virtues of the desire, and not of the virtues of the intelligence, yet something that is good can be found also in the intelligence. For knowing the truth is a kind of good. In this way, the dispositions that complete the intelligence to know the truth possess the character of virtue.

(14) Practical wisdom is, according to its essence, an intellectual virtue, but the matter it deals with is moral. That is why it is sometimes included among the moral virtues and sometimes as a mediator between the intellectual and the moral virtues.

(15) Although the intellectual virtues are distinguished from the moral virtues, they still belong to moral knowledge insofar as their activities are subject to the will. For we use knowledge and the other intellectual virtues when we want to do so. And something is called 'moral' because it is in some way within the scope of the will.

(16) The right reason of practical wisdom is not included in the definition of moral virtue as something that is part of its essence, but rather as a sort of efficient cause of it, in the sense that moral virtue participates

in it. For moral virtue is nothing other than a kind of participation of the desiring part in right reason, as we said above.

(17) The matter with which skills deal is things that are made *externally*; the matter of practical wisdom is things that are done *in us*. Just as skill requires a certain correctness in external things, because it organises them in accordance with a specific form, so practical wisdom requires the correct tendency of our emotions and feelings. That is why practical wisdom needs other moral dispositions in the desiring part, but skill does not.

We accept objection (18). For the desire of the intelligent part, that is, the will, can be for the universal good, which is grasped through the intelligence. This is not true, however, of the desire found in the sensory part because the senses do not grasp the universal.

(19) The desire does indeed naturally move towards the good that is apprehended. However, it needs some virtuous disposition in the desiring part in order to incline in an easy way towards the good that is pursued by reason, by means of a perfected practical wisdom. This is particularly so where true reason is deliberating and proving something good, while the desires are naturally and in themselves drawn in the opposite direction. For example, the sensual part is apt by nature to be attracted to sensual pleasures, and the aggressive part to vengeance; however, sometimes reason, after deliberation, forbids these things. Similarly, the will is apt by nature to seek for itself, for the necessities of life, whatever is available for human use. Sometimes, however, reason deliberates and commands that such things should be shared with someone else. That is why it is necessary to posit virtuous dispositions in the desiring part, so that it may obey reason with ease.

(20) Awareness relates directly to practical wisdom; however, activity relates to it indirectly, mediated by the virtues of the desiring part. That is why we need also to posit certain dispositions in the desiring power, and these are called moral virtues.

(21) In all moral matters (i) what is *true* has a single character, since in all moral matters the true is a contingent possible action; however, (ii) what is *good*, which is the object of virtue, does not have a single character. Therefore there is only one cognitive disposition for all moral matters, but more than one moral virtue.

(22) The mid-point is found in different ways in different domains of moral concern. Consequently, such differences in the matter of the moral

virtues cause differences of form, in keeping with which the moral virtues will differ in type.

(23) Some particular moral virtues, which are concerned with a particular domain, take on themselves what is common to every other virtue, and the other virtues are described in terms of them also. This is because something that is common to them all can be particularly difficult and praiseworthy in the context of a specific matter. For it is clear that every virtue (i) needs its actions to be modified according to due circumstances (for it needs to fit the mid-point for these); and (ii) is directed in an ordered way towards its end, or towards something external; and (iii) has some stability. For to act steadily is one of the criteria for virtue, as is clear from Aristotle [*NE* 2.4.3, 1105a35].

Now to persist stably is particularly difficult and praiseworthy where there is danger of death. That is why the virtue which has this as its matter wins the name of *courage* {cf. (iii)}. To hold back is particularly difficult and praiseworthy in the area of things pleasurable to touch. That is why the virtue that deals with this matter is called *temperateness* {cf. (i)}. In the use of external things, what is particularly needed and praiseworthy is correctness, because people use goods of this sort to share their lives together. That is why this is the good at which virtue aims in this area, because here we relate to others directly according to a kind of equality in respect of such goods. Because of this, the virtue in this area is called *justice* {cf. (ii)}.[34]

Therefore when we talk about the virtues, we use the names of courage and temperateness and justice not in the sense of particular virtues relating to a specific matter, but in the sense of those shared characteristics by which they may be described. That is why temperateness may be called 'courageous', i.e. having a certain stability, or courage may be called 'temperate', i.e. preserving a limit; the same reasoning applies to the other cases.

As regards practical wisdom, it is clear that it is in one sense general, in that it has all moral questions as its own domain, and in that all the moral virtues participate in it in some way, as I have shown. That is the reason why all moral virtue can be described as 'practically wise'.

---

[34] *Fortitudo* (courage) is literally 'strength' and *temperantia* (temperateness) literally 'restraint'. *Iustitia* (justice) is related to the verb *iungo*, 'to join together'.

(24) A virtue is called 'cardinal', i.e. fundamental, because other virtues depend upon it as a door does on a hinge {Latin: *cardo*}. And since a door is an entrance to a house, the *theological* virtues do not possess the character of cardinal virtues, since they are concerned with the ultimate end, and there is no way to move from the ultimate end and enter anything else. It suits the theological virtues that the other virtues rest on them as a solid base. That is why faith is called a 'foundation' in 1 Corinthians 3:11: 'For no one can make any foundation except the one already established'; while hope is called an 'anchor' in Hebrews 6:19: 'We have hope as the anchor of the soul'; again, Ephesians 3:17 describes charity as a 'root': 'rooted in and founded upon charity'.

Similarly, the *intellectual* virtues are not called 'cardinal', because some of them complete us for the *contemplative* life, for example, wisdom, knowledge, and intelligence. That life, though, is an end, and therefore does not have the character of a door. (The *active* life, by contrast, for which the *moral* virtues complete us, is like a door to the contemplative life.) *Skill* does not have virtues that are dependent upon it, and therefore cannot be called 'cardinal'. However, *practical wisdom*, which gives guidance in the active life, is counted among the cardinal virtues.

(25) In the rational part are found (i) a power of desire, which is called the will, and (ii) a power of apprehension, which is called reason. That is why there are two cardinal virtues in the rational part, *practical wisdom*, which belongs to reason, and *justice*, which belongs to the will. Then (iii) in the sensual part, there is *temperateness*, and (iv) in the aggressive part, *courage*.

(26) For each domain there ought to be a *cardinal* virtue that deals with whatever is most important in it. There are, however, virtues that deal with other elements of the matter, and they are called *secondary*, or additional, virtues.

For example, among the emotions of the *sensual* part, the principal ones are the sensual desires and the pleasures that come from touch, and temperateness deals with these. That is why *temperateness* is posited as the cardinal virtue in this domain. However, playfulness, which concerns the pleasure we get from playing games, can be classed as a secondary or additional virtue.

Again, among the emotions of the *aggressive* part, the most important concerns fear and daring in the face of mortal danger, which is the province of courage. That is why *courage* is posited as the cardinal virtue in the aggressive part. Gentleness, which deals with anger, is not, even though anger gives its name to this part of the soul because it is the last of its emotions.[35] Neither are greatness of spirit or humility cardinal virtues, relating as they do in some way to hoping and trusting in something great. The reason is that anger and hope do not affect us as deeply as the fear of death does.

Thirdly, in actions that relate to those *external* things that we use for living, the first and most important thing is that everyone is given what is his due. *Justice* ensures that. Indeed, if justice is not done, then there is no place for liberality or magnificence. That is why justice is the cardinal virtue and the others are additional.

Finally, in *rational* activity, the most important thing is to give instructions or to decide, and that is what *practical wisdom* does. For the part that consults, where good counsel is in charge, and judgement about the advice given, where good sense is in charge, are both ordered towards these. That is why practical wisdom is the cardinal virtue, and the others are additional.

(27) The other virtues that are additional and secondary are classed as parts of the cardinal virtues, but they are not integral or subjective parts of them since they have their own specific matter and their own activity. They are potential parts, as it were, in that they participate in a limited and imperfect way in the measure that belongs chiefly and completely to the cardinal virtues.[36]

Article 13: Whether virtue is found in a mid-point

Objections

It seems not, because:

(1) Aristotle says [*Heav* 1.11, 281a15], that virtue is the upper limit of a capacity. But an upper limit is not a mid-point but rather an extreme. Therefore virtue does not lie in a mid-point but in an extreme.

---

[35] See *ST* 1a2ae 25.4 ad 1: anger arises after other emotions of the aggressive part, e.g. hope and fear, and thus gives its name, *ira*, to the aggressive part, *irascibilis*.

[36] Integral parts are what we would ordinarily call parts: components or constituents. Subjective parts are species within a genus (for example, ox and lion are subjective parts of animal) or individuals within a species (for example, Socrates and Plato are subjective parts of human being). Aquinas's point here is that the secondary virtues are neither components nor subspecies of the cardinal virtues. Rather, they are what he calls potential parts: associated virtues that deal with matters closely related to the principal virtue but do not fully meet the definition of the principal virtue.

(2) Virtue has the character of something good: for it is a good quality, as Augustine says.[37] But good has the character of an end, because it is an upper limit, and therefore an extreme. Therefore virtue lies in an extreme rather than in a mid-point.

(3) Good is contrary to evil, and there is a mid-point between them that is neither good nor evil, as Aristotle argues [*Cat* 10, 12a25]. Therefore goodness has the character of an extreme. Thus, virtue, which makes its possessor good and what he does good [*NE* 2.6.2, 1106a17], does not lie in a mid-point, but in an extreme.

(4) Virtue is the good of reason, for what is virtuous is what accords with reason. However, reason is not in human beings as a mid-point, but as a pinnacle. Therefore the character of a mid-point does not fit virtue.

(5) All virtue is either theological or intellectual or moral, as is clear from what I have already said.

(i) Now *theological* virtue does not lie in a mid-point, because, as Bernard says [*LovGod* 1], the measure of charity is not to have a measure. Charity, though, is the chief of the theological virtues and their root.

(ii) Similarly, the character of a mid-point does not seem to fit the *intellectual* virtues. For a mid-point is between two contrary things. But things are not contraries insofar as they are in the intelligence, nor is the intelligence damaged by understanding something outstandingly good, as Aristotle says [*Soul* 3.4, 429b3].

(iii) Similarly, the *moral* virtues do not seem to lie in a mid-point. For some of them consist in a maximum: courage, for example, concerns the greatest of dangers, the danger of death; magnanimity concerns great honours; magnificence concerns great expenses; filial duty concerns the very great respect that is owed to parents, whom we can never adequately repay; similarly, piety deals with what is great in the worship of God, to whom we cannot give too much service. Therefore virtue does not lie in a mid-point.

(6) If the character of virtue is found in a mid-point, then more elevated virtues ought to come closer to the mid-point. Virginity and poverty are more elevated virtues, because they count as counsels, which have to be concerned with a higher good. Therefore it would follow that virginity and poverty lie in a mid-point. That seems false, because virginity consists of completely abstaining from its relevant matter, i.e. erotic love, and so

---

[37] See note 7.

it is an extreme; similarly, with poverty and its matter, i.e. possessions, since it renounces them completely. Therefore it does not seem to be part of the character of virtue to consist in a mid-point.

(7) Boethius proposes [*Ar* 2.42 ff.] three senses of 'mid-point':

(i) the *arithmetic* mid-point; for example, 6 is the mid-point between 4 and 8 because it is an equal distance between the two;

(ii) the *geometric* mid-point; for example, 6 is the mid-point between 9 and 4, because 6 is distant from 9 and 4 by the same ratio (namely, 3:2), although not by the same quantity;

(iii) the *harmonic*, or musical, mid-point; for example, 3 is the mid-point between 6 and 2, because the ratio of one extreme to the other {i.e. 6:2}, is the same as the ratio between 3, the difference between 6 and 3 {i.e. 6–3} and 1, the difference between 3 and 2 {i.e. 3–2}.

Virtue preserves none of these three sorts of mid-point. The mid-point of virtue need not be equidistant from extremes, whether measured by quantity {cf. (i)} or by the ratio between either terms {cf. (ii)} or by differences {cf. (iii)}. Therefore virtue is not found in a mid-point.

(8) *Rejoinder*: virtue consists in a mid-point according to *reason*, not one according to the *thing*, which is what Boethius is discussing. *But on the other hand* according to Augustine [*FC* 2.18], virtue is counted among the greatest goods, which no one can misuse. If, then, the good of virtue lies in a mid-point, it ought to be the case that the mid-point of virtue possesses the character of a mid-point to the greatest degree. But the mid-point of the *thing* possesses the character of a mid-point more completely than the mid-point according to *reason*. Therefore the mid-point of virtue is the mid-point of the thing rather than the mid-point of reason.

(9) Moral virtue deals with the emotions and the activities of the soul, which are indivisible. In indivisible things, however, there cannot be extremes or a mid-point. Therefore virtue does not lie in a mid-point.

(10) Aristotle says [*Top* 6.8, 146b17] that when it comes to sensual pleasure, it is better to be doing than to have done, or to be experiencing it than to have experienced it. Now there is a virtue that deals with sensual pleasures, and that is temperateness. Therefore since virtue always seeks something that is better, temperateness will always be seeking the present experience of sensual pleasure. But that is to hold to an extreme, not to a mid-point. Therefore moral virtue does not lie in a mid-point.

(11) We find a mid-point wherever we find less and more. We find less and more, though, also in vices: some people are more lustful or greedy

than others. Therefore in the area of greed or lust, and of the other vices too, we can find a mid-point. Therefore if it is the character of a virtue to be found in a mid-point, it seems that we must find virtue among the vices.

(12) If virtue consists in a mid-point, this can only be in the mid-point between two vices. This cannot be right for every moral virtue, since justice, for instance, is not between two vices, but has only one vice opposed to it: taking more than is yours is vicious, but having something that is yours taken away from you is not. Therefore it is not the character of moral virtue that it lies in a mid-point.

(13) A mid-point is equidistant from extremes. But virtue is not equidistant from extremes. For a courageous person is nearer to a daring one than to a coward, and a liberal person nearer to a prodigal one than to someone tight-fisted, and the same is obvious for the other virtues {cf. *NE* 2.8.6, 1109a1}. Therefore moral virtue does not consist in a mid-point.

(14) You can only cross from one extreme to another by way of the mid-point. If, then, virtue lies in the mid-point, there will be no way to cross from one vice to its opposite except via virtue. It is clear that this is false.

(15) The mid-point and the extremes of something belong to the same class. However, courage and cowardice and daring are not in the same class, because courage is in the class of virtue, while the others are in the class of vice. Therefore courage is not a mid-point between them. The same objection can be made for the other virtues.

(16) In the case of quantities, just as the extremes are indivisible, so is the mid-point. For both the mid-point and the end of a line are points. Therefore if virtue consists in a mid-point, it consists in something indivisible. This also seems to follow from what Aristotle says [*NE* 2.6.14, 1106b30] that it is difficult to be virtuous, just as it is difficult to hit the mark or to find the centre in a circle. If, then, virtue consists in what is indivisible, it seems that virtue cannot be increased or reduced. But that is clearly false.

(17) In things that are indivisible, there is no diversity. Therefore if virtue lies in the mid-point as something indivisible it seems that there can be no diversity in virtue, so that what is virtuous for one person would be virtuous for someone else. That is clearly false, for the same thing may be praised in one person but criticised in another.

(18) Whatever is extended even a little from an indivisible point, e.g. from the centre, is then outside the indivisible point and the centre. If,

then, virtue lies in a mid-point as in something indivisible, it seems that whatever falls away even a little from what is done in the right way is outside virtue. This would mean that we could only act very rarely in accordance with virtue. Therefore virtue does not lie in a mid-point.

But on the other hand

Every virtue is either moral or intellectual or theological. (i) Now *moral* virtue lies in a mid-point. For moral virtue, as Aristotle says [*NE* 2.6.15, 1107a1], is a disposition that chooses, consisting in a mid-point. (ii) *Intellectual* virtue also seems to lie in a mid-point, which is why St Paul says in Romans 12:3, 'Do not be wiser than you ought, but be wise as far as is sober.' (iii) Similarly, *theological* virtue seems to lie in a mid-point, since faith approaches the mid-point between two heresies, as Boethius says [*TwoNat* 7]. Hope is also a mid-point between presumption and despair. Therefore all virtue lies in a mid-point.

My reply

(i) The moral and (ii) the intellectual virtues lie in a mid-point, although in different ways. (iii) The theological virtues, however, do not lie in a mid-point, except maybe contingently.

To make this clear, we need to see that if something has a standard or measure applicable to it, the good of that thing consists in meeting the standard or measure in question. That is why we say that what is good is what is neither more nor less than it should be.

(i) Next we need to note that the domain of the *moral* virtues is human emotions and activity, just as the domain of skill is things that can be made. Now in the area of skill, what is good consists in whatever is made conforming to the measure that the skill in question demands; for skill is the standard for the things that are made. In just the same way, then, in the area of human emotions and activities the limits set by reason identify what is good; for reason is the measure and standard of all human emotions and activities. For since we are human by virtue of possessing reason, what is good for human beings ought to accord with reason. Conversely, when something in human emotions or activity exceeds or falls short of the limits of reason, this is bad.

Therefore since the good for a human being is human virtue, it follows that moral virtue consists in a mid-point between excess and deficiency, taking 'excess', 'deficiency', and 'mid-point' with reference to the standard given by reason.

(ii) Next, the *intellectual* virtues: these are found in the reason, and can be divided into (a) *practical*, i.e. practical wisdom and skill; and (b) *theoretical*, i.e. wisdom, knowledge, and intelligence. Human emotions and activities, or whatever needs to be made, are the matter of the practical virtues, while the matter of the theoretical virtues is necessary things.

Reason is related differently to each of these two. It relates to the things that it puts into effect {cf. (a)} as being *their* standard and measure, as I have said. By contrast, it relates to the things about which it reflects {cf. (b)}, as something that is measured and regulated relates to *its* standard and measure. For the good of our intelligence is what is true, and our intelligence attains that precisely by corresponding to the thing that it understands.

(a) As the moral virtues lie in a mid-point determined by reason, so the same mid-point is relevant to practical reason – the *practical* intellectual virtue in moral matters – to the extent that it finds the mid-point in the area of actions and emotions. Aristotle's definition of moral virtue [*NE* 2.6.15, 1107a1] makes this clear: it is a disposition that chooses, consisting in the mid-point as a wise man would reckon it. Therefore the mid-point for practical wisdom and for moral virtue is the same, but practical wisdom imposes the mid-point, while moral virtue has the mid-point imposed upon it. Similarly, the same correctness belongs to skill, which makes something correctly, and to an artefact that is correctly made.

(b) In the area of the *theoretical* intellectual virtues, the mid-point will be what is actually true, which is grasped to the extent that it matches up to its own measure. This mid-point does not fall between two things that are contrary with respect to the *thing*. The contraries on either side of the mid-point of virtue relate to *what is measured* {i.e. the intelligence} rather than to the *measure* {i.e. the true thing}. The question is: does the thing measured exceed or fail to reach the measure? This is clear from what was said about the moral virtues. Therefore we ought to understand the contraries on either side of the mid-point of the intellectual virtues as contraries with respect to the intelligence.

Aristotle makes clear [*Int* 14, 23b3] that the contraries found in the intelligence are opposites in the sense of affirmation and denial. The mid-point of the theoretical intellectual virtues, i.e. whatever is true, is found between opposing denials and affirmations. For example, it is true to say that something is, if it is, and that it is not when it is not. It will be false by excess to say that something is that is not; false by deficiency to say that it is not when it is. Thus it is only because we find in the intelligence contraries that belong to *it*, distinct from contraries in respect of the *thing*, that we can accept that there are a mid-point and extremes in the intellectual virtues.

(iii) Now it is clear that the *will* has no such contraries belonging to it (except in the sense that it can be ordered to contrary things that it might want). This is because, while the intelligence knows something as it is *in itself*, the will is moved towards something insofar as it is *in the will*. Therefore if there is any virtue in the will that relates to the standard and measure of the will itself, this virtue would not consist in a mid-point. For it cannot have extremes on the part of what is measuring {i.e. the will itself}, but only on the part of what is measured {i.e. the thing wanted}, when *that* exceeds or fails to reach the measure.

Finally, then, the *theological* virtues: these are ordered towards their own matter or object, which is God, by the mediation of the will. It is clear that this is true of charity and hope; we can say the same of faith. For although faith is found in the intelligence, however, it is there through being commanded by the will. For no one believes unless he is willing to.[38] Therefore since God is the standard and measure of the human will, it is clear that the theological virtues do not consist in a mid-point, speaking *per se*. Sometimes, it might happen that one of them consists in a mean for contingent reasons, as I will explain later on.

Replies to objections

(1) The upper limit of a capacity means the furthest that a capacity can extend. This is what is most difficult for it, because it is most difficult to find the mid-point, and easy to fall away from it. That is why virtue is called the upper limit of a capacity, which lies in the mid-point.

(2) What is good possesses the character of an upper limit in relation to the movement of the desire, but not in relation to the matter in which this goodness is instantiated. Therefore it ought to be found in a mid-point with respect to the matter, neither exceeding nor being exceeded by the appropriate standard and measure.

---

[38] By definition, for Aquinas, faith is an intellectual assent brought about not by the compelling character of the thing believed but by the will's choice.

(3) Considered in relation to the *form* that it derives from its measure, virtue has the character of an extreme. In this way it is opposed to what is bad as the formed is to the unformed, or the measured to the unmeasured. On the other hand, considered in relation to the *matter* on which this measure is imposed, virtue does consist in a mid-point.

(4) The argument understands 'pinnacle' and 'mid-point' with reference to the order of the capacities of the soul, not to the relevant matter; it is on the latter that the limit of virtue is set as a kind of mid-point.

(5) (i) Among the *theological* virtues, there is no mid-point, as I have said.

(ii) Among the *intellectual* virtues, there is a mid-point, not between contrary *things* insofar as they are in the intelligence, but between the contraries of affirmation and denial, as I have said.

(iii) As for the *moral* virtues, it is found to be common to all of them that they consist in a mid-point. As for the fact that some of them hit a maximum, they do so in its character as a mid-point, insofar as they hit this maximum by following the standard of reason. For example, brave people deal with the greatest of dangers in a rational way, that is when they ought, as they ought, and for the reasons that they ought. Excess and deficiency apply here with reference not to the quantity of the thing, but to the standard of reason. So, for example, it would be 'excessive' if someone were to face danger at the wrong time or for an inadequate reason; it would be 'deficient' if he failed to face danger when and in the way that he should have done.

(6) Although virginity and poverty are extremes with respect to the *thing*, they fall under a mid-point with respect to *reason*. Virgins abstain from all erotic love for an adequate purpose and in the way that they should. Their purpose is God, and they abstain as they do with pleasure. If, though, they were to abstain for a bad reason, for example, because they hated erotic love in itself, or the idea of having children or a spouse, then this would be an example of the vice of unfeelingness. But to abstain from all erotic love for a proper end is virtuous. Indeed, men who do this in order to devote themselves to warfare for the benefit of their country are praised for their civic virtue.

(7) The types of mid-point laid down by Boethius refer to *things*. For this reason they do not apply to the mid-point of virtue, which is a mid-point according to *reason*. The possible exception is justice, in which there is both a mid-point of the thing and a mid-point of reason, since

its rational mid-point is an arithmetical one when dealing with exchange, and a geometric one when dealing with distribution, as Aristotle makes clear [*NE* 5.4.1–3, 1131b25 ff.; {cf. *ST* 2a2ae 61.2}].

(8) The mid-point belongs to virtue not *qua* mid-point simply speaking, but *qua* mid-point according to reason, since virtue is the good of a human being, and this is to live in accordance with reason. That is why something is not closer to virtue by having to a greater degree the character of a mid-point, but only by being a mid-point *according to reason*.

(9) The emotions and activities of the soul are indivisible *per se*, but divisible *per accidens*, insofar as one can find different degrees in them in respect of different circumstances. It is in this sense that virtue keeps to a mid-point in emotions and activities.

(10) In the case of sensual pleasure, if we say that it is better to be experiencing it than to have experienced it, we use the word 'better' not with reference to the activity of honourable goodness, which is part of virtue, but of pleasurable goodness, which is part of sensual pleasure. For sensual pleasure is something we experience. When the essence of something lies in its actually being experienced, then when it is over, it no longer exists. That is why the good of sensual pleasure consists in present rather than in past experience.

(11) Not every type of mid-point belongs to virtue, but only the mid-point according to reason. This type of mean cannot be found in vices, because by their very character they are outside reason. And so virtue ought not to be found within vice.

(12) Justice fails to hit the mid-point in external things in the case where you take too much for yourself, because your will is not well ordered. Consequently that is an instance of vice. But when something is taken from what belongs to you, that is outside your will. That is why it does not in itself involve you in any disordered vice. But the emotions, with which the other virtues deal, are within us. That is why when excess or deficiency appears in them, it does make the person succumb to vice. That is also why the other moral virtues fall between two vices. Justice, though, does not. However, it does in its own domain hold to a mid-point that in itself belongs to virtue.

(13) The mid-point for a virtue is the mid-point according to *reason*, and not the mid-point of the *thing*. That is why it does not have to be equidistant from each extreme, but rather it should accord with reason.

Thus in cases where the good of reason particularly consists in restraining emotions, virtue comes closer to deficiency than to excess. This is clear in the cases of temperateness and gentleness. But in cases where it is good to go in the direction that emotion is pushing you, virtue is closer to excess, as is clear for courage.

(14) Just as Aristotle says [*Phys* 5.3, 227a7], where something is changing continuously, it changes into a mid-point before it changes into its ultimate state. Thus it is in only in cases where the movement is continuous that it is inevitable for something moving from one extreme to another to go through the mid-point. But a change from a vice to a virtue is not a continuous movement, and neither are changes in the will or the intelligence when they are drawn in different directions. Therefore it is not necessary that something goes through virtue on the way from one vice to another.

(15) Virtue, even if it is a mid-point with respect to the matter in which the mid-point is instantiated, is an extreme with respect to its form, i.e. as being placed in the class of what is good, as Aristotle says [*NE* 2.6.17, 1107a7].

(16) Although the mid-point in which virtue consists is something indivisible, however, virtue can become more or less intensive as someone is better or worse prepared for hitting that indivisible point, just as a bow can be more or less stretched for hitting an indivisible point on the target.

(17) The mid-point of a virtue is not the mid-point of a thing, but the mid-point according to reason, as I have said. This mid-point consists in having things and emotions properly proportional to and measured in accordance with the person. The appropriate measurement is different for different people. What is too much for one person is too little for someone else. That is why what is virtuous is not exactly the same for everyone {cf. *NE* 2.6.5, 1106a32}.

(18) Since the mid-point for a virtue is the mid-point according to reason, we should regard the indivisibility of this mid-point according to reason. But something that involves imperceptible distance such as cannot cause an error is regarded as indivisible according to reason, just as, for example, the earth as a whole is regarded as an indivisible point in relation to the whole of the heavens. That is how the mid-point of virtue has a certain breadth.

We accept what was said under *But on the other hand*, as far as the moral and intellectual virtues go, but not for the theological virtues. For it can happen that faith comes between two heresies; but it does not do so in itself, through its being a virtue. Similarly, we ought to say that hope may be between two extremes, but that is with respect to the tendency of its *subject* towards hoping for the things of heaven, and not in its relation to its *object*.

On Charity

Article 1: Whether charity is something created in the soul or is the Holy Spirit itself

Objections

It seems that charity is not something created in the soul, because:

(1) As Augustine says [*Serm* 15.5], just as the soul is the life of the body, so God is the life of the soul. But the soul is the life of the body without

105

any intermediary. Therefore God is also the life of the soul without any intermediary. Now the life of the soul results from its being in charity, because, to quote 1 John 3:14, 'Someone who does not love, remains in death.' Therefore someone is not in charity by means of an intermediary between God and human beings, but by means of God himself. Therefore charity is not something created in the soul, but God himself.

(2) *Rejoinder*: that comparison focuses on the way that the soul is the life of the body in the sense of moving it, not in the sense of giving it form. *But on the other hand* the more powerful an agent is, the less that the thing it is acting on needs the appropriate tendency. For example, an enormous fire is capable of burning even damp wood. Now God is an agent with infinite power. Therefore if he is the life of the soul in the sense of what moves it to love, it does not seem as if the soul, on its part, needs any created tendency.

(3) There is no mid-point between things that are the same. But the soul that loves God is the same as God, because, as 1 Corinthians 6.17 says, 'Whoever clings to God is one spirit with him.' Therefore no created charity comes as an intermediary between the soul that does the loving and God who is loved.

(4) The love with which we love our neighbour is charity. But the love with which we love our neighbour is God himself. For Augustine says [*Trin* 8.5.10], 'Whoever loves a neighbour, as a result loves love itself. But God is love. Therefore it follows that such a person particularly loves God.' Therefore charity is not something created, but God himself.

(5) *Rejoinder*: God is the love by which we love our neighbour in the sense of the love that *causes* this. *But on the other hand* Augustine says in the same place [*Trin* 8.5.10] and states this explicitly using John's words as his evidence, that brotherly love[1], with which we love one another, not only comes from God, but actually is God. Therefore God is love not only in the sense of causing love, but in the sense of *being* it.

(6) Augustine says [*Trin* 15.5.27–8, 31, 37], 'We will say that charity is called "God" because charity is the very substance that deserves the name of God, rather than because it is a gift of God – that is, in the way that we say of God, "You are my endurance", meaning that endurance comes to us from him. Indeed, "Lord, you are my charity" is not meant in this way; rather "God is charity" is meant in the way that we say, "God is a spirit".'

---

[1] Or 'the love from above'.

Therefore it seems that God is called 'charity' not only as causing it, but also as actually *being* it.

(7) God himself is not known simply by knowing his effects. But God himself is known through knowing brotherly love,[2] as Augustine says [*Trin* 8.5.12]: 'One knows the love by which one loves better than one knows the brother one is loving. See, then, that God can be better known to us than our brother. Embrace love and embrace God in love.' Therefore God is not said to be brotherly love only in the sense of causing it.

(8) *Rejoinder*: when we know brotherly love, we know God as if through his likeness. *But on the other hand* human beings are made in the substance of their own souls in the image and likeness of God. But that likeness is obscured through sin. Therefore all that is needed in order for us to be able to know God in the soul as in his likeness is for sin to be removed; there is no need for anything created to be added to the soul as well.

(9) Everything that is in the soul is either a capacity or an emotion or a disposition, as Aristotle says [*NE* 2.5.1, 1105b20]. But charity is not a capacity of the soul, because then it would be something natural. Nor is it an emotion, because it is not found in the sensory part, where all the emotions are found. Nor is it a disposition, because a disposition is difficult to shift, while it is easy to lose charity, since a single act of mortal sin can achieve this. Therefore charity is not a created thing in the soul.

(10) No created thing possesses infinite power. But charity has infinite power, because it joins things that are infinitely far apart, i.e. God and the soul, and because it merits an infinite good. Therefore charity is not a created thing in the soul.

(11) Every created thing is 'vanity' as Ecclesiastes 1 makes clear. But vanity cannot join anything to truth. Therefore since charity joins us to the first truth, it seems that it cannot be a created thing.

(12) Every created thing is a sort of nature, since it comes under one of the ten categories.[3] Therefore if charity is a created thing in the soul, it seems as if it is a sort of nature. Now it is through charity that we have merit. If charity is something created, it follows that the principle of merit is something natural. That is an error, and agrees with the opinion of Pelagius.[4]

---

[2] Or 'the love from above' (cf. note 1).
[3] The ten categories are the most general, irreducible classes into which all created natures fall.
[4] Aquinas characterises the heresy of Pelagius in his response to this objection.

(13) Human beings are nearer to God in their graced existence than in their natural existence. But God created us in our natural existence without any intermediary. Therefore neither does he use an intermediary, i.e. created charity, for our graced existence.

(14) An agent that acts without an intermediary is more complete than one that acts with an intermediary. But God is the most complete agent. Therefore he acts without an intermediary; therefore he does not use any created intermediary to make the soul just.

(15) A rational creature is more excellent than other creatures. But other creatures achieve their ends without needing anything extra. Therefore rational creatures ought far more to be moved by God to their own end without needing any extra created thing.

(16) *Rejoinder*: a rational creature does not correspond to its own end purely by means of natural things; that is why it needs something extra. *On the other hand* the end for human beings is an infinite good. But no created thing can correspond to an infinite good. Therefore human beings must be ordered towards their end by means of something other than a created good. Therefore charity is not some created thing in the soul.

(17) Just as God is the first light, so he is also the supreme good. But the light that is God is present in the soul, as Psalm 36.9 says about it, 'We will see light in your light.' Therefore the supreme good, which is God, is also present in the soul. But it is goodness through which we love something. Therefore that through which we love is God.

(18) *Rejoinder*: the good that is God is present in the soul not as its *formal* but as its *efficient* cause. *On the other hand* God is pure form. Therefore whatever he is in, he is in it as its form.

(19) Nothing is loved unless it is known, as Augustine says [*Trin* 10.1.1]. Therefore something is lovable insofar as it is knowable. But God is knowable through himself, as the first principle of knowing. Therefore he is lovable through himself. Therefore he is not lovable through some created charity.

(20) Each thing is lovable to the extent that it is good. But God is an infinite good. Therefore he is infinitely lovable. But no created love is infinite. Therefore since those who are in charity love him insofar as he is lovable, it seems that the love by which we love cannot be something created.

(21) God loves everything that exists, as Wisdom 11:24 tells us. But he does not love non-rational creatures by means of something extra added to them. Therefore neither does he do this with rational creatures. In this way, it seems that the charity and grace because of which human beings are loved by God are not some extra created thing added to our souls.

(22) If charity is something created, it must be an accidental quality. However, charity is not an accidental quality, because no accident is of more worth than its subject. But charity is of more worth than nature. Therefore charity is not some created thing in the soul.

(23) As Bernard says, we love God and our neighbour by the same law by which Father and Son love one another. But Father and Son love one another by uncreated love. Therefore we love God by uncreated love.

(24) Whatever brings the dead to life must have infinite power. But charity brings the dead to life, for 1 John 3:14 says, 'We know that we have been carried from death into life, because we love our brothers.' Therefore charity has infinite power. Therefore it is not some created thing.

But on the other hand

Everything that something receives, it receives in the manner appropriate to itself. Therefore if we receive love from God, we must receive it in a finite way, in the manner appropriate to us. But every finite thing is created. Therefore charity in us is a created thing.

My reply

Some people have held (i) that the charity in us, by which we love God and our neighbour, is nothing other than the *Holy Spirit*, as Peter Lombard makes clear [*Sent* 1.17.1.2]. In order to understand their opinion more fully, we need to know that Peter Lombard held that the act of love by which we love God and our neighbour was indeed a created thing in us, just like the acts of the other virtues. However, he held that there was this difference between the acts of charity and those of the other virtues: the Holy Spirit moves the soul towards the acts of the *other* virtues with the mediation of some of those dispositions that we call virtues, while the Spirit moves the soul towards acting with *love* (as Lombard explains [*Sent* 1.17.6.8]) by itself, without the mediation of any disposition. He is persuaded to hold this view both by the exalted nature of charity and by the passages from Augustine quoted in the objections and similar passages. (It would have been absurd, however, to say that the actual act of loving which we experience when we love God and our neighbour is the Holy Spirit.)

The opinion in question, though, cannot stand. For just as natural actions and movements derive from some interior principle (i.e. nature), so voluntary actions ought to derive from some interior principle. Now just as in natural things a natural inclination is called a natural desire, so in rational things the inclination that follows whatever the understanding grasps is an act of the will.

It is indeed possible for a natural thing to be moved in a certain direction by an exterior agent rather than an interior principle, as, for example, when a stone is thrown upwards. A movement or action of this sort, however, which does *not* proceed from an interior principle, cannot possibly be natural, because that would be intrinsically contradictory. Now not even divine power can make contradictory things coexist; therefore not even God can make a stone's moving upwards something natural, as long as that does not derive from an interior principle. He could, of course, give the stone a power that acted as an exterior principle, as it were, to enable it to move upwards in a natural manner. But he could not do this in such a way that the movement would actually be natural without changing the nature of the stone.

Similarly, even God cannot bring it about that a human movement that (whether interior or exterior itself) derives from an external principle is voluntary. That is why all the acts of the will ultimately derive as from their fundamental root from the thing that human beings want by nature, which is their ultimate end. As for the things that contribute to the end, we want these for the sake of the end. Consequently, such acts as exceed the entire natural abilities of human nature can only be voluntary if something interior is added to human nature that can complete the will in such a way that an act of this sort may arise from an interior principle.

If, therefore, acts of charity within someone do not derive from some interior disposition that is added to his natural capacities, but from the movement of the Holy Spirit, then one of two things will follow: either (a) the act of charity is not *voluntary*; but that is impossible, because to love something just is to want it; or (b) it does not *exceed* the abilities of our nature; but that is heretical.

Dismissing that option, then {i.e. (b)},[5] it will follow first (α) that acting with charity is not[6] an act of the *will*; secondly (β) that, if you grant that an action of the will could, like the action of a hand or a foot, come totally from something external, and if the act of charity comes only from an external principle that moves it, it will not be *meritorious*. This is because any agent that acts not in accordance with its own form, but only because it is moved by something else, acts only as an instrument, just as an axe does when the carpenter uses it. Consequently, if the soul acts in a charitable way not through a form of its own, but only because it is moved by some exterior agent, i.e. the Holy Spirit, it will follow that it is only related to this activity in the manner of an instrument. In this case, it will not be up to the person whether to perform this action or not; and therefore the action will not be meritorious. For the only actions that are meritorious are those that are in some sense up to us. As a consequence, all human merit will disappear, because love is the root of merit.

Thirdly, the mistaken conclusion will follow (γ) that someone who is in charity will not be *ready* to act in a charitable way, nor will he act with *pleasure*. For we find pleasure in virtuous activity because our dispositions suit us to this, and make us tend towards this in the manner of a natural inclination. Now acting with charity is something that someone who is in charity does very readily and with great pleasure; moreover, it makes everything else that we do or experience pleasurable.

The only possibility remaining, then, is (ii) that we must possess a *created disposition* of charity which can be the formal principle of an action of love. This does not prevent the Holy Spirit, who is uncreated charity, from dwelling in someone who possesses created charity, moving the soul to a loving action in the way that God moves each thing to those of its actions to which its own form makes it tend. That is how he organises everything in a way that gives delight, since he provides everything with the forms and the powers that make it tend towards the things to which he himself moves it, so that it inclines towards them of its own accord, rather than under compulsion.

---

[5] The structure of the argument is obscure, partly because of the variant reading in this sentence (see following note). I have taken this paragraph and the next to be expanding upon the argument following (a) in the previous paragraph. Readers should be aware that the bracketed numbers and letters are based on editorial interpretation and are not in Aquinas's text.

[6] A variant reading omits 'not'. See previous note.

Replies to objections

(1) God is the life of the soul as its *moving*, not as its *formal* principle.

(2) Indeed, for a moving cause to be effective, it does not need to presuppose a tendency in the subject. However, it does prove the effectiveness of a moving cause if it brings about a strong tendency in the thing that it is moving or affecting. For a powerful fire creates not only a substantial form, but also a strong tendency {to receive this}.[7] Therefore an agent that moves something to act in such a way that it also gives it the form by which it can act is more powerful than one that only moves something to act without giving it the relevant form.

That is why the Holy Spirit, as it is a very powerful moving cause, when it moves us to loving, does so in such a way that it also endows us with the disposition of charity.

(3) The words 'Whoever clings to God becomes one spirit with him' do not refer to being united in *substance*, but to being united in *affection*, such as exists between a lover and a loved one. In this union, the disposition of charity functions as a principle of love rather than as an intermediary between the lover and the loved one. For the action of loving passes directly to God, as the loved one, rather than indirectly through the disposition of charity.

(4) Although the love by which we love our neighbour is God, it is still possible to possess within us, as well as this uncreated love, also a created love, which is the formal means of our loving, as I have said.

(5) God is called love or charity in the sense not only of causing love (which is indeed the way he is called 'hope' or 'endurance'), but also of actually being love. However, this does not prevent us having within us a created love as well as the uncreated love which is what God of his essence is.

This also makes clear the answer to (6).

(7) This authoritative passage presents the same difficulty whether or not one posits a created disposition of charity within us. For when Augustine says that whoever loves a neighbour knows the love by which he loves more than the actual person whom he loves, he seems to mean the actual act of loving. But no one holds that that is something uncreated. Therefore one cannot conclude from this that the love that is known in

---

[7] That is, a powerful fire not only generates more fire (the 'substantial form') but also affects things in such a way that they are more likely to catch fire (the 'strong tendency').

this way is God, but rather that in perceiving the act of loving within us, we are aware that we are in some way sharing within ourselves in God; but this is because God is love, not because he is the actual act of loving that we perceive.

(8) The more perfected a creature becomes, the more it takes on the likeness of God. Now every creature possesses some likeness to God by virtue of being something good. A rational creature, however, is like God in one further respect, in that it is intelligent; and in yet a further respect when it is perfected. That is why God is more clearly perceived in the actions of charity, as in something that bears a closer likeness.

(9) Charity is indeed a disposition, and is difficult to shift. For although it can be lost through sin, someone who possesses charity does not easily tend to sin.

(10) Charity joins us to an infinite good acting not as an efficient, but as a formal, cause. Therefore it is not charity, but rather the *maker* of charity, that needs infinite power. Charity would possess infinite power if human beings were ordered by means of charity towards an infinite good in an infinite way. But this is clearly false: for the manner follows the form of a thing.

(11) A created thing is 'vanity' *qua* coming from nothing, not *qua* being the likeness of God. It is on account of the latter that created charity joins us to the first truth.

(12) The Pelagian heresy holds that the natural principles of a human being are sufficient to merit eternal life. It is not, however, heretical to say that we merit this through something created, which is a 'nature' in the sense of coming under a category. For it is clear that we gain merit through our acts, and since they are created, they come under one of the categories and are in that sense 'natures'.

(13) God created our natural existence without any *efficient* mediating cause, but not without a *formal* mediating cause. For he gave each thing the form that makes it what it is; similarly, he gives graced existence by means of an added form. However, there is a difference, for, as Augustine says [*Serm* 169.11.13], 'The one who created you without you will not justify you without you.' Hence for justification the person who is justified needs to do something, because in this case there is a formal active principle. The same is not true for creation.

(14) Those who act through an intermediary must be less effective at acting if they are using an intermediary because they need to. However, God does not make use of intermediaries when he acts because he needs

the help of any creature. Rather, he uses intermediate agents to preserve the order of things. But if we are talking of an intermediary that is a form, it is clear that the more complete an agent is, the more he is able to bestow a form; for an incomplete agent cannot bestow a form, but only a tendency (which will be weaker, the weaker the agent).

(15) Human beings and other rational creatures are able to achieve a higher end than other creatures. That is why, although they need more in order to achieve this end, they are still more complete. Similarly, someone who is able to gain full health by using a variety of remedies is in a better state than someone who cannot be completely healed, and for that reason only needs a few remedies.

(16) The soul is lifted by means of created charity beyond its natural potential so that it is more fully ordered towards the end than our natural faculties make possible. However, it is not ordered in this way towards attaining God in the fullest sense, in the way that he has the fullest enjoyment of himself. This is the case because no created thing can correspond to God.

(17) Even if the good that is God is present to the soul in itself, it still needs a formal intermediary for the soul to be fully ordered towards him; the need, however, is on the side of the soul not on the side of God.

(18) God is indeed a form that exists independently, but not in such a way that he is joined as its form to anything else.

(19) Let us grant that God can be known in himself by the soul (for this in fact can be questioned). Then he will be loved in himself in the same way that he is known in himself. But then the 'in himself' should be taken to refer to the object, not to the subject, of this love; for God is not loved by the soul on account of anything except himself. However, the soul still needs some formal principle in order to love God completely.

(20) We are not able to love God to the extent that he is lovable. That is why it does not follow that the love, i.e. charity, with which we love God is infinite. This would fail to follow in just the same way if we were talking about love as an *act* rather than as a disposition; yet no one could say that the loving *act* by which we love God is something uncreated.

(21) We need the disposition of charity in us insofar as we love God. That is something that other creatures do not do, although all creatures are loved by God.

(22) No accidental quality is of more worth than its subject in respect of its way of *being*, as a substance is a thing in itself, whereas an accident

is a thing in something else. However, nothing prevents an accident from being of more worth than a substance insofar as it is an *activity* and a *form* of the substance. For then the accident is related to the substance as an actualisation to its capacity, or as something that perfects to something capable of being perfected. It is in this sense that charity is of more worth than the soul.

(23) Although the law by which we love God and our neighbour is uncreated, the thing by which, as a formal cause, we love them, is something created. For the uncreated law is the first standard and measure of our love.

(24) Charity brings back to life those who are spiritually dead as a *formal*, rather than *efficient*, cause. That is why it does not need infinite power. Similarly with Lazarus's soul, which in a formal sense brought Lazarus back to life, in that Lazarus was brought back to life through its union with his body.

Article 2: Whether charity is a virtue

Objections

It seems not, because:

(1) A virtue deals with something difficult, as Aristotle says [*NE* 2.9.2, 1109a25]. But charity does not deal with difficult things. Rather, as Augustine says [*Serm* 70.3], 'Everything that is harsh and daunting, love makes easy and practically nothing.' Therefore charity is not a virtue.

(2) *Rejoinder*: whatever comes under virtue is difficult to *begin*, but easy to *complete*. *On the other hand* at the beginning it is not yet a virtue. If, then, something is only difficult at the beginning, difficult things will not be dealt with by virtue.

(3) What is difficult for virtues happens as a result of things that are contrary to them. For example, it is difficult to preserve temperateness, because of sensual desires that are contrary to it. But charity concerns the highest good, and there is nothing that is contrary to this. Therefore charity deals with something that is difficult neither at the beginning nor at the end.

(4) To have love or affection for something is to want it. But St Paul says in Romans 7:18, 'To want lies with me.' Therefore loving is something that 'lies with' us. Therefore we do not need any virtue of charity for this.

(5) In our minds there is nothing except understanding and desire. It is *faith* that raises the understanding to God, and *hope* that raises the feelings. Therefore we should not posit a third thing, the virtue of charity, to raise the mind to God.

(6) *Rejoinder*: hope *raises*, but does not *join*, the mind to God. Therefore charity is needed to do the joining. *But on the other hand* hope, because it does not join things together, always belongs to something that is still separate. That is why hope is inappropriate for those who are joined to God through enjoying blessedness. Therefore by the same reasoning, if charity joins us to God, it will not be possessed by those who are not yet joined to him, but are still on their journey. Virtue perfects us on our journey; for it is the tendency of something complete towards what is best {*Phys* 7.3, 246b2}. Therefore charity is not a virtue.

(7) Grace is sufficient to join us to God. Therefore we do not need the virtue of charity as a means to join us to God.

(8) Charity is a sort of friendship between human beings and God. However, the philosophers do not include friendships between human beings among the political virtues. Therefore charity towards God should not be included among the theological virtues.

(9) No emotion is a virtue; but love is an emotion. Therefore it is not a virtue.

(10) According to Aristotle [*NE* 2.6.15, 1107a1], virtue lies in a mid-point. But charity does not lie in a mid-point, because you cannot have too much love for God. Therefore charity is not a virtue.

(11) Sin corrupts the feelings more than it does the intelligence, because sin is found in the will, as Augustine said [*TwoSouls* 10–11]. But our intelligence cannot see God directly in himself while we are still on our journey. Therefore neither can our feelings love God directly in himself while we are still on our journey. But to love God in himself is a characteristic of charity. Therefore charity ought not to be numbered among the virtues which perfect us when we are on our journey.

(12) Virtue is the limit of a thing's capacity, as Aristotle says [*Heav* 1.11, 281a15]. But pleasure is the limit relevant to the feelings. Therefore pleasure ought to be a virtue rather than love.

(13) Every virtue has its due measure; that is why Augustine says [*NatGood* 3–4] that sin, which opposes virtue, is an absence of measure, type, and order. However, charity does not have a measure, as Bernard says

[*LovGod* 1]: the measure of charity is to love without measure. Therefore charity is not a virtue.

(14) One virtue is not described by using another, since all the types within a given class are distinguished by means of opposites. However, charity is described by using the other virtues, as 1 Corinthians 13:4 shows: 'Charity is patient and kind.' Therefore charity is not a virtue.

(15) According to Aristotle [*NE* 8.8.5, 1159b3], friendship consists in a sort of equality. But there is the greatest inequality between God and us, as between two things that are infinitely distant. Therefore God cannot have friendship towards us, nor can we towards God. Therefore charity, which implies friendship of this sort, does not seem to be a virtue.

(16) The love of the highest good is natural to us. But nothing natural is a virtue, because the virtues are not in us by nature, as Aristotle makes clear [*NE* 2.1.2, 1103a19]. Therefore love of the highest good, which is charity, is not a virtue.

(17) Love is a finer thing than fear. But fear is fine enough to count as a gift rather than a virtue (a gift, of course, is a finer thing than a virtue). Therefore charity is not a virtue, either, but rather a gift.

But on the other hand

The precepts of the law concern virtuous activities. But the law includes precepts about acting with charity. For Matthew 22:37–8 says that the first and greatest commandment is 'Love the Lord your God.' Therefore charity is a virtue.

My reply

There is no doubt that charity is a virtue: for a virtue is what makes its possessor, and whatever he does, good {*NE* 2.6.2, 1106a17}. It is clear therefore that human beings are ordered towards their distinctive good by a virtue distinctive of them.

Now we need to understand a human being's distinctive good in different ways, corresponding to the different ways we understand a human being:

(i) A human being's distinctive good *qua* human being is the good of reason, because to be a human being is to be a rational being.

(ii) The good of a human being *qua* craftsman is the good of skill. Similarly,

(iii) the good of a human being *qua* political is the common good of the city.

Since, then, virtue works towards the good, for someone to have virtue he must be disposed to work towards the good in a good manner, that is, willingly, readily, with pleasure, and also reliably. Such are the criteria for doing things in a virtuous way; they can only be met where those who are doing something love that good for the sake of which they are doing it. This is because love is the principle of all willing feelings. For when we love something, as long as we do not possess it, we long for it; when we do possess it, we take pleasure in this; anything that gets in the way of our possessing what we love distresses us. Moreover, whatever is done out of love is done reliably and readily and with pleasure. In this way, virtue needs the love of that good which virtue works towards.

Now the virtue of a human being *qua human being* works towards a good that is natural to human beings. That is why there exists naturally in our will the love of this good, which is the good of reason {cf. (i)}. But suppose we take the virtue of a human being under a different aspect, one that is not innate in human beings; then, for virtue of this sort, the love of the good to which virtue directs us will need to be something extra in addition to our natural will. In this way, a *craftsman* will only work well if he also has a love for that good which is the aim of exercising the skill in question {cf. (ii)}. Relatedly, as Aristotle says [*Pol* 8.1, 1337a20], in order to be a good *citizen*, you need to love the good of the city. Now if someone is allowed to share in the good of some city, he becomes its citizen and needs certain virtues for doing what a citizen does, and for loving the good of that city {cf. (iii)}.

In a similar way, when someone is, by divine grace, allowed to share in the blessedness of *heaven*, which consists in seeing and enjoying God, then he becomes a citizen and associate, so to speak, in that blessed society, which is called the heavenly Jerusalem in Ephesians 2:19: 'You are fellow-citizens of the saints and members of the household of God.' That is why someone who is in this way admitted to heavenly things is freely granted certain virtues, which are the *infused* virtues. For these to work as they should, they also require the love of the good of the whole society, that is the divine good; for that is the object of blessedness.

Now there are two senses of loving the good of some city: (i') to possess it; (ii') to preserve it. (i') Loving the good of some city in order to *possess* and to own it does not make a good citizen; that is how a tyrant loves the good of a city, in order to control it. In such a case, in fact, he loves himself more than the city, for he covets this good for himself rather than for the city. (ii') To love the good of a city in order to *preserve* and defend it is to love it in a real sense, and this makes someone a good citizen, in that some people are prepared to subject themselves to the risk of death in order to preserve or increase the city's good, and to ignore their own personal good.

Therefore to love for the purpose of possessing it or owning it that good in which the blessed share does not put someone in the right state for blessedness; indeed even the wicked covet this good. However, to love it in itself, wanting it to remain and spread, and wanting nothing to act against it, does put someone in the right state for the society of the blessed.

This, then, is charity, which loves God for himself and which also loves as themselves those neighbours who are capable of blessedness. It also resists everything that hinders this, whether in itself or in others. That is why it cannot coexist with mortal sin, which is an obstacle to blessedness.

From all this it is clear that charity is not only a virtue, but the most powerful of the virtues.

Replies to objections

(1) Virtue deals with things that are difficult in themselves, but become easy for someone who possesses the relevant virtues.

The answer to (2) is clear from this. The point is not proven. For the matter with which it deals remains difficult *in itself* even when virtue is present; it does, however, becomes easy *for the virtuous person*, thanks to the perfecting power of virtue.

(3) Difficulties arise not only from contrary impulses, but also where the object of the virtue is especially exalted. Similarly, something can be said to be difficult for us to understand with reference to the exalted nature of what is to be understood, rather than for any contradictions in it.

(4) The wanting that 'lies with' us by nature is weak and incomplete with respect to what is given to us freely through the spirit. That is why St Paul adds in the same place, 'For the good that I want I do not do' [Romans 7:19]. That is why we need the help of a freely given gift.

(5) Hope lifts human feelings towards *acquiring* the highest good; on top of this, however, the good of human beings requires us to *love* that good, as I said in my reply.

(6) It is part of the character of charity or love to join things *through feeling*. This type of joining can be understood in the sense in which you think of your friend as 'another yourself', and want the friend's good just as much as your own. However, it is not part of the character of charity to join in the sense of *actually connecting* two things. That is why we can love either something that we have or something that we do not have. When we do not have it, love makes us long for it; when we do have it, love gives us pleasure in having it.

(7) Grace joins us to God by making us like him. However, we still need to be united to him through the actions of our intelligence and feelings, and this happens through charity.

(8) Friendship is not held to be a virtue, but the *result* of a virtue. The reason is that when people possess virtue and love the good of reason, as a result, by virtue's own inclination, they love those who are like them, i.e. other virtuous people, in whom the good of reason flourishes. But friendship towards God, insofar as God is blessed and the cause of blessedness, needs to precede those virtues that order us towards blessedness. That is why, since it does not follow, but comes before, the other virtues, as I have shown, it needs to be a virtue in itself.

(9) Love is an emotion insofar as it is found in our sensory part; then it is love of a sensory good. That type of love, though, is not the love of charity. Therefore the argument does not follow.

(10) Aristotle's statement that virtue lies in a mid-point should be taken to apply to the *moral* virtues. It is not true of the *theological* virtues, which include charity, as I showed previously {*DQVirtGen* 13}.

(11) What moves the will is something understood as good. Now it is true that our intelligence understands God as the highest good only by means of intermediaries. However, by this means God moves the will in such a way that he can be *loved* directly, even though he is *known* through intermediaries. This is because the very things that the intelligence's understanding finds as its goal also move the feelings.

(12) 'Pleasure' does not refer to an activity, but to something that follows from activity. That is why, since virtue is a principle of activity, pleasure is not included among the virtues, but among the fruits of virtue, as is

clear from Galatians 5:22, 'The fruit of the Spirit is charity and joy, peace and endurance.'

(13) The object at which charity aims, i.e. God, transcends every human ability. That is why, however much the human will tries to love God, it will never succeed in loving him as he ought to be loved. As a result, we say that charity has no limit, because there is no fixed limit to the love of God, to overstep which would be against the character of virtue (as does happen with the moral virtues, which lie in a mid-point). Indeed, the measure of charity just is to have no measure, in this sense. Therefore we cannot conclude that charity is not a virtue, but rather that, unlike the moral virtues, it does not consist in a mid-point.

(14) Charity is called 'patient and kind', as if using other virtues to describe it because it brings about the acts performed by the virtues.

(15) Charity is not a virtue of human beings *qua human beings*, but insofar as, by sharing in grace, they become gods and the children of God, in keeping with 1 John 3:1, 'You see what charity the Father has bestowed on us, so that we are called, and have become, the children of God.'

(16) The love of the highest good, insofar as it is a principle of our natural existence, is in us by nature. But, insofar as the highest good is the object enjoyed by a blessedness that surpasses all the abilities of our created nature, it is not in us by nature, but over and above our nature.

(17) The gifts complete the virtues by lifting them beyond human limits; so, for example, the gift of intelligence does this to the virtue of faith, and the gift of fear to the virtue of temperateness (when someone refrains to a degree that surpasses human limits from whatever gives pleasure). But with regard to the love of God there is no shortfall that needs any gift to complete it. That is why love is not counted as a gift, but a virtue; however, it is a virtue that surpasses all the gifts.

Article 3: Whether charity is the form of the virtues

Objections

It seems not, because:

(1) A form gives the thing to which it belongs its being and its type. But charity does not give to each virtue its being and its type. Therefore charity is not the form of the other virtues.

(2) There is no form of a form. But all the virtues are forms, for they perfect things. Therefore charity is not the form of the virtues.

(3) A form is included in the definition of the thing to which it belongs. But charity is not included in the definition of the virtues. Therefore charity is not the form of the virtues.

(4) Things that are distinguished by being opposed are not related in such a way that one is the form of another. But charity is divided from the other virtues by being opposed to them, as is clear from 1 Corinthians 13:13, 'Now, though, there remain faith, hope, and charity, these three.' Therefore charity is not the form of the virtues.

(5) *Rejoinder*: charity is the form of the virtues, not as *intrinsic* to them, but as their *exemplar*. *On the other hand* an exemplar bestows its type on its copies. If charity were the form of the virtues as their exemplar, it would bestow on all the virtues their type. But then all the virtues would be the same in type, which is false.

(6) A form in the sense of exemplar is the basis of something else's coming into being. It is only needed, then, when a thing comes into being. Therefore if charity is the exemplary form of the virtues, it will only be needed for producing the virtues; when we already have them, we will no longer need charity. That is clearly false.

(7) Someone making something needs an exemplar, but not someone using something that is already made. For example, we need an exemplar for transcribing a book, but not for using a book that is already written out. Therefore if charity is the form of the virtues as an exemplar, it should belong not to us, who use the virtues, but rather to God, who makes the virtues in us.

(8) You can have an exemplar without any copies of it. If charity were the exemplary form of the virtues, then, it would follow that it could exist without any of the other virtues, which is false.

(9) Every virtue takes its form from its end and its object. Something that is formed through itself does not need to be given form by something else. Therefore charity is not the form of the virtues.

(10) Nature always makes what is better; how much more, then, does God? But it is better for something to be with form than without it. Since, then, God makes the virtues in us, it seems that he must make them already formed. Therefore they do not need to be given form by charity.

(11) Faith is a certain spiritual light. But light is the form of things that are seen by that light. Therefore just as physical light is the form of

colours, so faith is the form of charity and of the other virtues. Therefore this is not charity.

(12) The order of things that perfect follows the order of the things that are perfected. But the virtues perfect the capacities of the soul. Therefore the order of virtues follows the order of the capacities. But among the capacities of the soul, the intelligence is higher even than the will. Therefore faith is higher than charity; in this way, faith is more a form of charity than vice versa.

(13) The moral virtues are related to one another in the same way as the theological. But practical wisdom, which exists within the power of cognition, gives form to those other virtues that exist within the power of desire, i.e. justice, courage, temperateness, and so on. Therefore so should faith, which is found within our power of cognition, give form to charity, which is found within our power of desire, and not vice versa.

(14) The form of a virtue is its measure. But it is the job of reason to impose measure on desire, and not vice versa. Therefore faith, which is found in reason, should be the form of charity, which is found in the desiring part, rather than vice versa.

(15) On Matthew 1:2, 'Abraham begot Isaac and Isaac begot Jacob', the gloss comments that faith begot hope and hope begot charity. But everything that is begotten receives its form from its begetter. Therefore charity receives its form from faith and hope, and not vice versa.

(16) Within one and the same thing, an actualisation is preceded in time by the related capacity. Therefore if charity is related to the other virtues as their form and actualisation, in one person the other virtues ought to exist before charity does. But that does not happen.

(17) In moral matters, it is the end which gives the form. But all the virtues are ordered, as their ultimate end, towards the vision of God, which is our complete reward (as Augustine says [*Trin* 1.9.18]), and which follows faith. Therefore all the other virtues receive their form from the end proper to faith. Therefore it seems that faith must be the form of charity rather than vice versa.

(18) According to Aristotle [*Phys* 2.7, 198b25], the end, the efficient cause, and the form do not coincide in one and the same thing. But charity is both the end of the virtues and what moves them. Therefore it cannot be their form.

(19) The form is what gives something its principle of being. But the principle of spiritual existence is grace, according to 1 Corinthians 15:10,

'I am what I am by the grace of God.' Therefore the grace of God is the form of the virtues, and not charity.

But on the other hand

Ambrose says [according to *Sent* 3.23.3.2], 'Charity is the form and mother of the virtues.'

My reply

Charity is (i) the form of the virtues, (ii) their moving cause, and (iii) their root.

To prove this we need to know that our actions ought to be judged according to the relevant dispositions. Therefore when something that belongs to one disposition A functions as the formal cause of the actions of another disposition B, then A must be related to B as its form. But in all voluntary action what gives the form is what comes from the end. This is because each action receives its form and type in accordance with the form of the agent, for example, in the case of heating, in accordance with heat. Now the form of the will is its object, which is its good and end (in the way that what is intelligible is the form of the intelligence). Therefore whatever comes from the end ought to give form to the will's actions.

That is why an act of the same type when ordered towards one end may come under the form of a virtue, but when ordered to a different end may come under the form of a vice. The following example makes this clear: you can give alms for the sake of God, or for the sake of conceitedness. Again, the actions of one vice when they are ordered towards the end of another vice receive the form of the second: so, for example, someone who steals in order to fornicate is *materially* speaking a thief, but *formally* speaking intemperate.

It is clear, however, that the acts of all the other virtues are ordered towards the end that is distinctive of charity, which is charity's own object, i.e. the highest good. (a) This is clear with the *moral* virtues, because they deal with created goods, which are themselves ordered towards the uncreated good as their ultimate end. (b) This is also clear with the other *theological* virtues. As concerns faith, uncreated being is its object as something that is true; and that, *qua* something desirable, has the character of a good. In this way, faith directs itself towards its object *qua* desirable, because no one believes unwillingly. As for hope, its object, though it too is uncreated being, depends *qua* something good on the object of charity; for the object of hope is a good *qua* something that can be longed for and attained; and no one longs to pursue a good except because he loves it.

(i) Therefore it is clear that in the case of all the virtues their actions receive their form from charity. To this extent, charity is called the *form* of the virtues.

(ii) This makes it clear how it is also the *end* of all the virtues, in that all the actions of all the virtues are ordered towards the highest good as something loved, as I have shown. Since the precepts of the law concern virtuous actions, St Paul says in 1 Timothy 1:5 that 'the end of the precept is charity'.

(iii) It is also clear from this how charity is the *moving cause* of all the virtues, in that it commands the activities of all the other virtues; for every virtue or higher capacity is said to move a lower power by commanding it, in that the actions of the lower are ordered towards the goal of the higher. For example, the builder gives instructions to the bricklayer, because what is done through the bricklayer's skill is ordered towards the form of the house, and this is the end proper to the skill of the builder. So since all the other virtues are ordered towards the end of charity, charity itself commands the actions of all the virtues, and is therefore called their moving cause.

Because we use the word 'mother' of someone who conceives in herself, we call charity the 'mother' of all the virtues, insofar as it is the end proper to charity that conceives to produce the actions of the other virtues. For the same reason, charity is called the root of all the virtues.

Replies to objections

(1) Although charity does not bestow on each virtue its own distinctive type, it does give each one its *general* type, i.e. its being a virtue (at least now we are talking of virtue as the principle of deserving reward).

(2) There is no form of a form in the sense that one form stands as the subject of another. However, nothing prevents several forms coexisting in one subject if they follow a certain order, so that one is the form of another, as colour is the form of surface. In this way, charity can be the form of the other virtues.

(3) Charity is included in the definition of a meritorious virtue, as is clear from Augustine's definition,[8] which says that virtue is 'a good quality of mind by which we live rightly'. For living rightly must mean living in such a way that our life is ordered towards God, and charity brings this about.

(4) This argument is based on the sort of form that is integral to something's constitution. But charity is not called the form of the virtues in that sense, but in another, as I have explained.

(5) Since charity is the form common to the virtues, it draws the virtues into one *common* type. However, it does not make them all into one *distinctive* type in the strict sense (what is called a 'specific type').

(6) Charity can be described as the exemplary form of the virtues. However, this does not refer to a likeness in accordance with which they are *made*, but rather to their *acting* to some degree in its likeness. That is why, wherever it is necessary for virtuous activity to take place, it is necessary for there to be charity.

(7) Although creating the virtues belongs only to God, doing things in a virtuous way also belongs to human beings who possess virtue. That is why they need charity.

(8) Charity is related to virtuous activity not only as its exemplar, but also as the *effective* power that moves it. There is no effective exemplar without a copy, since the exemplar brings the copy into existence. That is why charity does not exist without the other virtues.

(9) Each virtue receives the form of its *type*, which makes it the virtue that it is, from its own distinctive end and object. But it receives a *general* form from charity, which makes it merit eternal life.

(10) God makes virtues in us that are formed according to both the form of their type and a common form. The former comes from their object and end, the latter from charity.

(11) Light is the form of colours insofar as they are actually visible through light. Similarly, faith is the form of the virtues insofar as they are knowable by us; we recognise through faith what is virtuous and what is contrary to virtue. But insofar as the virtues are something *practical*, they are given their form by charity.

(12) Intelligence is prior to will simply speaking, because the good as understood is the object of the will. However, the will is prior when it

---

[8] See *DQVirtGen* 2, n. 7.

comes to doing and moving. For the intelligence does not move anything unless the will is present. In this way, the will *qua* active moves the intelligence, for we make use of our intelligence when we want to. Hence, since believing is something the intelligence does when it is moved by the will (for we believe something because we are willing to), it follows that charity gives form to faith rather than vice versa.

(13) An act of the will follows the ordering of its agent towards things as they are in themselves. By contrast, an act of the intelligence follows the fact that the things understood are in the agent. Therefore (i) when things are *lower* on the scale than the person who understands them, the understanding of them is more valuable than the will to have them. For in this case, these things are higher on the scale when found in the intelligence than they are in themselves (for anything that exists in something else does so in the manner that that thing exists). However, (ii) when the things in question are *higher* on the scale than the person understanding them, then the will rises higher than the understanding can reach.

That is why in *moral* matters, which are lower on the scale than human beings, a cognitive virtue informs the desiring virtues, as practical wisdom does the other virtues. However, with the *theological* virtues, which concern God, the virtue of the will, i.e. charity, informs the virtue of the intelligence, i.e. faith.

(14) The power of reason provides a limit for the desire in things that are *lower* than us, but not in things that are *higher* than us, as I have explained.

(15) Faith precedes hope and hope precedes charity in the order of *coming into being*, in the way that what is imperfect precedes what is perfect. But in the order of *perfecting*, charity precedes faith and hope. That is why it is called their form, as the thing that perfects what is imperfect.

(16) Charity is not the form of the virtues in the sense of being a part of their *essence*, so that it must follow in time after the other virtues, or rather after some raw material for the virtues, as with the forms of things that come into being. It is their form in the sense that it *gives* them form; therefore it ought naturally to exist before the other virtues.

(17) This very vision, in that it is our end *qua* something good, is the object of charity.

(18) An intrinsic form cannot be the end of a thing, although it can be the end of a thing's coming into being. But charity is not an intrinsic form, as I have said. Rather, it forms the other virtues precisely by drawing them to its own end, as is clear from what I have said.

(19) The grace of God is said to be the form of the virtues in that it gives spiritual *being* to a soul, to make it receptive to virtue. But charity is the form of the virtues in that it gives form to what they *do*, as I said in my reply.

Article 4: Whether charity is a single virtue

Objections

It seems not, because:

(1) Dispositions are distinguished by their actions, and actions by their objects. But charity has two objects: God and neighbour. Therefore it is not one virtue, but two.

(2) *Rejoinder*: one of these objects is primary, i.e. God: for charity only loves a neighbour for the sake of God. *But on the other hand* Aristotle says [*NE* 9.8.7, 1168b9] that friendliness to another arises out of friendliness to oneself. But the preeminent thing in every class is its principle and cause. Therefore out of charity people love themselves as the principal object, and not God.

(3) 1 John 4:20 says, 'If you do not love your brother whom you see, how can you love God, whom you do not see?' Therefore it seems that we ought to love our neighbours more than we ought to love God. Therefore our neighbour is more lovable than God. Therefore our neighbour, rather, seems to be the primary object of charity.

(4) We do not love anything unless we know it, as Augustine says [*Trin* 10.1.1]. But we know our neighbour better than we know God. Therefore we love our neighbour better. Therefore it seems that charity is not a single virtue.

(5) Every virtue has its own distinctive measure, which it sets for its own actions. A just person, for example, not only does just things, but does them in a just way. Charity, however, provides two measures for its actions: for through charity we love God with our whole heart, but our neighbour as ourselves. Therefore charity is not a single virtue.

(6) The precepts of the law are ordered towards the virtues, because a lawmaker intends to make people virtuous, as Aristotle says [*NE* 1.13.2, 1102a8]. But two precepts are given concerning charity, i.e., 'You will love the Lord your God, and you will love your neighbour' [Matt 22:37–9]. Therefore charity is not a single virtue.

(7) Just as we love God and our neighbour, so we ought to honour them. But we honour God in a different way from our neighbour: we honour God with worship and our neighbour only with reverence.[9] Therefore the charity with which we love God is different from that with which we love our neighbour.

(8) Virtue is what enables us to live rightly. But loving God belongs to one sort of life and loving our neighbour to another. For loving God seems to belong to the life of contemplation, and loving our neighbour to the active life. Therefore charity towards God and towards a neighbour are not a single virtue.

(9) According to Aristotle [*Phys* 1.2, 185a21], something is said to be *one* in three ways: (i) by continuity, (ii) by indivisibility, and (iii) in meaning.

(i) But charity is not one by *continuity*, because it is neither a body nor the form of a body.

(ii) Nor is it one through being *indivisible*, because if so it would be neither finite nor infinite.[10]

(iii) Nor is it one in *meaning*, in the way that synonyms are, like 'clothing' and 'garment'. Therefore charity is not a single thing.

(10) Things that are one only in a proportional sense possess the character of oneness in the minimum sense. Consequently, if things are not even one in a proportional sense, then neither are they one in type or class or number, as Aristotle says [*Met* 5.6, 1016b31]. But charity concerns (i) what is eternal, i.e. God, and (ii) one's neighbour, and two such things cannot be proportional. Therefore charity cannot in any way be a single virtue.

(11) According to Aristotle [*NE* 8.3.8, 1156b25; 9.10.4, 1171a4] we cannot have friendship in the full sense with many people. But the charity by which we love God is friendship in the fullest sense. Therefore we cannot have it with many people. Therefore we do not love God and our neighbour with the same sort of charity.

(12) A virtue for which it is enough if its actions do not distress you is different from a virtue which brings pleasure when you do things; so, for example, courage differs from justice. But in acting charitably towards some objects, for example when we love our enemy, it is enough if this

---

[9] The word translated 'reverence' is *dulia*, the standard term for the kind of veneration shown to the saints.

[10] Because what is indivisible has no magnitude and so *a fortiori* has neither finite nor infinite magnitude.

does not distress us. In other cases, we ought actually to take pleasure in it, as when we love God or our friends. Therefore charity is not one single virtue, but different virtues.

But on the other hand

(1) If two things are related so that the one is included in the understanding of the other, then they are one thing. But love of God is included in our understanding of love of neighbour, and vice versa, as Augustine says [*Trin* 8.5.12]. Therefore the charity by which we love God and that by which we love our neighbour is the same.

(2) There is a single first moving cause in every class of things. But charity is what moves all the virtues. Therefore it must be single.

My reply

Charity is a single virtue. To prove this, we need to know that the unity of any capacity or disposition must be seen from its object. This is because the capacity is called the thing that it is from being ordered towards the thing for which it is a capacity, which is its object. Similarly, the character and the type of a capacity are given by its object. The same is true of a disposition, which is nothing other than the perfected tendency of a capacity towards its object.

We can consider the object, however, from the point of view either (i) of its form or (ii) of its matter. (i) The *formal* element in an object is that by which it is related to the relevant capacity or disposition; (ii) the *material* element is what this is grounded in. For example, if we talk about the object of the capacity of sight, its formal object is its colour, or something similar: for a thing is visible insofar as it is coloured. Its material object is the body to which the colour belongs.

This makes it clear that a capacity or a disposition relates *per se* to the formal character of an object, but only *per accidens* to its material element. Accidental attributes do not change what a thing is; only *per se* attributes can do that. That is why when the material object changes, the capacity or disposition does not; it only changes if the formal object does so: the capacity to see is the same whether we are looking at stones or people or the sky. That is because the object changes only *qua* matter, not *qua* form, i.e. what it is to be visible. On the other hand, the senses of taste and smell are different because flavour and scent are different things (though these are both *per se* perceptible).

We ought also to think about the following when it comes to charity. It is clear that I can love you in two senses: (i') for your own sake; (ii') for the sake of someone else. (i') I love you for your *own* sake when I love you for the sake of a good that is yours, for example, because you are honourable in yourself, or else pleasant company for me, or useful to me. (ii') I love you for the sake of *someone else* when I love you because you are connected to someone else whom I love. For when I love him in himself, I also love all his acquaintances, relations, and friends insofar as they are connected to him. In all these matters, however, there is a single *formal* character of love, that is, the good of the person whom we love for his own sake, and whom we love, in some sense, in all those other people.

In this way, we should say that charity loves God for his own sake, and loves other things for the sake of God, insofar as they are ordered towards God. In this way it loves God in some sense in every neighbour, because a neighbour is loved by charity either because God is in him, or so that God may be in him.

From all this, it is clear that it is the same disposition of charity which enables us to love God and our neighbour. But if we were to love our neighbours for their own sake, and not for the sake of God, this would derive from a different sort of love, whether natural or political, or one of the other sorts that Aristotle discusses [*NE* 8.3.2–5, 1156a15 ff.].

Replies to objections

(1) The neighbour is loved only for the sake of God. Therefore *formally* speaking both are a single object of love, though materially speaking they are two.

(2) Since love directs itself towards what is good, love differs as the good differs. Now (i) a human being *qua* individual person has his *own* good, and with respect to the love that looks to this good, each person is his own principal object of love. (ii) There is also a *common* good that relates to one person or another *qua* part of a whole; for example, to a soldier *qua* part of the army, or to a citizen *qua* part of the city. With regard to the love that looks to this good, the principal object of love is whatever the good principally resides in: for example, with an army, the commander, or with a state, the king. Consequently, it is part of the duty

of a good soldier to ignore even his own safety in order to preserve the good of the commander; similarly, you would naturally expose your own arm in order to protect your head.

In this way, charity looks towards divine goodness as its principal object; but that belongs to everyone insofar as they are able to share in blessedness. That is why we love with charity only those that are able to share with us in blessedness, as Augustine says [*CT* 1.35.39].

(3) John reasons from the greater, by negation,[11] not that a neighbour ought to be loved more, but that he is more *easily* loved. For we are more prone to loving what we can see than what we cannot see.

(4) Although we can only love what is known, it does not follow that what is better known is better loved. For something is not loved by reason of being *known*, but by reason of being *good*; that is why something that has more goodness is more to be loved, even if it is not better known. For example, people may love a slave, or even a horse, that they use all the time less than they love a good man of whom they know only by reputation.

(5) Charity looks towards divine goodness as its formal object, as I have argued. This good is differently related to God and to our neighbour. That is why there ought to be a different measure for the primary and the secondary object. But there is only one measure for the principal object.

(6) The precepts of the law deal with virtuous acts but not with dispositions. That is why different precepts do not imply different dispositions, only different acts. The latter, however, relate to one disposition because of their formal character.

(7) We honour also in our neighbours the good that is distinctive of them; that is why we owe a different sort of honour to God and to our neighbour.

(8) Both love of neighbour and love of God are included under the life of contemplation, as Gregory says [*HomEzek* 2.2.8]. For prayer, which seems to belong particularly to the contemplative life, is offered to God on our neighbour's behalf. At the same time, the principle of the active life is above all the love of God in himself. It does not follow, just because charity is the principle of different things, that it is not itself a single thing.

---

[11] This is technical language, classifying the argument in terms of the medieval doctrine of 'topics'. The non-technical upshot of this language is simply what Aquinas proceeds to say in the remainder of the reply.

(9) Charity is not one thing (i) by *continuity*. It can, however, be said to be one thing (ii) by *indivisibility*, in that it is one simple form; for it cannot in fact be called finite or infinite in respect of size, but only in respect of the amount of virtue. But that is not how we will deal with the virtue of charity here: rather, we will say that it is (iii) one in *meaning*. It is not, indeed, numerically one, like something that is both a tunic and a garment. However, it is one in type, as Socrates and Plato are one in that the meaning of 'human being' applies to them both.

(10) The argument would work if the temporal thing were the object of charity for its own sake and not for the sake of something eternal, as I have explained.

(11) We cannot have friendship in the full sense with many people, in the sense of having it with each person for his own sake. But the fuller a friendship is with one person for his own sake, the more it can, for his sake, be extended to others. In this way, charity, which is friendship in the fullest sense towards God, extends to all those who are able to see God, and not only to those we do not know, but even to our enemies.

(12) A virtue that acts with pleasure concerning a principal object may do things without pleasure, but also without distress, where some additional object is concerned. In this way, charity acts with pleasure concerning its principal object; with a secondary object, even though it may suffer some difficulty, it is enough in this case if it manages to act without distress.

Article 5: Whether charity is a specific virtue, distinct from the other virtues, or not

Objections

It seems not, because:

(1) Something that is included in the definition of every virtue is not a specific virtue, because virtue in general is included in the definition of any specific virtue. But charity is included in the definition of every virtue. For Jerome[12] says: 'To state concisely a general definition of virtue: virtue

---

[12] Actually it is Augustine who says something like this in a letter to Jerome (*Let* 167.4.15): 'And so as to state briefly the conception I have of virtue . . . virtue is the charity by which one loves what ought to be loved.' That charity is love of God and love of neighbour is a pervasive theme in Augustine.

is charity, by which we love God and neighbour.' Therefore charity is not a specific virtue, distinct from the others.

(2) The charity by which we love a neighbour is not a virtue distinct from the charity by which we love God, because charity makes us love a neighbour for the sake of God. But every virtue makes us love a neighbour for the sake of God. Therefore no virtue is distinguished from charity.

(3) Distinctions between dispositions derive from the activity of those virtues. But charity brings about the activity of all the other virtues: as 1 Corinthians 13:4 says, 'Charity is patient and kind.' Therefore charity is not a virtue distinct from the others.

(4) The good is an object shared generally by all the virtues: for virtue is something that makes its possessor and what he does good. But the object of charity is goodness. Therefore charity has a general object, and is therefore a general virtue.

(5) Each one thing that perfects something corresponds to one thing that is to be perfected. But charity perfects many different things, i.e. all the virtues. Therefore it is not one thing.

(6) The same disposition cannot exist in different subjects. But charity is found in different subjects: for we are told to love God with all our mind, all our soul, all our heart, and all our strength. Therefore charity is not a single virtue.

(7) Virtue is ordered towards removing sins. But charity is sufficient to remove all sins, since a tiny amount of charity can resist any temptation. Therefore charity does the job of all the virtues. Therefore it does not seem to be a particular virtue.

(8) Each particular virtue has a particular sin opposed to it. But all sins are contrary to charity, since any mortal sin destroys it. Therefore charity is not a particular virtue.

(9) Virtues are needed only for acting rightly. But charity alone is sufficient to make us act rightly; as Augustine says [*TEpJn* 7.8], 'Have charity and do whatever you wish.' Therefore there is no other virtue except charity. Consequently, charity is not a particular virtue distinct from others.

(10) The dispositions of the virtues are needed for someone to act readily and with pleasure. For no one is just who fails to take pleasure in doing things in a just way, as Aristotle says [*NE* 1.8.12, 1099a18]. But charity is sufficient for doing everything readily and with pleasure, since,

as Augustine says [*Serm* 70.3], 'Everything that is harsh and daunting, love makes easy and practically nothing.' Therefore no other virtue is needed besides charity.

(11) Things that can be distinguished from one another come into being and disappear separately. But charity and the other virtues do not come into being or disappear separately, because the other virtues are both infused and destroyed in us together with charity. Therefore charity is not a particular virtue.

But on the other hand

St Paul in 1 Corinthians 13:13 separates charity from other virtues, saying, 'Now, though, faith, hope, and charity remain, these three.'

My reply

Charity is a particular virtue, distinct from other virtues. To show this, we need to reflect that whenever an act depends on several principles which are interrelated in a certain order, for the act to be perfect requires every element of those principles to be so also. The act will be imperfect if there is any imperfection in the first or last of the principles, or in any intermediate ones. Similarly, whether a craftsman lacks experience of his skill, or whether there is something wrong with his tools, either way his work will be imperfect.

(i) We need to think about this point also in relation to the *capacities* of the soul. If the reason, which moves the lower powers, is in good order, but the sensual desire is out of kilter, someone will act in accordance with reason, but his action will be imperfect. This is because it will be hindered by the sensual desire pulling in the opposite direction. This is clear from the case of self-control.[13] That is why, in order to behave as we should with regard to sensual pleasures, we need not only practical wisdom, which brings reason to perfection, but also temperateness, if we are to act readily and without hindrance.

(ii) Then we need to consider the same point in relation not only to different capacities, where one moves another, but also to different

---

[13] The self-controlled person (*continens*) acts in accordance with reason but must overcome some contrary desire in order to do so. In someone who has the virtue of temperateness, by contrast, desire has been brought under the guidance of reason, so there is no contrary desire to be overcome.

objects, where one is ordered towards another as its end. For one and the same capacity, insofar as it is concerned with that end, not only moves other capacities, but also moves itself to whatever contributes towards the end. That is why in order to do things rightly, we need to be well disposed not only towards the end, but also towards the things that contribute to the end. If not, we will be hindered in what we do. This is clear in the example of someone who is well disposed towards desiring health, but poorly disposed to take the measures needed to become healthy.

In this way, it is clear that those who are disposed through charity to have the right attitude towards the ultimate end, also need to possess other virtues in order to be properly disposed towards whatever contributes towards the end. Therefore charity is different from the virtues that are ordered towards what contributes to the end. Yet the virtue that is ordered towards the end is preeminent and architectonic {cf. *NE* 1.1.4, 1094a14} in relation to those that are ordered towards the things that contribute to the end: compare medicine in relation to pharmacy or soldiering in relation to horsemanship. Therefore it is clear that charity needs to be a particular virtue distinct from the other virtues, but in relation to them their principle and moving cause.

Replies to objections

(1) The definition refers to the cause, insofar as charity is the moving cause of all the other virtues.

(2) In loving a neighbour, charity has God as the object formally defined, and not only as its ultimate end, as is clear from what I have already said. However, the other virtues have God not as their object formally defined, but as their ultimate end. That is why, when charity is said to love a neighbour because of God, the 'because of' refers not only to the final cause but also, in one sense, to the formal cause. However, when we say about the other virtues that we exercise them because of God, the 'because of' refers *only* to the final cause.

(3) Charity does not bring about the acts of the other virtues by drawing them out, but only by *commanding* them. For a virtue only draws out those acts that are done by reason of its own form, for example, with justice acting correctly, or with temperateness acting temperately. But a

virtue is said to 'command' all those actions that it summons towards its own end.

(4) It is not the common good that is the object of charity, but the highest good. That is why it does not follow that charity is a general virtue, but is rather the highest of the virtues.

(5) Charity perfects the other virtues as something not intrinsic, but rather extrinsic, to them, as I said above. Therefore the argument does not follow.

(6) The only capacity that possesses charity is the will. But the will moves the other capacities by commanding them. That is why we are told to love God with our whole mind and heart, so that all our powers may be summoned to obey God's love.

(7) Just as charity commands the actions of the other virtues, so, by giving commands, it excludes the sins opposed to them. In this way, charity resists temptations. But we still need the other virtues, because they exclude sins directly and by drawing out their opposite.

(8) Just as the acts of the other virtues are ordered towards the end which is the object of charity, so the sins that are contrary to the other virtues oppose the end that is the object of charity. That is why the things that are contrary to the other virtues, i.e. sins, also drive out charity.

(9) It is true that charity is capable, by giving commands, of governing us in all areas of a life lived rightly; but in order for us to act readily and without hindrance, we still need other virtues that carry out the commands of charity, by drawing out actions.

(10) Something that is difficult and distressing in itself is indeed sometimes done for the sake of a further end: someone may, for example, willingly swallow a bitter medicine for the sake of health, even though he finds actually drinking it very unpleasant. Charity, then, makes everything pleasurable from the point of view of its end. However, it needs the other virtues in order to render virtuous activities pleasurable *in themselves*, so that we can act more easily.

(11) Charity comes into being together with the other virtues not because it is not distinct from them, but because God's deeds are perfect. Therefore when he infuses charity into us, at the same time he also infuses into us everything that is needed for salvation. Charity disappears at the same time as the other virtues because the same things are contrary to both charity and to the other virtues, as I have said.

Article 6: Whether charity can coexist with mortal sin

Objections

It seems so, because:

(1) Origen says [*Prin* 1.3.8], 'I do not think that any one of those who stand on the highest and best possible level can immediately be emptied and fall, but it is necessary that they slip down gradually, bit by bit.' However, someone can commit a mortal sin immediately simply by consenting to it. Therefore someone who is in the best possible condition because of charity cannot fall from charity through a single act of mortal sin. Therefore charity can coexist with mortal sin.

(2) Bernard[14] says that when Peter denied Christ, his charity was not extinguished, but only put to sleep. But Peter committed a mortal sin by denying Christ. Therefore charity can remain along with mortal sin.

(3) Charity is stronger than a morally virtuous disposition. But a morally virtuous disposition is not removed by one vicious act, since it is not created by one single act. For virtue comes into existence and is destroyed by doing the same acts, but in the opposite way, as Aristotle says [*NE* 2.1.6, 1103b8]. Therefore much less will the dispositions of charity be removed by a single mortal sin.

(4) One thing opposes one thing. But charity is one particular virtue, as I have shown. Therefore it has one particular vice that opposes it. Therefore it is not removed by other sorts of mortal sin. In this way, it seems that mortal sin can coexist with charity.

(5) Opposites are only incompatible if they relate to the same subject. But some sins are found in a different subject from that of charity: for charity is found in the higher part of the reason, when it is turned towards God. But mortal sin can exist in the lower part of reason, as Augustine says [*Trin* 12.11.16–12.17]. Therefore not every mortal sin is incompatible with charity.

(6) Something very strong cannot be driven out by something very weak. But charity is very strong: as the Song of Solomon 8:6 puts it, 'Love is as strong as death.' Sin, however, is very weak, because evil is weak and powerless, as Dionysius says [*DivNames* 4.18–35]. Therefore mortal sin does not exclude charity; therefore they can coexist.

---

[14] Actually William of Saint Thierry, in *On the Nature and Dignity of Love*, ch. 6.

(7) We identify dispositions by their actions. But the actions of charity can coexist with mortal sin: for a sinful person can still love God and neighbour. Therefore charity can coexist with mortal sin.

(8) Charity above all makes us take pleasure in the contemplation of God. But nothing is contrary to the pleasure of thinking about things, as Aristotle says [*Top* 1.15, 106a36]. Therefore nothing is contrary to charity. Therefore charity cannot be excluded by mortal sin.

(9) Something that moves things generally can be blocked in moving one thing but not another. Charity moves all the virtues generally, as I have said. Therefore if it is blocked by some sin from moving one virtue, this need not stop it moving the others. Therefore charity can remain alongside a sin that opposes, say, temperateness, in that it can still move the other virtues.

(10) Faith and hope as well as charity have God as their object. But faith and hope can exist in an unformed way. Therefore by the same reasoning so can charity: it can coexist with mortal sin, because every virtue that can exist in an unformed way can coexist with mortal sin.

(11) Everything that lacks the completeness that it is apt by nature to have is unformed. But while we are on our journey, charity still lacks the completeness that it is by nature apt to have when it reaches our homeland. Therefore it is unformed, and so it seems to be able to coexist with mortal sin.

(12) We identify dispositions by their actions. But the actions of someone who possesses charity may be imperfect, for very often even those who possess charity are motivated by impatience or conceitedness. Therefore the disposition of charity can be imperfect and unformed. In this way, charity seems to be able to coexist with mortal sin.

(13) Just as sin opposes virtue, so ignorance opposes knowledge. But not every sort of ignorance removes knowledge completely. Therefore not every mortal sin will remove virtue completely. That is why, although charity is the root of the virtues, it does not seem that every mortal sin must remove it.

(14) Charity is the love of God. But even while having love for something, it is possible to act against that thing through lack of self-control. For example, even if we love ourselves we can still through lack of self-control act against our own good. Similarly, even if we love another community, it is possible through lack of self-control to act against it, as Aristotle says

[*Pol* 5.9, 1309b11]. Therefore it is possible to act against God by sinning, even while still possessing charity.

(15) You may be in the right state as regards the universal, but go wrong about something in particular: for example, those without self-control have a correct rational belief about a universal question, holding, for example, that fornication is bad. But they still choose fornication here and now as if it were a good, as Aristotle says.[15] But charity gives us the right attitude as regards the universal end. Therefore while still possessing charity, someone could sin in a particular instance. In this way, charity could coexist with a mortal sin.

(16) Contraries are found within the same class. But sin comes under the class of an act: for a sin is something that is said or done or desired in contradiction of the law of God. But charity comes under the class of dispositions. Therefore sin is not the contrary of charity. Therefore it is not incompatible with it. Therefore it can coexist with it.

But on the other hand

(1) Wisdom 1:5 says, 'The Holy Spirit of teaching will flee from what is false and will turn away from your unintelligent thoughts and will be rebuked' (that is, driven out) 'by the wickedness that is present.' But we have the Holy Spirit within us as long as we possess charity; for the Spirit of God dwells in us through charity. Therefore charity is driven out by wickedness when it appears. Therefore it cannot coexist with mortal sin.

(2) Anyone who possesses charity is worthy of eternal life, according to St Paul in 2 Timothy 4:8: 'For the rest, a crown of justice is laid up for me which God will give me on that day, as the just judge. Not only to me, but also to those who love his appearing.' But whoever commits a mortal sin is worthy of eternal punishment, according to Romans 6:23: 'The wages of sin are death.' But no one can be worthy simultaneously of eternal life and of eternal punishment. Therefore we cannot possess charity at the same time as mortal sin.

My reply

Charity cannot at all coexist with mortal sin. To show this we need first to reflect that every mortal sin is directly opposed to charity. Whenever

---

[15] The reference is presumably to *NE* 7.3.9–10, 1147a25 ff., although Aristotle's actual example there is of overindulgence in sweets, not fornication.

someone chooses A in preference to B, he loves A more than B. Consequently, as we love our own lives and their continuance more than sensual pleasure, we would withdraw from a sensual pleasure, however great it were, if we reckoned that it would certainly kill us. Hence Augustine says [*83DQ* 36.1] that there is no one who does not fear pain more than he loves sensual pleasure. Sometimes we see that even the fiercest animals withdraw from enormous pleasures for fear of pain.

Someone sins mortally by choosing something else in preference to living in accordance with God and to clinging to him. Therefore it is clear that those who sin mortally, by that very fact love some other good more than God. Indeed, if they loved God more, they would choose to live according to God rather than to possess any sort of temporal good. The character of charity means that God is loved above everything else, as is clear from the above. Therefore all mortal sin is contrary to charity.

Now charity is infused in us by God. Whatever is infused by God needs God's action not only at its beginning, to bring it into being, but the whole time that it lasts, to keep it in being. Similarly, the air needs the sun to be present for it to be illuminated, not only when this first happens, but also as long as it continues. That is why if some obstacle gets in the way and prevents the air from looking directly at the sun, so to speak, the air ceases to be lit. A similar thing happens when mortal sin occurs, because it prevents the soul from looking directly at God. When people choose something else ahead of God, the inflow of charity is blocked and they cease to possess charity, in keeping with Isaiah 59:2, 'Your sins have made a division between you and your God.' But when their minds return to look straight at God, by loving him above all else (which cannot happen without God's grace), they themselves return once more to a state of charity.

Replies to objections

(1) Origen's words should not be taken to mean that those, however completely good, who sin mortally do not immediately lose charity, but rather that it does not happen *easily* that those who are completely good will commit a mortal sin straight away and at once. Rather, they will first become disposed to this through carelessness and various venial sins, so that finally they slip into mortal sin.

(2) Bernard's claim does not seem sustainable, unless we understand 'charity was not extinguished in Peter' to mean that it was very quickly resurrected. For things that are separated by very little seem to have no distance between them at all, as Aristotle says [*Phys* 2.5, 197b30].

(3) Moral virtue, which we acquire through activity, consists in the inclination of a capacity to be activated. This inclination is not completely removed by a single act. The inflow of charity from God, on the other hand, *is* blocked by a single act; that is why a single sinful act can remove charity.

(4) The opposite of charity, speaking generally, is hatred, but indirectly all sins are opposed to charity insofar as they are connected with scorning God, who ought to be loved above all else.

(5) (i) The higher reason, where charity is found, moves the lower. That is why sin, insofar as it opposes charity's moving of the lower part, is incompatible with charity.

(ii) Or perhaps we ought to respond that mortal sin requires consent, and this belongs to the higher part of reason, where charity is found.

(6) Sin does not drive out charity through its own power, but by the fact that a person willingly submits to the sin.

(7) Those who sin mortally do not love God above all else, as he ought to be loved from charity. Rather, they prefer something else to the love of God, and scorn the commands of God on account of this.

(8) The pleasure we take in thinking about something is not contrary to something in the same class; at least, thinking about something else is not incompatible with it. That is because the *concepts* of two contrary things in the intelligence are not themselves contraries. So, for example, to take pleasure in thinking about whiteness is not incompatible with taking pleasure in thinking about blackness. But because the activity of the will consists in the soul's moving towards something, if two things are contrary in themselves, the movements of will towards them will also be contrary: so, for example, a longing for something sweet is contrary to a longing for something bitter. It is in this way that the love of God is incompatible with the love of sin, which keeps us from God. Thinking does indeed not have a contrary; but thinking is not, strictly speaking, an activity of charity in the sense of being *drawn out* by charity. Rather, it is something *commanded* by charity as its effect.

(9) When charity, which is the general moving cause of the virtues, is blocked in connection with one virtue through mortal sin, it is then

blocked in respect of its object in general. For this reason it is blocked in general, in every respect. This is a different case from when something that is moveable in general is blocked in respect of one particular effect, without being blocked in connection with its power in general.[16]

(10) Although faith and hope have God for their object, it is not their role to be the form of the other virtues, which is the role of charity, for the reasons given above. Therefore although charity cannot exist in an unformed state, faith and hope sometimes can.

(11) It is not just any lack of completeness that makes a virtue unformed, but only that sort of lack that prevents its being ordered towards its ultimate end. That ordering does exist in charity when we are on our journey, even though it does not yet possess the completeness it will have in our homeland, which will result from enjoying as completely as possible its own proper object.

(12) Someone who has charity can indeed act in an imperfect way, but the actions in question will not be done *from* charity. For not every action of a given agent is an action of every form that exists in the agent. This is particularly true in the case of a rational nature, which has the freedom to use or fail to use the dispositions that it possesses.

(13) It is true that not every sort of ignorance of particular principles excludes a whole branch of knowledge; however, the ignorance of its *general* principles does. For someone ignorant of those must be ignorant of the skill itself, as Aristotle says [*SR* 11, 172a27]. Now the ultimate end functions as an utterly general principle. That is why someone who, through mortal sin, ceases to be ordered towards the ultimate end will lose charity entirely. However, if they fail to be so ordered only in a particular area this will not happen, as is clear with venial sins.

(14) Those who through lack of self-control act against a good that they love must in fact reckon that they will not lose that good completely by acting in this unselfcontrolled way. For if those who loved some city or the safety of their own bodies were to reckon that they would lose one of these through a certain action, then either they would avoid the action entirely, or else they must love the thing they do more than their own safety or the city. In this way, when people know that they will lose God through mortal sin (which is what it is to know that one is sinning mortally), but

---

[16] The argument here is obscure.

still act without self-control, it is demonstrable that they love what they are doing more than they love God.

(15) Charity requires not only that we accept in general that God is to be loved above all else, but also that our *actual* choosing and willing are directed towards this as something that ought in particular to be chosen. But you cannot choose both one particular thing and something incompatible with it, in the way that sin is incompatible with God.

(16) It is true that in a *direct* sense one act is contrary to another, in the way that in a direct sense one disposition is contrary to another. However, in an *indirect* sense one act can also be contrary to a disposition, because it conforms with a disposition contrary to it. This is because dispositions are brought into being through actions akin to them, and they cause acts that are akin to them. This is true even though not all dispositions are caused by actions.

Article 7: Whether the object that is to be loved through charity is a rational nature

Objections

It seems not, because:

(1) When A is x because of B, B is also more x than A.[17] But human beings are loved through charity because of virtue and of blessedness. Therefore virtue and blessedness, which are not rational creatures, should be loved more out of charity than human beings. Therefore it is not rational creatures that are the object, in the strict sense, of charity.

(2) It is through charity that we conform most closely to God in our loving. But God loves everything that exists, as Wisdom 11:24 says, through charity, by loving himself, who is charity. Therefore everything ought to be loved through charity, and not only rational natures.

(3) Origen says [*CommSS* prol 2.35] that to love God and to love whatever is good is one and the same. But God is loved out of charity. Therefore since all creatures are something good, all of them should be loved out of charity, and not only rational natures.

(4) It is only the love of charity that is meritorious. But we may gain merit by loving all sorts of things. Therefore we may love all sorts of things out of charity.

---

[17] Cf. *PostAn* 1.2, 72a25; *DQVirtGen* 6 s.c.3.

(5) God is loved[18] from charity. Therefore whatever he most loves ought to be loved rather out of charity. But among all created things what God loves most is the good of the universe, which embraces everything. Therefore all things ought to be loved out of charity.

(6) Loving is more closely related to charity than believing is. But charity 'believes all things' as 1 Corinthians 13:7 says. Therefore far more must it love all things.

(7) Rational nature is found most fully in God. Therefore if rational nature is the object of charity, we ought to love God out of charity. But this seems impossible, because the love of charity is love in the fullest sense. But we cannot love God fully in this life, since in this life we do not know God fully; for we do not know what God is, only what he is not. Loving, though, presupposes knowing: for you cannot love something you do not know. Therefore rational or intelligent nature is not the object, in a strict sense, of charity.

(8) God is further than any creature is from human beings. Therefore if we do not love other creatures out of charity, we are far less able to love God in this way.

(9) The angels also possess intelligent natures. But the angels are not to be loved out of charity, it seems. Therefore intelligent natures are not the objects, in a strict sense, of charity.

To prove the middle premise: friendship consists in sharing a life; for it is distinctive of being friends that you live with one another, as Aristotle says [*NE* 9.10.3, 1171a2]. But we do not seem to share our lives with the angels. For we do not share our *natural* life with them, as they possess a far finer nature than we do. Nor do we share our *glorified* life with them, as gifts of grace and glory are given by God according to the virtue of the receiver, as Matthew 25:15 says: 'He gave to each one according to his own virtue.' But an angel's virtue is far greater than a human being's. Therefore angels do not share either type of life with us.

(10) The person who is loving out of charity also possesses a rational nature. But we ought not to love ourselves out of charity, or so it seems. Therefore the object of charity is not rational nature.

---

[18] *diligit* (loves) for *diligitur* (is loved) gives a much simpler argument. As it stands, the argument relies on the thought that we ought to love more from charity those things that are loved more by those whom we love from charity. If we change *diligit* to *diligitur*, the argument relies on the thought that we ought to imitate God.

To prove the middle premise: there are precepts of the law that prescribe virtuous actions. But there is no precept of the law that prescribes loving oneself. Therefore to love oneself is not to act with charity.

(11) Gregory says [*HomGosp* 17.1], 'You cannot have charity between less than two people.' Therefore one cannot love oneself out of charity.

(12) Just as justice consists in sharing, so does friendship, according to Aristotle [*NE* 2.7.11, 13; 1108a10–14, 27–8]. But strictly speaking one cannot be just towards oneself, as Aristotle also says [*NE* 5.11.1, 1138a4]. Therefore nor can one be friends with oneself, nor, therefore, have charity towards oneself.

(13) Nothing that can be counted as a vice is an act of charity. But loving oneself can be counted to one as a vice, according to 2 Timothy 3:1–2, 'Dangerous times will afflict us, and there will be people who love themselves.' Therefore loving oneself is not acting with charity. Therefore rational nature is not the object, in a strict sense, of charity.

(14) The human body is a part of a rational nature, that is, of human nature. But we do not seem to have to love human bodies out of charity, because, as Aristotle says [*NE* 9.8.4, 1168b15], those who love themselves only in their external nature are blamed for this. Therefore rational nature is not the object of charity.

(15) No one who possesses charity shuns whatever is loved from charity. But the saints who possess charity shun the body, according to Romans 7:24, 'Who will free me from the body of this death?' The body, then, is not to be loved out of charity. So the same conclusion follows as in the last objection.

(16) We are not obliged to fulfil obligations when we cannot know if we are doing so. But we are not able to know that we possess charity. Therefore we are not obliged to love rational creatures out of charity.

(17) When we say that a rational creature is loved out of charity, the preposition 'out of' picks out some causal relation. But it cannot pick out (i) a *material* causal relation, because charity is something spiritual rather than material. Nor, again, (ii) a *final* causal relation, because the end of loving out of charity is God and not charity. Nor, similarly, (iii) an *efficient* causal relation, because it is the Holy Spirit that moves us to love, according to Romans 5:5, 'The charity of God is poured into our hearts through the Holy Spirit, who has been given to us.' Nor, again, (iv) a *formal* causal relation, because charity is not an *intrinsic* form (since it does not belong to a thing's essence), nor is it an *extrinsic*, exemplary,

formal cause, because then everything that is loved by charity would be assimilated to the type of charity, in the way that copies are assimilated to the type of the original.

Therefore, rational creatures are not to be loved out of charity.

(18) Augustine says [*CT* 1.30.31] that our neighbour is whoever bestows a kindness on us. But God bestows kindnesses on us. Therefore God is our neighbour. Therefore Augustine's claim that *both* God *and* neighbour are to be loved out of charity seems badly expressed.

(19) Since Christ is the mediator between God and human beings, it seems as though we ought to posit something else that is lovable besides God and neighbour. In this way, there would be five things that we ought to love out of charity, and not only four, as Augustine says.[19]

But on the other hand

The gloss comments on Leviticus 19:18, 'You shall love your neighbour as yourself', as follows, 'Our neighbour does not mean only a blood-relation, but anyone united with us by reason.' Therefore we ought to love things out of charity insofar as they are united with us in possessing rational nature. Therefore rational nature is the object of charity.

My reply

When we inquire about things that are dealt with by the activity of a given capacity or disposition, then we need to determine the *formal character of the object* of that capacity or disposition. For how things are dealt with by that capacity or disposition will be determined by their relation to that formal character. For example, whether things are said to be visible *per se* or *per accidens* will be determined by their relation to the formal character of the visible.

Now since the object of love understood generally is the good understood as something common, it is necessary for there to be a particular good as the object of any particular love. For example, the distinctive

---

[19] See *CT* 1.23.22: 'There are four things to be loved: one that is above us, another that is we ourselves, a third that is in company with us, and a fourth that is below us.' He means, respectively, God, ourselves, our neighbours (including angels as well as other human beings), and our bodies. (See the response for further details.) The objection speculates that if there is a mediator between the first two items on the list, there needs to be an additional item, and so there will be five things rather than four that ought to be loved.

object of the natural friendship we have for our family is such natural good as we derive from our parents. For political friendships, on the other hand, the object is the good of the community. In this way, charity too has its own particular good as its distinctive object, that is, the good of *divine blessedness*, as I said above. How things are to be loved by charity is determined by the way that they relate to this good.

We need to reflect, though, that when we talk of loving, which is wishing the good for someone, something can be loved in two ways: (i) as the thing for which we want the good; or (ii) as the good which we want for someone. In the first sense (i), things can only be loved from charity if we want the good of eternal life for them. These can only be things that are by nature apt to possess the good of eternal blessedness. That is why, since only intelligent natures are by nature apt to possess the good of eternal blessedness, only an intelligent nature can be loved by charity, in the first sense of loving.

For this reason, Augustine distinguishes [*CT* 1.23.22] four types of thing that can be loved by charity, with reference to the different ways that they can possess eternal blessedness. (a) One thing has eternal blessedness through its own being, and this is God. Other things have it through participation, and these are (b) those rational creatures that are doing the loving; and (c) other creatures that are associated with these in sharing blessedness. Different again are (d) things that can possess eternal blessedness only by a sort of 'overflow', like our bodies, which are glorified through the glory of the soul overflowing into them.

(a) *God* is to be loved out of charity as the root of blessedness. Human beings ought to love (b) *themselves* out of charity as sharing in blessedness; and then (c) their *neighbour* as a companion in the sharing of blessedness; and then (d) their own *body* in that blessedness overflows into it.

In the second sense (ii), i.e. when we say that we 'love' the good things that we want for others, we can love any good out of charity insofar as it is a good for someone who is capable of possessing blessedness. For all creatures are there for human beings on their journey, to incline them towards blessedness. Again, all creatures are ordered towards the glory of God insofar as divine goodness is displayed in them. In this way, we are able to love everything out of charity if we order it towards things that either possess blessedness or could do so.

We ought also to bear in mind that types of love are related to one another in the same way as the goods that are their objects. That is why, since all human goods are ordered towards eternal blessedness as to their ultimate end, love in the sense of charity includes all types of human love, except those based upon sin, which cannot be ordered towards blessedness. In this way, the mutual love of family members, or fellow-citizens, or fellow-pilgrims, and so on, can, through charity, be meritorious. But if people love one another because they are allies in robbery or adultery, this can be neither meritorious nor out of charity.

Replies to objections

(1) We love virtue and blessedness out of charity in that we want them *for* those capable of possessing blessedness.

(2) God loves everything out of charity not in the sense of wanting blessedness for them, but in ordering them towards himself and towards other things that can possess blessedness.

(3) All good things are in God as their first principle. That is what Origen meant by saying that to love God and whatever is good is one and the same.

(4) We are able to love all things meritoriously by ordering them towards whatever is capable of blessedness, but not by wanting blessedness for them.

(5) Rational nature is included within the good of the universe as its chief good, as it is capable of blessedness, while other creatures are ordered towards it. In this way, it is fitting, both for God and for us, out of charity to love the good of the universe very greatly.

(6) Just as charity believes everything that ought to be believed, so it also loves everything to the extent that it ought to be loved out of charity.

(7) We are not able here to love God as fully as we will love him in our homeland, when we will see him in his own being.

(8) The reason why other creatures are not loved out of charity is not their distance from us, but the fact that they are not capable of blessedness.

(9) The angels do not share with us in our *natural* life in respect of their type, but only in respect of the class of rational natures. We are, however, able to share the life of *glory* with them. The words 'gave to each one according to his own virtue' should not be taken to mean only the 'virtue' of nature, since it is a mistake to say that the gifts of grace and of glory are given in accordance with the degree of anything natural. 'Virtue' must be taken to refer to something that is also graced, because grace is bestowed

in order to enable human beings to merit a glory equal to that of the angels.

(10) (i) The written law was given to assist the law of nature, which was obscured by sin. However, it was not so obscured that it no longer moved us to love in the sense of loving *ourselves and our bodies*. It was obscured insofar as it failed to move us to love *God and our neighbour*. That is why the written law had to provide precepts about loving God and neighbour.

(ii) In any case, those precepts also include our loving ourselves, since when we are led to love God, we are led to long for God, and through this we love ourselves very greatly, as we want for ourselves what is the supreme good.

(iii) Again, the precept about loving our neighbour says, 'You will love your neighbour as yourself.' This, then, includes love of oneself.

(11) Although one cannot be friends with oneself in the strict sense, one can love oneself. For, as Aristotle says [*NE* 9.8.1, 1168a30], friendliness to another person comes from friendliness to oneself. Insofar as charity means love, one can certainly love oneself out of charity. But Gregory is speaking of charity in the sense that involves the idea of friendship.

(12) Although friendship, like justice, involves sharing with someone else, love is not necessarily related to someone else, and love is enough for the idea of charity.

(13) Those who love themselves are blamed insofar as they do so more than they ought. This cannot happen with respect to spiritual goods, because no one can love too much having the virtues. With respect to exterior and corporal goods, one can love oneself excessively.

(14) People are not blamed for loving themselves in their external nature, but for seeking external goods beyond the limit that is virtuous. In this way, we are able to love our bodies out of charity.

(15) Charity does not shun the body itself, but the perishable nature of the body, in keeping with Wisdom 9:15, 'A body, which is perishable, weighs down the soul.' That is why St Paul talks in a figurative way of 'the body of this death'.

(16) Just because we do not know for certain that we possess charity, it does not follow that we cannot love out of charity, but only that we cannot *judge* whether we are loving out of charity. Thus we can be required to love out of charity, but not to judge that we do so. That is why St Paul says in 1 Corinthians 4:3–4, 'I do not judge myself; he who judges me is the Lord.'

(17) When we say that someone loves a neighbour out of charity, the preposition 'out of' picks out the final, efficient, and formal causal relations. (i) The *final*, in that the love of neighbour is ordered towards the love of God as its end; that is why 1 Timothy 1:5 says, 'The end of the precept is charity'; since the love of God is the purpose of keeping the precept. (ii) The *efficient*, in that charity is a disposition that tends towards loving, and is related to the activity of loving in the way that heat is related to heating. (iii) The *formal*, in that an act takes its type from the disposition in question, as heating does from heat.

(18) Both the one who bestows a kindness and the one who receives it match the description of 'neighbour'. However, we ought not to describe everyone who bestows a kindness as a neighbour; it is also necessary for neighbours to be part of a shared order. That is why God, even though he bestows kindnesses, cannot be called our neighbour. Christ, however, *qua* man, is called our neighbour insofar as he bestows kindnesses upon us.

The answer to (19) is clear from this.

Article 8: Whether loving our enemies belongs to the fullness of a counsel

Objections

It seems not, because:

(1) Something that falls under a precept does not belong to the fullness of a counsel.[20] But loving our enemies falls under a precept, i.e. 'You shall love your neighbour as yourself.' For 'neighbour' should be taken to mean 'any person', as Augustine says [*CT* 1.30.31]. Therefore loving our enemies does not belong to the fullness of a counsel.

(2) *Rejoinder*: love of enemies belongs to the fullness of a counsel with reference to actually *showing* friendship and the other practices of charity. *But on the other hand* we are bound to love all our neighbours out of charity. But the love of charity does not exist only in the heart, but also in what we do: 1 John 3:18 says, 'Let us not love in words or speech,

---

[20] *sit de perfectione consilii*, in other words, 'is a requirement appropriate only to the very high standards set by "counsels" rather than to the less demanding standards set by "precepts" '. Precepts are obligatory for everyone; counsels are followed by those, particularly members of religious orders, who freely undertake to aim at Christian perfection.

but in deeds and truth.' Therefore the love of enemies comes under a precept also with respect to the *practices* of charity.

(3) Matthew 5:44 says similarly, 'Love your enemies and do good to those who hate you.' Therefore if loving our enemies falls under a precept, then doing good to them also falls under a precept, and this relates to the practices of charity.

(4) The Old Law did not hand down anything relevant to the fullness of counsels, for, as Hebrews 7:19 puts it, 'The Law made nothing perfect.' But the Old Law handed down that we should not only have *feelings* of love for our enemies, but also engage in *practices* of love towards them. See, for example Exodus 23:4, 'If you come across a stray ox or ass belonging to your enemy, take it back to him'; Leviticus 19:17, 'Do not hate your brother in your heart, but reprove him openly, so that you do not sin in relation to him'; Job 31:29–30, 'Suppose that I rejoiced at the fall of those who hated me, and celebrated because misfortune had come upon them; indeed, I did not give my throat to sin'; Proverbs 25:21, 'If your enemy is hungry, feed him. If he is thirsty, give him water to drink.' Therefore loving our enemies in the sense of openly practising charity does not belong to the fullness of a counsel.

(5) A counsel should not conflict with a precept of the Law. That is why the Lord, when he was about to hand over the New Law, which brings fullness, said first in Matthew 5:17, 'I have not come to abolish the Law, but to fulfil it.' However, loving our enemies seems to conflict with a precept of the Law, as Matthew 5:43 says, 'You will love your friend and hate your enemy.' Therefore the love of enemies does not come under the fullness of a counsel.

(6) Love has as its own distinctive object the thing towards which it tends, since, as Augustine puts it [*Conf* 13.9.10], 'My weight is my love.' But our enemy does not seem to be the distinctive object of our love, but rather to repel our love. Therefore it does not belong to the fullness of a counsel that we should love our enemies.

(7) The fullness of virtue does not conflict with the inclination of nature; rather, the inclination of nature is fulfilled through virtue. Nature, though, moves us to hate our enemies; for every natural thing fights against its contrary. Therefore it does not belong to the fullness of a counsel to love our enemies.

(8) The fullness of charity and other virtues consists in being like God. But God loves his friends and hates his enemies, according to

Malachi 1:2–3, 'I loved Jacob and I held Esau in hatred.' Therefore it does not belong to the fullness of a counsel that we should love our enemies, but rather that we should hold them in hatred.

(9) The love of charity looks directly towards the good of eternal life. But we ought not to want the good of eternal life for certain enemies, because they are already damned and in hell, or while still alive already rejected[21] by God. Therefore loving our enemies is not part of the fullness of charity.

(10) We cannot lawfully kill those whom we are obliged to love from charity, nor can we want their death nor want anything bad to befall them, since it is part of the character of friendship that we want our friends to exist and to live. But we are lawfully allowed to kill some people, because, as St Paul says in Romans 13:4, 'The secular power is the minister of God, and has vengeance to the point of anger on those who act badly.' Therefore we are not bound to love our enemies.

(11) Aristotle teaches [*Top* 2.7, 112b32] that reasoning in the case of contraries works as follows: if it is good to love our friends and do good to them, then to love our enemies and do good to them is bad. But nothing bad possesses the fullness of charity, nor does it come under a counsel. Therefore to love our enemies is not part of the fullness of a counsel.

(12) Friend and enemy are contraries. Therefore to love our friends and to love our enemies are contraries. But contraries cannot coexist. Since, then, we are obliged to love our friends out of charity, it cannot come under a counsel that we should love our enemies.

(13) Counsels cannot require something impossible. But loving an enemy seems impossible, because it contradicts our natural inclinations. Therefore loving our enemies does not fall under a counsel.

(14) It is the role of the fully virtuous to fulfil counsels. The apostles were the most fully virtuous, but they did not love their enemies as regards both the feelings and practices of charity: we can read that blessed Thomas the Apostle cursed someone who struck him a blow on the cheek, with the result that the latter's hand was carried off by dogs during a feast.[22]

---

[21] Aquinas uses the technical term *reprobatus*, which applies to someone who by divine decree is already marked out for damnation.

[22] The story is found in the apocryphal *Acts of Thomas* 1.8, and quoted by Augustine against the Manichees, who treated that text as authoritative (*SermMount* 1.65; *AA* 17.2; *AF* 22.79). Aquinas appears less sceptical than Augustine about the text's authority.

Therefore loving one's enemies with respect to *both* feeling and practice does not come under the fullness of a counsel.

(15) Uttering harmful curses against people, especially for their eternal damnation, is opposed to love, from the point of view of both feeling and practice. But the prophets uttered harmful curses against their opponents. For example, Psalm 69:28 says, 'May they be removed from the Book of Life and not be listed there with the just'; while Psalm 55:15 says, 'May death come upon them, and may they descend alive into hell.' Therefore loving our enemies does not belong to the fullness of charity.

(16) It is part of the character of true friendship that friends are loved for themselves. Charity, though, includes friendship in the way that something full includes something less full. However, to love our enemies for themselves is contrary to charity, according to which only God is loved for himself. Therefore it does not belong to the fullness of a counsel that we should love our enemies.

(17) Something that falls under the fullness of a counsel is better and more meritorious than something that falls under the necessity of a precept. But to love an enemy is not better or more meritorious than to love a friend, which clearly falls under the necessity of a precept. This is because, if it is good to love something good, then it is better and more meritorious to love something that is even better. A friend, though, is better than an enemy. Therefore to love our enemies does not belong to the fullness of a counsel.

(18) *Rejoinder*: loving our enemies is more meritorious because it is more difficult. *But on the other hand* to love an enemy is more difficult than to love God. Therefore by the same reasoning, it is more meritorious to love our enemy than to love God.

(19) It is a sign that we possess the relevant dispositions when we take pleasure in doing something, as Aristotle says [*NE* 2.3.1, 1104b5]. But loving a friend is more pleasurable than loving an enemy. Therefore it is more virtuous, and consequently more meritorious. Thus loving our enemies does not come under the fullness of a counsel.

But on the other hand

Augustine says [*Hand* 19.73], 'It is the role of the fully virtuous children of God to love their enemies; everyone ought to show himself faithful in this respect.'

My reply

Loving our enemies comes under the necessity of a precept in one way and under the fullness of a counsel in another. To show this, we must recall that, as I said above, God is the object of charity strictly speaking and *per se*. Whatever is loved out of charity is loved with reference to its relation to God (in the way that if we love one person, we therefore love all those connected with him, even if they are enemies to us). It is agreed that all human beings are related to God insofar as they are created and capable of blessedness, which consists in the enjoyment of God. It is clear, therefore, that the reason for loving to which charity responds is found in all human beings.

In this way, then, we discover two things about those who practise hostility towards us: (i) a reason for *loving* them, which relates to God; and (ii) a reason for *hating* them, because they are our adversaries. Wherever we discover reasons both for loving and for hating, if we abandon the love and turn ourselves to hatred, it is clear that the reason for hating has outweighed in our hearts the reason for loving. In this way those who have hatred for their enemy allow the hostility in their hearts to outweigh the love of God. Therefore they are hating their enemy more than they are loving God. We only hate something, however, insofar as we love the good of which our enemy deprives us. We conclude, then, that everyone who hates an enemy loves some created good more than God, and that is contrary to the precept of charity. To have hatred for an enemy, then, is contrary to charity. Now, given that we are obliged by the precept of charity to let the love of God in us outweigh the love of any other thing – and consequently the hatred of its opposite – it must then follow that we are obliged by a necessary precept to love our enemies.

We also need to bear in mind, however, that when we are obliged by the precept of charity to love our neighbours, this does not mean that we should *actively* love every single neighbour in particular, or do good to each one in particular, because no one is capable of thinking about every other person in such a way as actively to love each one in particular, and no one is capable of doing good to or assisting each one individually.

We are, however, bound to love and to help in particular those who are bound to us by some other reason of friendship; for all other lawful loves are included under charity, as was said above. That is why Augustine says

[*CT* 1.28.29], 'Since you cannot help everyone, you ought to care most for those who are nearest to you in the circumstances of time or place or whatever, as if they have been allotted to you. For you should think of those more closely connected to you in a temporal sense as allotted to you, and for this reason you should prefer to give to them.'

This makes it clear that by the precept of charity (i') we are not obliged to be moved in terms of either the feelings of love or practical activity to help *in particular* someone who is not connected to us by any other tie (except perhaps at a certain time and place, for example if we were to see someone in urgent need who could be helped only by us). (ii') We are, though, obliged with respect to both the feelings and the practice of the charity with which we love *all* our neighbours and pray for *all* of them, not to exclude those who are not connected to us by any particular tie, as, for example, those living in India and Ethiopia.

Now the only thing that unites us to our enemies is charity; therefore we are bound by the necessity of a *precept* to love them in general both in feelings and in practice, and in particular when they are threatened by a situation of serious need. However, suppose that one were for the sake of God to show towards one's enemies as particular individuals such particular feelings and practice of love as one shows towards others who are close to one; that would be part of the fullness of charity, and come under a *counsel*. For it is through the fullness of charity that charity can by itself move us towards our enemy, in the way that both charity and particular love move us towards a friend.

It is clear, though, that a consequence of the fullness of an active virtue is that what the agent does extends further: a fire has fuller power if it can heat not only what is near, but also what is further away. In this way, charity that is fuller moves us to love and do good not only to those near to us, but also to those further away, and finally to our enemies, and not only in a general, but also in a particular, way.

Replies to Objections

(1) The love of enemies is included under a precept, in the way that I have explained.

(2) We ought to love our enemies in practice as well as in feelings, as I have explained.

From this the answer to (3) is clear.

(4) Those Old Testament authorities are speaking of cases of serious need, when we are bound by a precept to do good to our enemies, as I have explained.

(5) (i) The words 'You shall have hatred for your enemy' are not found anywhere in the Old Testament. They come from the tradition of the scribes, who thought they should add this, because the Lord instructed the children of Israel to persecute their enemies.

(ii) Or else, we should say that the words 'You shall have hatred for your enemy' are not to be taken as an order to someone just, but as a concession to someone weak, as Augustine says [*SermMount* 1.21.70].

(iii) Or else, as Augustine also says [*TEpJn* 8.10], it is not our enemies themselves that we ought to hate, but their vice.

(6) An enemy is not the object of love *qua* enemy, but *qua* related to God. That is why we ought to hate in our enemies the fact that they hate us, and wish for them to love us.

(7) By nature, one human being loves every other one, as Aristotle too says [*NE* 8.1.3, 1155a23]. But the fact that someone is an enemy results from something *added to* his nature, and this ought not to make us destroy our natural inclination. Therefore charity, when it moves us to love our enemies, is fulfilling our natural inclination. The case is different with things that are in their own natures incompatible, like fire and water, or wolves and sheep.

(8) God does not hate what is his own in anything, whether its natural good or anything else, but only what is not his own, i.e. sin. We too, then, ought to love in human beings what comes from God, and hate what is foreign to God. That is also the way to interpret Psalm 139:22, 'I hated them with the fullest hatred.'

(9) (i) On the one hand, those who are foreknown and damned: we ought not to love them, in the sense of hoping for their eternal life, because they are already completely excluded from that by God's decree. However, we can love them as we love other works of God in which divine justice is made manifest; for that is the way in which God loves them.

(ii) On the other hand, those who are foreknown but *not yet* damned: we ought to love them, in the sense of hoping for their eternal life, because we cannot be certain in such a matter. In any case, they are not excluded by God's foreknowledge from the possibility of attaining eternal life.

(10) The person to whom this duty attaches can lawfully punish and even kill wrongdoers while still loving them out of charity. For Gregory

says [*HomGosp* 34.2] that the just do initiate persecution, but out of love; for even if for the sake of discipline they pile on reproaches externally, they still, through charity, maintain a kindly attitude internally. Now when we love people out of charity, we may want for them or inflict on them some temporal evil for three reasons: (i) for their correction; (ii) because sometimes if a few people are very successful in a temporal sense, this can damage the mass of people, or even the whole Church, as Gregory says [*MorJob* 22.11.23]: 'It can often happen that we rejoice in an enemy's fall without abandoning charity, or regret his triumphs without being guilty of envy. This is when we think that his collapse will lift up other people, or we fear that his success will mean that many people are unjustly oppressed'; (iii) to preserve the order of divine justice, as Psalm 58:10 says, 'The just will rejoice when they see his vengeance.'

(11) Propositions of the sort from which Aristotle is reasoning should be construed as *per se*. Just as to love a friend *qua* friend is something good, so it is bad to love an enemy *qua* enemy. But it is good to love an enemy *qua* related to God.

(12) Loving a friend *qua* friend and loving an enemy *qua* enemy are contraries. But loving a friend and loving an enemy, both *qua* belonging to God, are not contraries, any more than are seeing black and seeing white, both *qua* something coloured.

(13) To love an enemy *qua* enemy is difficult or even impossible. But to love an enemy for the sake of something which you love more, is easy. In this way charity towards God[23] makes easy something which *per se* seems impossible.

(14) St Thomas did not effect the punishment of his assailant out of enthusiasm for revenge, but in order to reveal God's justice and power.

(15) The curses we find in the prophets should be interpreted as prediction, so that 'let them be destroyed' should be interpreted as 'they will be destroyed'. They use this mode of expression because they are conforming their will to God's justice as it has been revealed to them.

(16) To love others for their sake can be understood in two ways: (i) as loving them as the ultimate end; and in fact only God should be loved for his own sake in this sense; (ii) in the way that we love someone whose good we want, as happens in the honourable sort of friendship. That is not the same as wanting some good for *ourselves*, as happens with the

---

[23] *caritas Dei*: either 'charity towards God' or 'the charity that God bestows'.

pleasurable and the useful sorts of friendship.[24] In their case, we love a friend as something good for us, not because we are seeking something pleasurable or useful *for the friend*, but because we are seeking something *from* the friend that is pleasurable or useful *for us*. That is also the way that we love other things that are pleasurable or useful to us, such as food or clothes. By contrast, when we love others on account of virtue, we want what is good for them; we do not want them for us. This occurs especially in friendship based on charity.

(17) It is better to love an enemy than a friend only because it reveals a fuller charity, as I have explained. But if we consider the two activities simply speaking, it is better to love a friend than an enemy, and better to love God than a friend. For the difficulty of loving an enemy only relates to the idea of merit in that it reveals the fullness of the charity in question, which overcomes that difficulty. It follows, though, that if the charity were so full as to overcome the difficulty entirely, that would be even more meritorious. But now we are talking about someone who loves a friend out of the fullest charity, and this will also extend to loving an enemy; however, it will be more intensively at work in loving the friend. *Per accidens*, though, loving an enemy might need more intensive effort, in that resisting something may require a greater effort, just as in natural things warm water needs to be frozen more intensively than cold.

This makes clear the answers to (18) and (19).

Article 9: Whether there is some ordering within charity

Objections

It seems not, because:

(1) Charity is related to things we should love in the way that faith is related to things we should believe. But faith believes everything we should believe to an equal degree. Therefore charity loves everything we should love to an equal degree.

(2) Ordering relates to reason. However, charity is found not in the reason but in the will. Therefore ordering is unrelated to charity.

---

[24] Aquinas follows Aristotle in identifying three sorts of friendship: those based on pleasure, those based on the friends' usefulness to each other, and those based on the virtuous or honourable character of the friends.

(3) Whenever there is order, there are degrees. Bernard says [*SermSS* 83.1.3], however, that 'Charity knows no degrees and takes no notice of status.' Therefore there is no ordering within charity.

(4) The object of charity is God, as Augustine tells us [*CT* 1.27.28]. For charity loves nothing in our neighbour except God. However, God is not greater in himself than he is in our neighbour, nor greater in one neighbour than in another. Therefore charity does not love God more than our neighbour, nor one neighbour more than another.

(5) The reason for loving is likeness, according to Ecclesiasticus 13:15, 'Every animal loves what is like it.' But one human being is more like a neighbour than like God. Therefore the ordering within charity that Ambrose gives, whereby God is loved first,[25] must be incorrect.

(6) 1 John 4:20 says, 'If you do not love your brother, whom you see, how can you love God, whom you do not see?' He argues from the love of neighbour to the love of God by negation. An argument based on negation, though, begins from what is greater, not from what is less. Therefore our neighbour should be loved more than God.

(7) Love is a force that unites, as Dionysius says [*DivNames* 4.12]. But nothing is more united to anything else than to itself. Therefore we ought not to love God out of charity more than we love ourselves.

(8) Augustine says [*CT* 1.28.29] that all human beings are equally to be loved. Therefore one neighbour ought not to be loved more than another.

(9) We are instructed to love our neighbours as ourselves. Therefore all neighbours are equally to be loved.

(10) We love someone more if we want a greater good for them. But out of charity we want the same good for all our neighbours, i.e. eternal life. Therefore we ought not to love one neighbour more than another.

(11) If the ordering is a feature of charity, it ought to fall under a precept. But it does not seem to do this, because provided that we love each person as much as we ought, it does not seem to be a sin if we love someone else more. Therefore this ordering is not a criterion of charity.

(12) Charity on our journey imitates charity in our homeland. But in our homeland, we will love more those who are better, not those more closely related to us. Therefore it seems that if there is in fact an ordering within charity, while we are on our journey too we ought to

---

[25] Cf. Origen, *Homilies on the Song of Songs* 2.8.

love more those who are better rather than those who are more closely related to us. This contradicts Ambrose,[26] who says that we ought to love God first, then our parents, then our children, then members of our household.

(13) God is the reason why we love someone out of charity. But sometimes non-relations are closer to God than our relations, and even our parents. Therefore they ought more to be loved out of charity.

(14) As Gregory says [*HomGosp* 30.1], 'The proof of love is its being shown in what we do.' But sometimes the practice of charity, i.e. doing good, is shown more to a stranger than to a neighbour, as is clear in the distribution of ecclesiastical benefices.[27] Therefore it does not seem that in charity we should have more love for those close to us.

(15) 1 John 3:18 says, 'Let us not love in words or speech, but in deeds and truth.' But sometimes we ought to show the deeds of love to others more than to our parents. For example, a soldier obeys his military commander more than his father; and a son ought to pay back his benefactor rather than his father if there is an equal degree of need. Therefore we ought not to love our parents more.

(16) Gregory says that we ought to love those we have received from holy baptism[28] more than those we have produced from our own flesh. Therefore there are some who are unrelated to us whom we ought to love more than our relations.

(17) If it is more blameworthy to break off a friendship, then the friend in question must be more worthy of love. But it seems to be more blameworthy to break off those friendships where we chose the friends of our own accord than those with our relations, whom we acquired by the lot of nature rather than our own choice. Therefore we ought to love certain other friends more than our relations.

(18) If we ought to love more someone who is closer to us, then a wife, who is of one flesh [Gen 2:24], or a child, who is part of its parent, is closer to us than our parents. Therefore it seems that we ought to love a wife or child more than a parent. In that case, we ought not to love our parents most of all. Therefore the ordering within charity indicated by the saints seems incorrect.

---

[26] See note 25.
[27] That is, positions of responsibility within the Church, particularly those that are remunerative.
[28] I.e. our godchildren.

But on the other hand

Song of Solomon 2:4 says, 'The king led me into the banqueting-room and ordered charity within me.'

My reply

There is no doubt that according to all teaching and to the authority of scripture we ought to preserve an ordering within charity such that *God* is to be loved above everything else in both how we feel and what we do. As for loving our *neighbours*, here some used to be of the view that the ordering within charity concerns how we *feel* rather than what we *do*. They were inspired by Augustine's saying [*CT* 1.28.29] that we ought to love everyone equally, but 'since you cannot help everyone to the same degree, you ought to care most for those who are closest to you in place and time and opportunity in whatever way, as if they have been linked to you by lot'.

This position, however, seems unreasonable. For God provides for each person what his situation requires. That is why God bestows upon things that tend towards a natural end the love of and desire for that end, in accordance with the way that their condition requires them to tend towards that end. In this way, if something has a stronger natural movement towards a certain end, it will have a stronger inclination towards it; this is known as natural 'desire', and it can be seen in both light and heavy objects.

Desire or natural love, then, is an inclination placed in natural things towards their own natural ends; similarly, love in the sense of charity is an inclination infused into rational natures to make them tend towards God. Inasmuch as it is necessary for something to tend towards God, this inclination arises out of charity.

Now those things that tend towards God as their end stand in need above all of God's help; secondly, of help that comes from themselves; and thirdly of cooperation from their neighbour. Again, in this last category, there are degrees of cooperation. Some cooperate with us in a general way; others who are more closely connected with us, in a particular way: for everyone could not cooperate with everyone else in particular ways. Our body also assists us, though only in an instrumental way, as does whatever the body needs.

All this explains why our human *feeling* ought, through charity, to make us tend to love *God* first and chiefly; then secondly *ourselves*; then thirdly our *neighbours*; and, among them, those especially who are more closely connected to us and are apt by nature to help us more. (Those who hinder us, however, whoever they are, *qua* hindering us should be hated. Hence the Lord's words in Luke 14:26, 'Anyone who comes to me and does not hate his mother and father, cannot be my disciple.') Last of all, we should love our *bodies*.

Thus, too, when it comes to *acting* in a way drawn out by charity, here too we ought to observe the order that corresponds to our feelings in loving our neighbours. But we also ought to consider, as I have said above [articles 7 and 8], that other lawful and honourable types of love which arise from other causes can also be ordered towards charity. This allows charity to command the *activities* of loves of that sort. In this way, whatever one loves more on the basis of a love of that sort, one also loves more out of charity, when charity is commanding this.

It is clear too that natural love leads us to have stronger *feelings* of love for our relations, while social love does the same for our close friends, and so on for other types of love. This makes it clear that from the point of view of feeling, one neighbour is to be loved more than another out of charity also, when that is commanding the activities of other lawful types of love.

Replies to objections

(1) The object of faith is truth. Something ought to be believed more, therefore, insofar as it happens to be more true. Now truth consists in the intelligence's becoming equal with the thing. If we consider truth with reference to the character of *equality*, which does not admit of more or less, then something cannot be more or less true. On the other hand, if we consider it with reference to the thing's actual *being*, which gives the truth its character, as Aristotle says [*Met* 2.1, 993b30], then things are disposed in the same way in respect of being and of truth. Thus things that are greater in respect of being are greater in respect of truth.

For this reason even in the demonstrable branches of knowledge principles are believed more than their conclusions. This also happens in the area of faith. That is how St Paul in 1 Corinthians 15:12–19 proves the future resurrection of the dead from the resurrection of Christ.

(2) The ordering by reason is the ordering of the one that *orders*; the ordering of the will is the ordering of the one *being ordered*. It is in this latter way that it is appropriate for charity to be ordered.

(3) Charity does not recognise different degrees between the one who loves and the one who is loved, because it unites the two. However, it does recognise different degrees among things that are to be loved.

(4) Although God is not greater in one thing than in another, it is true that he exists more fully in himself than in some creature, and in one creature than in another.

(5) Wherever one loves *oneself* as the principal object of one's love, then the likeness between lover and beloved will indeed increase the love; this is the case for natural love. But for love in the sense of charity, the principal object is *God* himself. That is why we ought to love more out of charity whatever is more closely united to God, other things being equal.

(6) St John's reasoning is based on those who cling particularly to what they can see, for they love what they can see more than what they cannot see.

(7) By *nature*, nothing is more united with us than we are ourselves. However, through *feeling*, which has good as its object, we ought to be united more closely with the supreme good than with ourselves.

(8) All human beings are to be loved equally in the sense that the *good* that we ought to want for them is equal, i.e. eternal life.

(9) We are told to love our neighbour *as* ourselves, but not *as much as* ourselves; consequently, it does not follow that all neighbours are to be loved equally.

(10) We are said to love more not only when we want for others a greater good, but also when we hope with a more intensive feeling that they will have that good. In this way, although we hope for the same good for everyone, i.e. eternal life, we do not love everyone to an equal degree.

(11) It is not possible to bestow on one person what out of love we ought to, when there is someone else whom we ought to love less than this person, but whom in fact we love more. For in a situation of serious need we might end up helping the second person more, to the disadvantage of the first, whom we ought in fact to be loving more.

(12) Those who are in the *homeland* are already joined to the ultimate end. For this reason their love is governed only by that end itself. For them, then, the ordering of charity need only take notice of someone's degree of closeness to God. That is why those who are closer to God will

be loved more. But when we are on our *journey*, we need to direct ourselves towards our end; for this reason the ordering of love also responds to the degree of assistance that we are given by others in directing ourselves to our end. Consequently, it is not always the case that those who are better should be loved more; the degree of closeness must also be taken into account. Reasoning about the relative degree of love must be based on both of these considerations taken together.

This makes clear the reply to (13).

(14) A prelate does not distribute benefices *qua* Peter or Martin, but *qua* a teacher in the Church. For this reason, when distributing benefices, one ought to take notice not of a person's closeness to oneself, but of his closeness to God and of his usefulness to the Church. Similarly, when someone is responsible for distributing the goods of a household, he ought to distribute his master's property with an eye to service rendered to his master rather than to himself. With his own property, on the other hand, as for example with goods he has inherited or acquired for himself through his own labours, he ought to make distributions with an eye to the order of closeness, and of benefits, to himself.[29]

(15) (i) With respect to things that relate to you strictly as a private person, you ought to do more out of love for a parent than for someone unrelated; the only exception would be where the common good depended on the latter's good, since one ought to prefer that even to oneself. (So, you might expose yourself to danger of death in order to save the commander in a war, or the city's ruler in a city, because the safety of the whole community depends on them.)

(ii) By contrast, with respect to things that relate to you by reason of something additional, for example, insofar as you are a citizen or a soldier, you have more obligation to obey the city's ruler, or the commander, than your father.

(16) The authoritative text from Gregory should be interpreted with respect to matters relating to spiritual rebirth, where we are obliged to those whom we have received from holy baptism.

(17) The argument works with regard to things relating to social life, which is the basis of friendship with those outside the family.

(18) (i) With respect to the love by which someone loves *himself*, he loves a wife or children more than parents, for the wife is a part of the husband,

---

[29] The text is problematic at this point.

and the son a part of the father. That is why the love that someone has for a wife or son is more integrated into the love he has for himself than is the love he has for his father. But this is a case of love of his son not for the son's sake, but for his own sake. (ii) But with regard to the kind of loving by which we love *others for their sake*, then we should love a father more than a son, in that we have received a greater benefit from our father, and insofar as a son's honour depends more on his father's honour than vice versa. That is why in showing respect, in obedience, in responding to his wishes, and in similar matters, we are obliged to love a father more than a son. However, in providing necessities, we are obliged to care for a son more than a father, because parents ought to store up treasure for their children, and not vice versa, as 2 Corinthians 12:14 says.

Article 10: Whether it is possible in this life to possess complete charity[30]

Objections

It seems so, because:

(1) God does not give us impossible precepts, as Jerome says [*CommMatt* 2, on Matt 5:44]. But complete charity is included under a precept, as Deuteronomy 6:5 makes clear: 'You shall love the Lord your God with all your heart.' For whole and complete are the same. Therefore it is possible to have complete charity within this life.

(2) Augustine says [*TrueRel* 48.93] that complete charity requires us to love better things more. But this is possible within this life. Therefore we can have complete charity in this life.

(3) The character of love consists in some kind of union. But charity in this life can involve the greatest unity, since 'Whoever clings to God is one spirit', as 1 Corinthians 6:17 says. Therefore charity can be complete within this life.

(4) A complete x is as far removed as possible from the contrary of x. But charity can in this life resist all sin and temptation. Therefore charity in this life can be complete.

(5) In this life our feelings are drawn to God through love without an intermediary. Now when our intelligence will be drawn to God without

---

[30] The argument of this and the next article often depends on the range of meaning of the Latin words *perfectus* and *perfectio*, for which the translation uses several different words. It would be helpful to consult the Glossary under *perfectus* at this point.

an intermediary, then we will know him completely and wholly. Therefore we already love God completely and wholly. Therefore complete charity does exist in this life.

(6) Our will governs our actions. But loving God is an activity of the will. Therefore the human will can be wholly and perfectly drawn to God.

(7) The object of charity is God's goodness, which gives the greatest pleasure. But it is not difficult to carry on continuously and without a break when doing something pleasurable. Therefore it seems that in this life it would be easy to possess complete charity.

(8) If something is simple and indivisible, if you possess it at all, you must possess it wholly. But love in the sense of charity is simple and indivisible, both on the part of the soul that does the loving and on the part of its object, i.e. God. Therefore anyone who possesses charity in this life does so wholly and completely.

(9) Charity is the finest of the virtues, according to 1 Corinthians 12:31, 'I shall show you a still more excellent way', i.e. the way of charity. But the other virtues can be complete in this life; therefore so can charity.

But on the other hand

(1) Since all sins conflict with charity, as has been said [*DQChar* 6], complete charity requires a person to be without any sin. But this is not possible in this life, according to 1 John 1:8, 'If we say we have no sin, we deceive ourselves.' Therefore we cannot have complete charity in this life.

(2) Nothing can be loved if it is not known, as Augustine says [*Trin* 10.1.1]. But God cannot be known completely in this life, according to 1 Corinthians 13:9, 'Now we know in part.' Therefore neither can he be completely loved.

(3) Something that can always make progress is not yet complete. But charity in this life can always make progress, as the saying goes. Therefore charity in this life can never be complete.

(4) 'Complete charity casts out fear', as 1 John 4:18 says. But no human being can be without fear in this life. Therefore no one can possess complete charity.

My reply

'Complete' has three meanings: (i) complete simply speaking; (ii) complete in relation to a thing's nature; (iii) complete in relation to a stage of time. (i) Something is said to be complete *simply speaking* if it is so in all respects, and lacks no type of completeness. (ii) Something is said to be complete in relation to a thing's *nature* if it lacks nothing that is naturally possessed by that nature. For example, to say that a person's intelligence is complete does not mean that he understands everything intelligible, but that he understands everything that human beings naturally understand. (iii) We call someone complete in relation to a *stage of time* when he possesses everything that is naturally possessed at that stage: we can call a child 'complete' if it possesses whatever a human being needs to possess at its age.

We have to conclude that only God possesses complete charity simply speaking {cf. (i)}. Human beings may possess charity complete in relation to their nature, but not in this life {cf. (ii)}. Even in this life, we can possess charity complete in relation to the stage of time {cf. (iii)}.

To show this, we need to know that since both actions and dispositions take their type from their object, what it is for them to be complete also derives from that. The object of charity is the supreme good. Charity is complete simply speaking, then, when it is drawn to the supreme good to the extent that that is something lovable. Now the supreme good is infinitely lovable, because it is infinitely good. For this reason a creature, which must be finite, must also be unable to possess complete charity, simply speaking. Only the charity with which God loves himself can be called complete in this sense {cf. (i)}.

We can talk of charity as complete in relation to the nature of a rational creature {cf. (ii)} when that creature is turned towards loving God as wholly as it is able. In this life, three things prevent us from having our minds totally focused on God:

(a) the contrary inclinations of the mind. When the mind, through sin, turns towards some changeable good as its end, it turns away from the good that does not change;

(b) being engaged in the business of the world. St Paul says in 1 Corinthians 7:33–4 [Vulgate], 'Anyone who has a wife is worried about the things of the world, how to please his wife; he is divided'; that is, his heart does not move only towards God;

(c) the weakness of this present life, which means that we must engage with, and be distracted by, necessities so that our mind cannot be actively focused on God; I mean sleeping, eating and doing whatever is necessary to live this present life. Furthermore, the soul is dragged down by the very weight of the body so that it cannot see the divine light in its own being, and thus, by seeing this, have its charity made complete. According to St Paul in 2 Corinthians 5:6–7, 'As long as we are in the body, we are pilgrims away from God, for we walk by faith and not by sight.'

Now we can in this life be without mortal sin, which turns us away from God {cf. (a)}. Again, we can avoid engaging with affairs of the world, as St Paul says in 1 Corinthians 7:32: 'Anyone who has no wife can concern himself with the things of God, how to please God' {cf. (b)}. But we cannot, in this life, be free from the burden of our vulnerable flesh {cf. (c)}. Consequently, charity can be complete in this life insofar as we can remove the first two obstacles, but not insofar as we can remove the third. For this reason no one can possess in this life the completeness of charity that will exist after this life. The one exception is Christ, since it was distinctive of him that he was both travelling and in possession of his destination at the same time.

Replies to objections

(1) The words, 'You shall love the Lord your God with your whole heart' should be taken as a precept insofar as wholeness excludes everything contrary to divine love. However, insofar as it excludes everything that hinders our clinging completely to God, it is not a precept, but rather the goal of the precept. For it points us not to what we should do but to where we are going, as Augustine says [*CT* 1.32.35].

(2) We are not able to love the better things by as much as their goodness demands, and so we cannot possess complete charity, as I have said.

(3) We can find many levels of union between someone who loves and someone who is loved. Our mind will only be completely one with God when it is always actively drawn to him. That is not possible in this life.

(4) The completeness that belongs to something on account of its type belongs to it at every stage of time. For example, a man is complete in his rational soul at any time or age. Therefore the completeness that charity possesses at every time is the completeness that belongs to it on account of its type. Now the character of charity is that it loves God above all things, and does not love any other creature in preference to him. That is why, since temptation always originates with the love of some created good, or the fear of a contrary evil (which also derives from love), charity at every stage is, because of its type, able to resist any temptation to the

extent that the temptation will not lead us to mortal sin, but not so much that we are not affected by temptation at all. The latter will be true only with the completeness proper to our homeland.

(5) In our *homeland* God will be wholly seen and wholly loved in the same way, as follows. The 'wholly' can refer (i) to the *person* who loves and sees, because he will be involved in loving and seeing God to the limit of his powers as a creature. We can also take it (ii) that *God* will be wholly seen and loved in the sense that there will not be some *part* of him that is not seen and loved, because he is not composite, but simple. In another sense, however, God will be neither wholly loved nor wholly seen, since he will be neither seen nor loved by any created thing to the *degree* that he can be seen and loved.

But in *this life* God cannot be wholly loved and seen in even the first and second ways, because {cf. (ii)} he is not seen in his own being and {cf. (i)} it is not possible for a human being in this life to live in such a way that his feelings are actually focused on God without interruption. However, God can be wholly loved by human beings in this life in a certain sense, if their feelings include nothing that is contrary to divine love.

(6) (i) The will governs our actions in doing what we do, but not in persevering continuously in one thing, since the conditions of this life require our wills actually to focus on many different things.

(ii) Or else we can say that the will governs our actions in those things that are natural to human beings, but that complete charity, which will exist most fully in our homeland, is higher than a human being, especially if we are thinking of the human condition in this present life.

(7) An activity can cease to be pleasurable not only (i) from the side of the object, but also (ii) from the side of an agent that is short of the power needed for that activity. (i) We need, then, to say that being actively focused on God is always a pleasurable thing from the side of the *object*, (ii) but from *our* side there cannot in this life be such continual pleasure. The reason for this is that the human mind's activity of contemplation requires the exercise of the imaginative power and the other bodily powers;[31] these inevitably tire when they are exercised for a long time, because of the weakness of the body, and that is what hinders the pleasure. For this reason, Ecclesiastes 12:12 says, 'Frequent meditation wearies the flesh.'

---

[31] Cf. *ST* 1a 84.7. Aquinas holds that in the conditions of this present life, in which our intelligence is conjoined with the body, we cannot engage in intellectual thought without engaging the physical powers that produce and store images.

(8) Charity becomes complete not by growing in quantity, but by intensifying in quality. This intensiveness is not incompatible with the simple nature of charity.

(9) The object of the other, moral, virtues are *human* goods, which do not exceed human powers; for that reason we can attain them completely, in every sense, in this life. But the object of charity is an *uncreated* good, and this does exceed human powers. That is why the reasoning differs in the two cases.

Responses to arguments under 'But on the other hand'

(1) It is possible to live this life without *mortal* sin, but not without *venial*. The latter does not conflict with charity that is complete in relation to our journey, but only with that which is complete in relation to our homeland. For there, complete charity means having one's mind always actively focused on God. However, venial sin does not remove the disposition of charity, but only hinders its activity.

(2) We cannot know God completely in this life in the sense of knowing about him what he is. We can, however, know what he is not, as Augustine says [*Trin* 8.1.2], and this is what counts as complete knowledge while we are on our journey. Similarly, in this life we cannot love God perfectly in the sense of always actively focusing on him; but we can in the sense of never having our minds focused on something contrary to him.

(3) In this life charity cannot be complete either (i) simply speaking or (ii) in relation to human nature, but only (iii) in relation to the stage of life. Whatever is complete in this way is still able to grow, as is clear from children. In this way, charity in this life is always able to grow.

(4) Complete charity casts out the *slavish* fear that we have to begin with; it does not, though, cast out chaste or filial fear, nor even natural fear.

Article 11: Whether we are all obliged to possess complete charity

Objections

It seems so, because:

(1) Everyone is obliged by something that counts as a precept. But complete charity does count as a precept, since Deuteronomy 6:5 says, 'You shall love the Lord your God with all your heart.' Therefore everyone is obliged to possess complete charity.

(2) It seems to be part of complete charity that we refer all our actions to God. But we are all obliged to do this, since 1 Corinthians 10:31 says, 'Whether you eat or drink, or do anything else, do everything for the glory of God.' Therefore everyone is obliged to possess complete charity.

(3) *Rejoinder*: St Paul's precept entails that everything should be referred to God not *actively*, but rather *by disposition. But on the other hand* the precepts of the law deal with virtuous actions. Dispositions do not come under a precept. Therefore St Paul's precept should be taken to imply not a disposition that refers our actions to God, but the actions themselves.

(4) The Lord fulfils the precepts of the Old Law, saying in Matthew 5:17, 'I have not come to abolish the law, but to fulfil it.' Salvation requires the law to be fulfilled, as is clear from the words he adds, 'If your justice does not exceed that of the scribes and Pharisees, you will not enter the kingdom of heaven.' Everyone, though, is obliged to do whatever is required for salvation, and therefore to observe the fulfilment of the law in question. But this fulfilment is part of being perfect; that is why the Lord ends by saying, 'Be perfect, as your father in heaven is perfect.' Therefore everyone is obliged to possess complete charity.

(5) It is only the counsels that do not oblige everyone. But completeness of life or of charity is not achieved through the counsels. For we have been given a counsel about poverty, but it does not follow that the poorer someone is, the more perfect. We have also been given a counsel about virginity, but there are many virgins who possess charity less completely than other people. It seems, then, that completeness of charity does not depend on the counsels. Therefore no one is excepted from the obligation to possess complete charity.

(6) The status of a bishop is more elevated than that of a member of a religious order; otherwise, no one would be able lawfully to be transferred from the life of a religious to that of a prelate. That is why Dionysius says that bishops are more elevated; monks, however, are more completely devoted to their virtues; he also says that monks ought to lift themselves up to the elevated level that they see in bishops. Bishops, however, are not obliged to observe the counsel of poverty and related matters. Therefore complete charity does not lie in these.

(7) The Lord imposed on the apostles many obligations that are part of a perfect life: not to carry two tunics, or sandals, or a staff, or anything of that sort. But what he urged on the apostles, he urged on us all, according

to Mark 13:37, 'What I say to you, I say to everyone.' Therefore everyone is obliged to follow a perfect way of life.

(8) Anyone who possesses charity loves eternal life more than temporal life. But everyone is obliged to act with charity. Therefore everyone is obliged to put eternal life before bodily life. But, as Augustine tells us [*TEpJn* 5.4], when charity has attained completeness, it says, 'I am longing to be dissolved and to be with Christ' [Phil 1:23]. Therefore everyone is obliged to possess complete charity.

(9) Augustine says [*TEpJn* 5.4] that complete charity means that someone will be ready even to die for his brother. But we are all obliged to this; for 1 John 3:16 says, 'We know the charity of God in this, that he laid down his soul for us, and we ought to lay down our souls for our brothers.' Therefore everyone is obliged to possess complete charity.

(10) Everyone is obliged to avoid sin. But everyone who is without sin is confident about the day of judgement. As 1 John 4:17 says, 'Charity between God and us is complete in this, so that we can have confidence on the day of judgement.' Therefore we are all obliged to possess complete charity.

(11) Aristotle says [*NE* 9.1.7, 1164b3], 'We cannot give back to God or to parents as much as we have received; it is enough that everyone gives them as much as he can.' But complete charity consists in one's doing what one can for God, for no one does more than he can. Therefore everyone is obliged to have complete charity.

(12) Members of religious orders make profession of a perfect way of life. Therefore they seem to be obliged to possess complete charity, and everything that is included in a perfect way of life.

But on the other hand

We are not obliged to achieve something that is not in our power. But it is not in our power to possess complete charity: this comes from God. Therefore it cannot come under a precept.

My reply

We can take the solution to this question from our previous argument. For we have shown above (i) that there is a completeness that corresponds to charity as the type of thing that it is, inasmuch as it consists in taking away any inclination that is contrary to charity. Again, (ii) there is a second sort of completeness without which charity can still exist, but which is part of its existing well, and this consists in getting rid of worldly engagements, which hinder human feelings from moving freely towards God. (iii) There is a third type of completeness of charity, which is not possible for human beings in this life, and (iv) a fourth, which in fact no created nature can ever achieve, as is clear from my earlier argument.

It is clear, moreover, that we say that everyone is obliged to do whatever is needed for achieving salvation. No one can reach eternal life without charity, and if we have it, we will come to eternal salvation. Consequently, we are all obliged to possess complete charity in sense (i), as we are obliged to possess charity itself. We are not obliged to possess complete charity in sense (ii), for without it we can still possess charity, and charity of any sort is sufficient for salvation. Much less are we obliged to possess complete charity in senses (iii) or (iv), since no one is obliged to do something impossible.

Replies to objections

(1) That 'wholeness', insofar as it comes under the precept about charity, relates to that completeness {cf. (i)} without which charity cannot exist.

(2) It is not possible in this life *actively* to refer everything to God, just as it is not possible always to be thinking about God. For this belongs to the completeness proper to our homeland. But as for *effectively*[32] referring everything to God, that belongs to complete charity in sense (i), which we are all obliged to possess.

To show this, we need to consider that, just as with efficient causes the power of the primary cause remains in all the subsequent causes, so too the aim of the primary end remains effective in all the secondary ends. That is why whenever anyone is *actively* aiming at some secondary end, *effectively* he is aiming at the primary end. For example, a doctor while he is collecting herbs is actively aiming at making a medicine, and he may not be thinking at all about health; effectively, however, he is aiming at the health for which he is making the medicine. In this way, when one orders oneself towards God as one's end, the aim of the ultimate end – that is,

---

[32] In this and the next reply, Aquinas distinguishes between *actu*, 'actively', *virtute*, 'effectively' and *habitu*, 'dispositionally'.

God – remains effective in everything that one does for his sake. That is why, if we possess charity, anything we do can deserve reward. That is the sense in which St Paul instructs us to refer everything to the glory of God.

(3) Referring things to God (i) effectively is a different thing from referring them (ii) dispositionally. (ii) You can refer something to God *dispositionally* even when you are neither doing anything nor actively aiming to do anything, as when you are asleep. (i) Referring something to God *effectively*, though, means that you act for an end that is ordered towards God. Therefore to refer things to God dispositionally does not come under a precept, but to refer everything to God effectively does come under the precept of charity, since this is nothing other than having God as our ultimate end.

(4) The words 'be perfect' seem to need referring to love of our enemies, which is governed in one way by the fullness of a counsel, and in another by the necessity of a precept, as I have said above.

(5) A perfect life consists (i) in some things principally and *per se*, and (ii) in others secondarily and *per accidens*. (i) Principally and *per se* it consists in things that pertain to one's inner tendency of mind, and especially in active charity, which is the root of all the virtues. (ii) Secondarily, though, and *per accidens*, it consists also in exterior things, for example, in virginity, poverty, and similar matters. These are said to be a part of perfection in three ways:

(a) In that they remove from us those occupations that hinder us, such that when they are removed, our mind can be drawn more freely to God. That is why when the Lord says in Matthew 19:21 'If you want to be perfect, go and sell all you have and give to the poor,' he then adds, 'And come, follow me' to show that poverty is only connected with perfection insofar as it disposes us to follow Christ; and we follow him not with the experiences of our bodies, but with the feelings of our minds. In the same way, St Paul in 1 Corinthians 7:32 gives the counsel about not marrying, because someone who is a virgin 'thinks about the things of God, about how to please God'. The reasoning is the same for the other similar matters.

(b) In the sense that they can be the effects of charity. For those who love God completely withdraw themselves from whatever might distract them from being free for God.

(c) In the sense of completeness of repentance, because no other compensation for sin can be as adequate as religious vows; through these, people consecrate themselves to God: their soul through the vow of obedience, their body through the vow of celibacy, and their possessions through the vow of poverty.

In the light of all this, {cf. (i)} in things that are connected with perfection principally and *per se*, it follows that the perfection is greater where these are more to be found; thus someone who possesses greater charity is more perfect. However, {cf. (ii)} in things that are connected with perfection because of their consequences and *per accidens*, so to speak, it does not follow that where they are more to be found, there will be greater perfection, simply speaking. That is why it does not follow that the poorer someone is, the more perfect. Perfection in such matters needs to be measured by its relation to the things that constitute charity simply speaking. So, for example, one can be called more perfect when one's poverty takes one away from earthly business and makes one more freely available for God.

(6) The difference between the *honourable* and *pleasurable* types of friendship is that in the second a friend is loved for the sake of pleasure; in the first, a friend is loved for himself, but pleasure follows as a consequence. A *perfect* honourable friendship includes one's having from time to time, for the friend's sake, even to go without the pleasure that one has in his company, because one is busy doing something to help him. In this type of friendship, it shows greater love to be apart from the friend for his sake than to be unwilling to give up his company even for his sake. But if one willingly and easily separates oneself from the friend's company and takes more pleasure in other things, then it is evident that one loves him hardly or not at all.

We can consider the following three levels within charity towards God, who is most of all to be loved for himself. (i) Some people willingly and without any great difficulty separate themselves from their leisure for contemplating God, so that they can involve themselves in worldly business. They appear to have little or no charity. (ii) Others take so much pleasure in the leisure they have for contemplating God that they are unwilling to give it up even to devote themselves to God's service for the salvation of their neighbours. (iii) Others have reached such a peak of charity that they will abstain even from contemplating God, although that brings them the very greatest pleasure, in order to serve God in the salvation of their neighbours. This degree of perfection is found in St Paul, who says in Romans 9:3, 'I was willing to be cut off' (i.e. separated) 'from Christ for my brothers', and in Philippians 1:23–4, 'I am longing to be dissolved and to be with Christ, but it is necessary to remain in the flesh for your sake.'

This third level of perfection is the one that belongs in a distinctive way to prelates and preachers and anyone else who is engaged in securing the salvation of others. That is why Jacob's ladder symbolises them by means of the angels who ascend in order to contemplate and descend in order to care for their neighbours' salvation.[33] It takes nothing away from the elevated status of the prelate if some abuse this, and seek the position for the sake of temporal goods, as though they are not attracted by the sweetness of contemplation. Similarly, as Romans 3:3–4 tells us, the unbelief of the majority does not nullify the faith of God.

(7) In the teaching of the gospels (i) some things are said to the apostles as representing all the faithful, and these are part of what is necessary for salvation. That is why Mark 13:37 says, 'What I say to you, I say to everyone: stay awake.' For 'wakefulness' there means the concern that *everyone* ought to have not to be found by Christ unprepared. (ii) Other things are said to the apostles that are connected to a perfect way of life or to the duties of a prelate, and the words 'What I say to you, I say to everyone' cannot be applied to those words.

We need to know, though, that the Lord's words to the disciples in Luke [9:3, cf. 10:4] 'Take nothing on the journey', and so on, are not connected with a perfect way of life, as Augustine explains. Rather, they are connected with the authority that belongs to their standing *as apostles*. This enabled them to carry nothing with them and live by being served by those to whom they were preaching the Gospel. That is why it says in the same passage that a workman is worthy of his hire, or his food [Luke 10:7]. This, then, was neither a precept nor a counsel, but a concession. Because of this, St Paul, who carried what he needed with him, and did not make use of the concession, was being extra generous, like a soldier who fights at his own expense, as 1 Corinthians 9:3–18 makes clear.

(8) Human beings possess two types of feeling: (i) that of charity, which makes the soul long to be with Christ, and (ii) that which is natural, which makes the soul shrink from being separated from the body. The second is so much part of our nature that not even old age took it away from Peter, as Augustine says [*TGJn* 123.5].

---

[33] Aquinas here defends the mixed life of the friars, including his own Dominican order, as superior both to the purely active and to the purely contemplative life.

The combination of these two means that the soul would like to be joined with God without being separated from the body, in keeping with St Paul's words in 2 Corinthians 5:4, 'We do not want to be stripped, but to put on another garment, so that what is mortal will be absorbed by life.' But because this is impossible – 'for as long as we are in the body we are pilgrims away from the Lord' [2 Cor 5:6] – a certain conflict arises between the feelings in question. The more complete that charity is, the more perceptibly the feeling of charity overwhelms the natural feelings; this is part of complete charity. That is why St Paul adds in 2 Corinthians 5:8, 'However, we are confident and we have a good will, more to be pilgrims apart from the body, and to be in the presence of the Lord.'

With those who possess charity in an *incomplete* way, even if the feeling of charity wins out, the conflict with natural feeling will mean that the victory of charity is not felt. Therefore it belongs to *complete* charity to say openly, without hesitation, and with confidence (as St Paul puts it) 'I am longing to be dissolved and to be with Christ' [Phil 1:23]. The *basic necessity* for charity is that the soul should in some way prefer enjoying God to being united with the body, even if this is not felt.

(9) To lay down one's 'soul', i.e. the present life, for one's brothers is a part in one way (i) of what is *necessary* for charity and in another (ii) of what makes charity *complete*. (i) For we are bound to love our neighbours more than our own body; that is why in a situation where we are obliged to care for our neighbour's safety, we are also obliged to expose our bodily lives to danger for the sake of that. (ii) But it is part of complete charity to expose our bodily lives to danger for our neighbours even in cases where we are not obliged to them.

(10) Although everyone is obliged to be without mortal sin, not everyone is able to feel safe in this respect, but only the perfect, who have their sins entirely under control.

(11) We are obliged wholly to repay our parents, and much more God, insofar as we can; that, though, means in the way usual within human life. Someone can indeed sometimes be more generous than that; however, we are not obliged to be so by the necessity of a precept.

(12) No one makes profession of perfect charity. But some people make profession of a perfect *state of life*, which consists of elements like poverty and fasting that are ordered instrumentally towards perfect charity. One

is not obliged to engage in all of these, but only those which one professes. However, perfect charity does not come under the vow such people take, but is rather their end, which they are trying to attain through the vows they have made.

Article 12: Whether charity once possessed can be lost

Objections

It seems not, because:

(1) 1 John 3:9 says, 'All those who are born of God do not commit sin, since God's seed remains in them. And they cannot sin because they are born of God.' But only the children of God possess charity, for that is what differentiates the children of the kingdom from the children of perdition, as Augustine says [*Trin* 15.18.32]. Therefore no one who possesses charity can lose it by sinning.

(2) Every virtue that is lost by sinning also withers through sin. But, as Augustine says [*TEpJn* 3.12], 'Charity is an invisible anointing, which will be the root of anything in which it is found, which cannot wither, is fed by the heat of the sun and does not wither.' Therefore charity cannot be lost through sin.

(3) Augustine says [*Trin* 8.7.10] that if love is not truly love it should not be called love. But he also says, 'Charity which can be lost was never truly charity.'[34] Therefore it was not charity at all. Therefore anyone who possesses charity cannot lose it by sinning.

(4) Prosper says [*ContLife* 3.13], 'Charity is right will, inseparably joined to God, without stain, innocent of corruption, liable to no flaw of changeability; with it no one ever was or will be able to sin.' Therefore charity once possessed cannot be lost through sin.

(5) Gregory says [*HomGosp* 30.2], 'The love of God does great things, if it is present.' But no one can lose charity by doing great things. Therefore if charity is in someone it cannot be lost.

(6) We love God through charity more than we love ourselves through natural love. But we never lose love of ourselves by sinning. Therefore neither do we lose charity.

---

[34] The quotation is actually from *De salutaribus documentis ad quemdam comitem*, 7, by Paul of Friuli (Paul the Deacon), a monk of Monte Cassino.

(7) Free judgement does not tend towards sin except through some other motivation to sin. However, the motivation of all sin is love of oneself, which, as Augustine says [*CG* 14.28], 'makes the city of Babylon'. But charity excludes this, because, as Dionysius says [*DivNames* 4.13], 'Divine love causes ecstasy, and does not allow you to love yourself.' Similarly, greed is held to be the root of all evils, as St Paul says [1 Tim 6:10]. But charity also excludes greed, as Augustine says [*83DQ* 36.1]. Therefore someone who possesses charity cannot lose it by sinning.

(8) Anyone who has charity is led by the Spirit of God, according to Galatians 5:18, 'If you are led by the Spirit, you are not under the law.' But the Holy Spirit, since it has infinite power, cannot fail in its activity. Therefore it seems that someone who possesses charity cannot sin.

(9) One cannot sin in contradiction of a disposition which has its being in what it does: for Aristotle says [*NE* 7.3.5, 1146b32] that we cannot sin against active knowledge but only against dispositional knowledge. But charity always consists in doing something; for Gregory says [*HomGosp* 30.2], 'The love of God is never at rest.' Therefore no one can sin against charity so as to be able to lose it through sin.

(10) If anyone loses charity, he loses it either while he has it or while he does not have it. But he cannot lose it through sin while he has it, because if that were the case, sin could coexist with charity. Nor, though, can he lose it while he has not got it, because someone cannot lose what he does not have. Therefore there is no way that someone can lose charity.

(11) Charity exists in the soul as an accidental quality. An accidental quality can be lost in four ways:

(i) because the *subject* is destroyed; charity cannot be lost in this sense, because the human soul, the subject of charity, is indestructible;

(ii) because its *cause* fails, as when the air lacks light because there is no sun. But charity cannot be lost in this way because its cause, i.e. God, never fails;

(iii) because its *object* fails, as when the death of a son makes someone cease to be a father. But charity cannot be lost in this way, because its object is eternal goodness, i.e. God;

(iv) through *the action of something contrary to it*, as when water loses its coldness because of the action of heat upon it. But charity cannot be lost in this way either, since it is stronger than sin, which, it seems, is what acts in a way contrary to it; as Song of Solomon 8:6–7 puts it, 'Love is as strong as death', and again, 'Many waters cannot extinguish charity.'

Therefore charity cannot fail in any of these ways in someone who possesses it.

(12) Sin is a sort of rational evil. But evil is active only in virtue of something good, as Dionysius says [*DivNames* 4.18–35]. However, good is not contrary to good, as Aristotle tells us [*Cat* 11, 13b35]; and so good cannot destroy good, since each thing is destroyed by its contrary. Charity, then, cannot be destroyed through sin.

(13) If charity is lost through sin, it must be through a sin that either (i) exists or (ii) does not exist. (i) But it is not lost through an *existing* sin, because mortal sin cannot coexist with charity; (ii) nor again through a sin that does *not exist*, since something non-existent cannot do anything. Therefore there is no way that charity can be lost through sin.

(14) If charity is lost through sin, then charity and sin both exist in the soul either (i) at the same instant or (ii) at different ones. (i) But not at the *same* instant, because then they would coexist. (ii) Nor, though, at *different* ones, because then there would have to be some time between, in which the person would possess neither sin nor charity. That cannot be right. Therefore charity cannot be lost through sin.

(15) Peter Lombard says [*Sent* 3.31.1.9], that complete charity cannot be lost through sin. But complete and incomplete charity share the same type. Therefore incomplete charity cannot be lost through sin.

(16) The intelligence stands to knowing the truth in the same way as the will does to loving the good. But the intelligence, by knowing something true, knows the first truth; therefore by loving something good, it loves supreme goodness. But no one sins[35] except by turning in love to a changeable good. Therefore in every sin the person loves the supreme good and love of this is charity. Charity, then, can never be lost through sin.

(17) Just as in the class of efficient cause an agent can be either universal or particular, so also in the class of final cause. But a particular agent always acts by virtue of the universal agent. Therefore a particular end always moves the will by virtue of the ultimate and common end, which is God. Thus the conclusion is the same as in (16).

(18) Charity is a sign that someone is a true disciple of Christ, according to John 13:35, 'In this they will all know that you are my disciples, because you have love for one another.' But you can only be a true disciple of Christ if you are always his disciple. That is why Augustine says [*TGJn* 27.8],

---

[35] Omitting *qui amat*.

when explaining John 6:66, 'Many of his disciples left him and went away', that these people were not true disciples of Christ. Also, the Lord says in John 8:31, 'If you abide by my words, you will be true disciples of mine.' Therefore someone who does not always abide in love never possessed charity in the first place.

(19) Every movement follows the pressure of whatever is in control. But in the heart of someone who possesses charity, charity is in control, because it takes hold of the whole heart, according to the command in Deuteronomy 6:5, 'You shall love the Lord your God with all your heart.' Therefore every movement of someone who possesses charity is in accordance with charity. Therefore charity cannot be lost through sin.

(20) Differentiating features of a class or a type cannot qualify numerically the same thing. But 'destructible' and 'indestructible' make a difference of type, as Aristotle says [*Met* 10.10, 1058b26]. Since, then, charity on our journey and charity in our homeland are numerically the same, it seems that since charity in our homeland cannot be destroyed, then neither can charity on our journey.

(21) If charity is destroyed, it turns either (i) into something else, or (ii) into nothing. (i) But not into *something else*, because this only happens to those forms that are drawn out of the capacity possessed by matter. (ii) Nor, however, can charity be reduced to *nothing*, because God never destroys charity, and God alone can make nothing from something, just as God alone can make something from nothing; for there is the same distance between the two in each case. Therefore it seems that charity cannot be destroyed.

(22) Something through which sin is removed cannot be destroyed by sin. But sin is removed through charity, according to 1 Peter 4:8, 'Charity blots out a multitude of sins.' Therefore charity cannot be lost through sin.

(23) The gloss, quoting Augustine, comments on Psalm 27:2, 'While evil men seize me to devour my flesh', as follows: 'If the gift is removed, the giver is defeated.' But God, who is the giver of charity, cannot be defeated. Therefore charity cannot be removed through sin.

(24) The soul is united to God through charity as a bride, in a sort of spiritual marriage. But physical marriage cannot be dissolved just because disagreement afflicts the marriage. Therefore charity cannot be removed through sin, which makes the mind disagree with the things of God.

But on the other hand

(1) Revelation 2:4: 'I have a few things against you, because you have abandoned the charity you first had.'

(2) Gregory says [*HomGosp* 30.2], 'God comes into some people's hearts but does not make his dwelling there, because while through remorse they pay regard to God, then in the time of temptation they return to committing sins as if they hardly deplored them.' But God does not come into the hearts of the faithful except through charity. Therefore someone can lose charity after possessing it, through subsequent sin.

(3) 1 Samuel 16:18 says of David that the Lord was with him. But afterwards he sinned mortally by committing both adultery and murder. God, though, is with a person through charity. Therefore someone can sin mortally after possessing charity.

(4) Charity is the life of the soul, according to 1 John 3:14, 'We know that we have been carried from death to life, because we love our brothers.' But natural life can be lost through natural death. Therefore the life of charity can be lost through the death of mortal sin.

My reply

Peter Lombard holds [*Sent* 1.17.1.2] that charity in us is the Holy Spirit. He did not mean, however, that the activity of our love is the Holy Spirit, but that the Holy Spirit moves our soul to love God and neighbour, just as it moves it to other virtuous activity. But it moves the soul to other virtuous activity by means of certain dispositions of infused virtues; while in his view it moves us to the action of loving God and neighbour without any intermediary disposition.

Peter Lombard's opinion was true, then, in as far as he held that the soul is moved by the Holy Spirit to love God and neighbour; but it was incomplete in that he did not hold that we have in us a disposition, something created, which completes the human will so that it can act with love of this sort. For, as I argued above [in article 1], we should hold that there is such a disposition in the soul.

We can, then, consider charity in four ways:

(i) from the side of the *Holy Spirit*, which moves the soul to love God and neighbour; here we have to say that the movement of the Holy Spirit always effects whatever it intends to. 'For the Holy Spirit works in the soul, distributing to individuals as it wishes', as 1 Corinthians 12:11 puts it. (a) That is why when the Holy Spirit, as it judges best, wishes to give to certain people an *enduring* movement of love towards God, it is not possible for them to have in them any sin that would exclude charity. (I mean, not possible from the side of the moving power. It could be possible, though, from the side of free judgement, which can change.) Such things are 'the gifts of God, by which, without doubt, those who are set free are set free', as Augustine says [*GPers* 14.35]. (b) The Spirit may also as it judges best, grant to other people to be moved *temporarily* by a movement of love towards God, but not grant them to persevere in this to the end, as is also clear from Augustine [*AdGr* 6.10].

(ii) We can consider charity with reference to its *power*. From this point of view, no one who possesses charity can sin, that is, not by the power of the charity itself, as something that possesses a form x cannot act against x by the power of x. For example, something hot cannot cool anything, or be cold, by the power of being hot. However, it can lose its heat and then both cool down itself and cool other things. For this reason, Augustine can say [*SermMount* 2.24.79] the following, explaining Matthew 7:18, 'A good tree cannot produce bad fruit': 'In the same way, something that was snow can stop being snow, but it cannot be warm snow. Similarly, someone who was bad can stop being bad, but it cannot happen that someone who is bad does things well.' The same reasoning holds concerning what is good in respect of any virtue, since no one can use a virtue badly.

(iii) We can consider charity from the side of the *will*, insofar as the will is the subject of charity as matter is of form. (a) Here we must notice that when a form fulfils the matter in question to the limits of its capacity, the matter will have no more capacity to possess further form. Hence it will possess the form in such a way that it cannot lose it, as is clear from the matter of the heavenly bodies. (b) Some forms do not, however, fulfil the matter's capacity to its limit, and then there remains some capacity to possess further form. Then that form is possessed in such a way that it can be lost, from the side of the matter or of the subject. This is clear with the forms of the elements.

Now charity fulfils the capacity of its subject by leading its subject to act with love. For this reason in our *homeland*, where rational creatures actively love God with their whole heart, and love nothing else except by actively referring it to God, charity is possessed in such a way that it cannot be lost {cf. (a)}. When we are on our *journey*, however, charity does not fulfil the capacity of the soul to its limit {cf. (b)}, because the soul is not always actively moved towards God, referring everything to him with an active intention. For that reason, we possess charity on our journey in such a way that it can be lost, that is, from the side of the subject.

(iv) We can consider charity from the side of the *subject* insofar as it is, because of its type, related to charity as a capacity is related to a disposition. We need to consider here that the disposition of a virtue makes us tend to act correctly insofar as it allows us to evaluate the end correctly, since, as Aristotle says [*NE* 3.5.18, 1114b15], 'How the end appears to one will correspond to what one is like.' For just as with the taste of an object the judgement that our tastebuds make depends on whether their condition is good or bad, so with things valuable to us as human beings, we evaluate them as good in accordance with the condition of the dispositions inherent in us, whether that is good or bad. What disagrees with that, we find bad and off-putting. Hence St Paul's words in 1 Corinthians 2:14, 'An unspiritual person does not grasp the things that belong to God's Spirit.'

However, it can happen sometimes that something can appear in a certain way to someone according to the inclination of his dispositions, but appear differently according to something else. For example, the pleasures of the flesh might seem good to someone who is lustful according to the inclination of his own disposition, but might seem bad to the same person according to rational reflection or the authority of scripture. For this reason, someone who possesses the disposition of lustfulness sometimes acts in a way contrary to it by evaluating something in this manner. Conversely, someone who possesses a virtuous disposition sometimes acts against the inclination of his own disposition, when something appears differently to him in some other way, for example, through some emotion or other temptation.

Therefore, when no one is able to evaluate the end and the object of charity except in a way that accords with the inclination of charity, then no one will be able to act against the disposition of charity. This will be the case in our homeland, when we will see the very being of God, which is also the very being of goodness. Hence, just as no one can in this present life want anything except under the general character of goodness, and something that is good cannot, *qua* good, not be loved, similarly, then, no one will be unable to love the good that is God. For that reason, no one who sees God in his own being can act against charity. That is why charity in our *homeland* will not be able to be lost.

But now our mind cannot see the very being of divine goodness, but only some of its effects. These can seem good or not depending on how they are considered. For example, a spiritual good may not seem good to those who are affected by sensual desire for the pleasures of the flesh, insofar as it is incompatible with these. That is why charity on our *journey* can be lost through mortal sin.

Replies to objections

(1) St John's words are to be understood according to the power of the Holy Spirit, which moves the soul and acts unfailingly as it wishes.

(2) Augustine is speaking there about charity according to the power of charity in itself. Of *itself*, it possesses enough for it never to wither. But sometimes it can be lost because of the changeability of its *subject*, as I have argued.

(3) True love of its own character is such that it is never lost. For if you love someone truly, you will aim in your mind never to lose that love. But sometimes your aim changes and then the love, which was true, disappears. However, if someone had the aim of ceasing to love at some point, then that would not be true love. From this it is clear that charity cannot be lost according to its own power, but can be lost according to the power of a changeable subject.

(4) The authoritative text from Prosper speaks about charity according to its own power and not according to the power of the subject.

(5) Charity as long as it exists has an inclination to do great things. It wants and aims at this according to the character of its own power. But sometimes it fails in this because of the changeability of the subject.

(6) Since human beings have a double nature, i.e. the intelligent, which is more fundamental, and the sensory, which is lesser, true love of oneself involves loving oneself for a rational good. If you love yourself for a sensory good contrary to a rational good, strictly speaking you are hating rather than loving yourself. As Psalm 11:5 puts it, 'Someone who loves wickedness hates his own soul.' Aristotle says the same [*NE* 9.4.8, 1166b6]. It follows that true love of oneself is lost through a sin that is contrary to it, as is the love of God.

(7) Charity, according to its aim, excludes all motivation to sin. For it is part of the character of charity that one does not want to have excessive sensual desire or love oneself in a disordered way. But the contrary

sometimes happens because our nature is changeable and damaged, in keeping with St Paul's words in Romans 7:19, 'For I do not do the good that I want, but I do the evil that I hate.'

(8) As long as one follows the movement of the Holy Spirit, one does not sin. When one resists, then one sins.

(9) The *being* of charity does not always consist in doing things; if so, then those who were asleep would not possess charity. The words 'The love of God is never at rest', though, refer to the *aim* of charity, which is that one should give oneself wholly to God.

(10) Loss stands to the thing that is possessed as destruction to the thing that exists. Now destruction begins with something that exists and ends with its not existing, because there is a change from being to not being; in the same way, therefore, loss, since it is a change from possessing to not possessing, begins with possessing and ends with not possessing. That is why the process of losing charity begins at a time when charity is possessed, and ends at a time when it is not possessed.

(11) Charity ceases to exist in the soul in all four different ways, as follows:

(i) Although the substance that is the *subject* of charity is indeed indestructible, that subject can become unfitted for this form through a contrary tendency to sin.

(ii) Again, although the *cause* of charity is indestructible, its influence can be hindered through sin, which separates us from God.

(iii) For the same reason, charity can fail on the side of the *object*, whenever the will turns away from the unchangeable good.

(iv) It can also disappear through the *contrary motivation* to sin, which, although strictly speaking it is weaker than charity, can in a specific situation be stronger, i.e. when charity is not actively at work and a sinful motive actively moves us to carry out some specific activity. Similarly, Aristotle also shows [*NE* 7.7.8, 1150b20] that knowledge can be overcome by emotion, even though it is very strong, when it is not actually active, but there as a disposition which emotion incapacitates. While knowledge is very strong in general, an emotion can be so in the case of a particular deed; similarly, charity is very strong as regards the ultimate end, but a sinful motive can be strong for some particular action.

(12) Aristotle says that the good of one *virtue* cannot be contrary to the good of another. This is what he means in the discussion in the *Categories* [11, 13b35] and in the *Ethics* [2.3.7, 1104b30]. But in *natural* things one

good can be contrary to another, for each of two contraries is a sort of natural good. In this way, the good that moves the desire towards sin is contrary to the divine good, which is the object of charity in that the end of charity lies in this. In this way, there cannot be more than one ultimate end, just as, in a kingdom where there can only be one king, someone who makes himself king acts contrary to the king, as John 19:12 tells us: 'Everyone who makes himself a king opposes Caesar.'

(13) Sin does not act as an *agent* in driving out charity, but as a *contrary*. That is the sense in which the arrival of sin means the departure of charity, just as the arrival of the light means the departure of darkness. For light drives out sin simply by coming into existence as itself. But the motive to sin drives out charity by pre-existing in the perception of the soul.

(14) When one consents to mortal sin, one does so with some rational deliberation; for it is not mortal sin if there is no deliberative consent. However, deliberation is a sort of movement, and takes a measurable time; at the last instant of this period of time sin exists in the soul. But it is not possible to posit an instant directly preceding the final instant, when charity is there. This is because instants do not stand in a sequence; instead time is continuous. Therefore charity is in the soul during the whole preceding time that finishes with the final instant, and sin is there first at that final instant. Therefore we cannot give a final instant when charity is there, but only an ultimate time, as Aristotle makes clear [*Phys* 8.1, 251b18].

(15) If Peter Lombard is meaning complete charity, which is the charity of our *homeland*, it is true that it cannot be lost, for the reasons given above. But if he is meaning charity on our *journey*, in whatever way it is complete, it is not true that it can become unlosable through the way that it inheres in its subject. It can, however, become unlosable through the Holy Spirit's power to effect change. That is how we can use the word 'confirmed' of those who have been confirmed in charity.[36]

(16) When we know any true thing we know the first truth as the first exemplar, in its image or its traces. Similarly, when we love any good thing, we love the supreme good. But this love of the supreme good is not enough for the character of charity: that also requires the supreme good to be loved *as* the object of blessedness.

---

[36] The good angels and the blessed dead are said to be 'confirmed' (*confirmatus*: literally, strengthened, resolute, proved) in goodness, so that they are incapable of sinning.

This also makes clear the answer to (17).

(18) Augustine comments as follows when explaining John 10:27, 'My sheep listen to my voice and do not listen to the voice of anyone else': 'Christ has a voice that is heard only by those who are his own sheep through predestination; it is his voice saying, "Whoever perseveres to the end will be saved."' From this, he takes it that whoever does not remain in Christ's words is not *truly* his disciple, because he has not learnt effectively from him how to persevere. However, one can be a disciple *temporarily*, with a love of God and neighbour that is only of a temporal nature.

(19) As long as charity is *actively* in control in us, then we will not be moved by any contrary movement, but follow the movement of charity. That is why the supreme remedy for sin is for one to return to one's heart, and turn that towards the love of God. But when one is not actively being moved according to charity, then sometimes the contrary movement of sin arises.

(20) Being destroyed and coming into existence, or becoming something, both happen in the strict sense to things that have being: I mean only things that subsist in themselves. Accidents, and forms that do not subsist in themselves, are called 'beings' not because they do have their own being, but because something else exists for them. That is why strictly speaking it is not accidents or forms that come into being and are destroyed, but their *subjects*. For example, when a body becomes white, that is just what it is for whiteness to 'become', just as when a body is white, that is just what it is for whiteness to 'be'. The same reasoning works for destruction. Hence, 'destructible' and 'indestructible' are attributed *per se* not to accidents, but to *substances*. That is why nothing prevents charity on our journey from being numerically the same as charity in our homeland, even though the former can be lost but the latter cannot.

(21) As I have just said, charity strictly speaking is not destroyed, but the subject ceases to share in it. Therefore one cannot say strictly that charity is reduced either to something or to nothing.

(22) Because of the changeability of the subject, just as charity that comes upon sin destroys it, so sin that comes upon charity drives it out. For contraries drive each other out.

(23) If a gift were removed by violence, it would seem that the giver was defeated, because it is his role to preserve the gift for the person to whom he gave it. But if the receiver *voluntarily* throws it away, then the

giver does not appear to be defeated, since it is not his role to force people into virtue.

(24) Through marriage, a woman loses the power over her own body. But the soul does not through charity lose the power of free judgement. Therefore the reasoning does not follow.

Article 13: Whether charity is lost through a single act of mortal sin

Objections

It seems not, because:

(1) Origen says [*Prin* 1.3.8], 'Sometimes people who remain on the highest and perfect level might feel they have had enough. If so, I do not think that they can suddenly be emptied and fall, but it will be necessary for them to slip down gradually, bit by bit. In this way, it can sometimes happen that those who slip briefly, and quickly come back to their senses, do not seem to collapse completely.' But someone who loses charity, collapses completely, according to St Paul in 1 Corinthians 13:2: 'If I do not possess charity, I am nothing.' Therefore charity is not lost through a single mortal sin, which can sometimes happen suddenly.

(2) Bernard[37] says that when Peter denied Christ, charity was not extinguished in him, but put to sleep. However, when he denied Christ, this was a mortal sin. Therefore charity is not lost through a single act of mortal sin.

(3) Pope Leo says in a sermon on the Passion [*Serm* 60.4], addressing Peter, 'The Lord did not see in you either defeated faith or deserted love, but rather your steadfastness that was shaken. Your tears overflowed as your feelings had not dried up. This fountain of love washed away the words of fear.' Therefore the love of charity did not disappear in Peter through an act of mortal sin.

(4) Charity is stronger than acquired virtue. But acquired virtue is not destroyed by a single act of sin, just as it is not generated by one. For Aristotle says [*NE* 2.1.6, 1103b8] that virtue is destroyed and generated by the same things. Therefore much less will charity be lost by a single act of mortal sin.

---

[37] Actually William of Saint Thierry, in *On the Nature and Dignity of Love*, ch. 6.

(5) One contrary is only driven out by the corresponding contrary. However, the opposite of the disposition of charity is not a sinful action, but a sinful disposition, and this cannot be generated by a single action. Therefore charity is not lost through a single sinful action.

(6) Charity stands to the many things that should be loved with charity in the way that faith stands to the many things that should be believed. But someone who believes the opposite of one article of faith does not thereby lose faith in all the others. Therefore someone who sins against one thing that charity should love does not thereby lose charity in respect of the other things that should be loved. In this way, charity is not lost through a single mortal sin.

But on the other hand

1 John 3:17 says, 'If anyone has sufficient of this world's goods and sees a brother in a state of need and closes his heart against him, how can God's charity remain in him?' Therefore it seems that one can lose charity by a sin of omission. But a sin of commission is no less serious than a sin of omission. Therefore charity can be removed by whichever type of sin.

My reply

There is no doubt that the *disposition* of charity is destroyed by any act of mortal sin. Otherwise, it would not be called a *mortal* sin, if one did not die spiritually through it. That cannot happen when charity is present, for charity is the life of the soul. Similarly, mortal sin also makes a person worthy of eternal death, according to Romans 6:23, 'The wages of sin are death.' Anyone who possesses charity, though, merits the possession of eternal life: for the Lord promises to reveal himself to those who love him, and eternal life consists in just that. Therefore we have to say that someone loses charity through any act of mortal sin.

Now it is clear that every *act* of mortal sin involves turning away from the unchanging good, to which charity unites us; thus any act of mortal sin is opposed to charity. But since an act is directly contrary not to a disposition, but to another act, it could seem to someone that an act of mortal sin would hinder an opposed act of charity, but not so as to remove the disposition itself. This is the case for the acquired virtues: we do not lose the disposition of speaking grammatically by making one grammatical error.

But the case is different with the disposition of charity. For this does not depend on a cause that is in its subject, but is totally dependent on an *external* cause. For 'charity is poured into our hearts through the Holy Spirit, who has been given to us', as Romans 5:5 says. Moreover, God does not cause charity in the soul in the sense of only being the cause of its coming into existence, and not of its continuing; i.e. he is not like a builder who only causes a house to come into existence, so that when he goes away the house still stays there. Instead, God causes charity and grace both to *come* into existence and to *remain* in the soul, i.e. in the way that the sun causes light in the air. Consequently, just as the light in the air disappears if some obstacle gets in the way, so the disposition of charity in the soul disappears when the soul turns itself away from God through sin. This is what Augustine means when he says [*LCG* 8.12]: 'God, when he justifies us, does not make us just in such a way that if he leaves, when he has gone what he has done will still be there. Rather, just as the air is not *made* luminous by the presence of light, but instead *becomes* luminous, so too, we are enlightened when God is present in us, but when he goes away, we are immediately in the dark again.'

Replies to objections

(1) (i) Origen's words can be understood to mean that someone who is in a condition of perfection does not *suddenly* move to commit a mortal sin, but only through first being inattentive. (ii) But because he adds the point about, 'those who slip briefly', it seems better to say that by 'be emptied and fall' he means fall by sinning *out of ill-intention*.[38] That cannot happen immediately from the beginning, because, as Aristotle says [*NE* 5.9.16, 1137a17], it is not easy for a just person all at once to do something unjust in the same way that an unjust person would do it, i.e. simply by deciding.

Therefore it is possible to lose charity by a single act of mortal sin. However, as long as one does not in fact lose charity through ill-intention, a few traces of the perfection one previously had will remain.

(2) Charity can be lost in two ways, (i) directly and (ii) indirectly. (i) It is lost *directly* through actually scorning God, as happens with those who say to God, 'Leave us alone, for we do not want to know your ways', to quote Job 22:17. (ii) It is lost *indirectly* when someone who is not thinking about

---

[38] Cf. *DQChar* 6 ad 1.

God consents, because of some emotion of fear or excessive sensual desire, to doing something against a precept, and as a consequence loses charity.

Bernard's meaning, therefore, is that charity was not extinguished in Peter in the first sense, but only lost in the second sense, and he calls this 'going to sleep'.

(3) We should interpret Pope Leo's words in the same way. This is clear from what follows: 'The remedy of washing away sin can be speedy where the will's judgement was not involved.' For Peter's denial was forced out of him through fear rather than being based on the will's deliberate judgement. This makes clear the answer to (3).

(4) Acquired virtue is caused by its subject and is not wholly dependent on something external as charity is. Therefore the reasoning works differently.

(5) In the case of contraries that are not contradictories one can disappear without the other one appearing. The dispositions of virtues and vices are contraries but not contradictories. That is why Aristotle says [*Cat* 10, 12a25] that there is something in the middle between good and evil, which is neither good nor evil. Hence someone can lose the disposition of a virtue without immediately acquiring the disposition of the opposite vice.

(6) A disposition in itself corresponds to the object in its *formal* character rather than to the object in the sense of matter. For this reason, if the formal character of the object is removed, then that type of disposition cannot remain. Where faith is concerned, the object in its formal character is the first truth *as revealed through the teaching of the Church*, in the same way that in the case of knowledge, its formal character consists in the intermediate stages of the proof. Now those who memorise the conclusions of geometrical proofs do not thereby know geometry, if they do not accept these conclusions because of the intermediate arguments; they will, rather, hold the conclusions just as opinions. In the same way those who hold the contents of faith, but do not assent to them because of the authority of catholic teaching, will not possess the disposition of faith. For those who assent to one thing because of catholic teaching will assent to everything else held by catholic teaching. Otherwise, they would be believing themselves rather than the teaching of the Church. From all this, it is clear that someone who stubbornly fails to believe one article of faith does not have faith in the other articles – I mean faith in the sense of an infused disposition – but holds the contents of faith only as opinions.

On Brotherly Correction

The first question is whether there is a precept about brotherly correction.[1]

The second is whether there is a precept about the order for brotherly correction.

Article 1: Whether there is a precept about brotherly correction

Objections

It seems not, because:

(1) Divine precepts are not contraries of one another. But we find a divine precept about not reproving sinners in Proverbs 9:8, which says, 'Do not reprove someone who scoffs, in case he comes to hate you.' Therefore there is no precept about brotherly correction.

(2) *Rejoinder*: that passage prohibits us from reproving a scoffer who scorns being corrected, and therefore becomes a yet worse person. *But on the other hand* sin is a weakness of the soul, according to Psalm 6:23, 'Have mercy on me, Lord, because I am weak.' But the person who has responsibility for caring for the weak ought not to omit to do so even in the face of being contradicted or scorned, since when someone refuses his medicine, he is in even greater danger. That is why doctors do whatever they can to heal those who are mad. How much more then should someone who has an obligation to heal his errant brother by rebuking him make

---

[1] The two articles of this question are a commentary on Matthew 18:15–17. For the patristic authorities which Aquinas uses, see *Catena aurea ad loc.*

sure that he does not omit to correct him, however much the brother might scorn this.

(3) We should not ignore a divine precept because someone else scorns it. After all, we are not excused from living out the truth for fear of scandalising anyone, as Jerome makes clear [*CommMatt* 3, on Matt 18:5]. Therefore, if there were a precept about correcting a brother, we ought not to ignore this just because of someone else's scorn.

(4) We ought not to do evil so that good may come of it, as St Paul makes clear in Romans 3:8. Therefore, by parallel reasoning, we ought not to omit good things to avoid evil coming from them. If brotherly correction were a good that came under a precept, we ought not to omit to do it because of the evil of scandal or the scorn of the person who is corrected.

(5) We ought as far as we are able to imitate God in what we do, in accordance with Ephesians 5:1, 'Be imitators of God, as his very dear children.' God, however, does not omit the good of infusing into us a rational soul, even though we might then incur the stain of original sin, which is subject to condemnation. Therefore in a similar way human beings ought not to omit the good of correcting one another, if this comes under a precept, even though the other person might then scorn the correction and become even worse.

(6) The Lord says in Ezekiel 3:19, 'If you make a proclamation to the impious and they are not converted from their impiety, they will die in their own wickedness. However, you will have freed your own soul.' Therefore we must not omit correction even in those cases where it may not succeed in reforming the person who needs rebuking.

(7) It is more helpful to correct than to punish an offender. But a judge does not refrain from punishing an offender just because the punishment will not reform him. Therefore, if there were a precept about brotherly correction, one would not have sometimes to refrain from correcting someone else for fear of scandalising or being scorned by him. Therefore it seems that there is no precept about brotherly correction.

(8) Divine precepts do not oblige us to do what is impossible. But it is impossible to correct every single offender, since 'the foolish are infinite in number', as Ecclesiastes 1:15 puts it. Therefore there is no precept about brotherly correction.

(9) *Rejoinder*: we do not have an obligation to correct those who need correction but do not cross our path. *But on the other hand* if there is a precept about brotherly correction, it follows from this precept

that each person is in debt to a brother, owing it to him to correct him. Someone who owes someone else a physical debt ought not to wait to run into him, but ought to look for him in order to pay him back what he owes. How much more then, if there is a precept about brotherly correction, ought someone to look for the person whom he should correct, and not just wait to run into him?

(10) If there were a precept about brotherly correction, an improper failure to carry this out would be a mortal sin. That, though, is not true, since we can even find holy men on occasion avoiding doing this: Augustine says [*CG* 1.9] that not only the weaker,[2] 'but even those who have a higher state in life refrain from criticising others, because they are held by chains of selfishness rather than out of their duty of charity. This, in consequence, seems to me to be a major reason why even good are lashed along with the wicked.' Therefore there is no precept about brotherly correction.

(11) Someone who disobeys a precept commits a mortal sin, even if he does not act directly against charity; so, as Bernard[3] tells us, even when Peter was denying Christ, his charity was not completely extinguished. Therefore, if there were a precept about brotherly correction, we would sin mortally if we ignored this, even if we did not do so in scorn,[4] acting directly against the precept.

(12) All the precepts of the divine law can be derived from the precepts of the Ten Commandments [Ex 20:2–17, Deut 5:6–21]. But brotherly correction does not fall under any of the precepts of the Ten Commandments, as is clear just by running through them. Therefore there is no precept about brotherly correction.

(13) Whatever is included in a divine precept enables human beings to achieve their end. However, admonishing a brother is not enough to reform him; not even a speech of admonishment can achieve this, as Aristotle tell us [*NE* 10.9.5, 1179b16] and as Ecclesiastes 7:14 says, 'Consider the works of God, because no one can offer correction if God has looked down on him.' Therefore there is no precept about brotherly correction.

(14) If it is not up to you to judge something, you ought not to interfere in it. But if someone sins against God, it is not up to us to judge this, as

---

[2] Following Augustine's own text; an alternative text reads 'inferiors'.

[3] Actually William of Saint Thierry, in *On the Nature and Dignity of Love*, ch. 6.

[4] To act in scorn of the precept would involve explicitly having a thought like 'What do I care for this commandment? I will act however I please to act.'

Jerome says [*CommMatt* 3]. Therefore no human being ought to interfere in such matters. Hence there is no general precept about rebuking a brother.

(15) No one is excused from observing a precept because of sin. However, someone who is a sinner ought not to correct anyone else; for Isidore says [*Sent(Is)* 3.32.1] that someone who is subject to vices ought not to correct other people's vices. Therefore there is no precept about admonishing a brother.

(16) No one incurs damnation for observing a divine precept. But some people incure damnation by rebuking others, according to Romans 2:1, 'You condemn yourselves on the very point on which you judge others.' Therefore there is no precept about brotherly correction.

(17) We ought not to arrogate to ourselves duties that do not belong to us, according to 2 Corinthians 10:13, 'We, though, do not boast in a measureless way, but according to the standard of the measure which God has measured for us.' But to rebuke offenders seems to be the duty of someone higher up: in the human body the higher parts move the lower, and in the universe the higher bodies move the lower. Therefore people other than superiors[5] are not obliged to offer brotherly correction.

(18) If we ought to bestow something on our neighbour because it is owed by charity, we ought to bestow this on everyone. But we do not have to bestow correction on everyone; for 1 Timothy 5:1 says, 'Do not take someone senior to task.' The gloss comments on this, 'To avoid his being insulted by being rebuked by someone junior and becoming angry.' That is why Dionysius criticises the monk Demophilus for correcting a priest. Therefore brotherly correction is not something that is owed by charity.

(19) The divine precepts are ordered to charity and peace, according to 1 Timothy 1:5, 'The end of the precept is charity.' However, the correction of a brother frequently disturbs charity and peace, in keeping with the saying of Terence [*Andria* 1.1.41], 'Truth produces hatred.' Therefore there is no precept about brotherly correction.

But on the other hand

(1) Augustine says [*Serm* 82.4.7] that if you fail to offer correction, you become worse than the person who sinned. The person who sinned acted

---

[5] For example, bishops with respect to their priests, or abbots with respect to their monks.

against a precept. Therefore the person who fails to correct him also acts against a precept. Therefore there is a precept about brotherly correction.

(2) Matthew 18:15 says, 'Rebuke him between the two of you alone.' The gloss comments here, 'In this way, those who see that their brother has sinned and say nothing sin themselves, just as much as if they fail to pardon a sinner.' But someone who fails to pardon a sinner acts against a precept. Therefore someone who does not offer correction also acts against a precept.

(3) We ought to conform ourselves to God in fulfilling the precept of charity, as Ephesians 5:1 says, 'Be imitators of God, as his very dear children.' But according to Proverbs 3:12, 'The Lord rebukes those whom he loves.' Therefore, since we are obliged by the Lord's precept to love, it seems that we are obliged by precept to correct our brothers.

(4) Ecclesiasticus 17:14 says, 'God has charged each person with caring for his neighbour.' Therefore, there is a precept that each of us should exercise concern for our neighbour's salvation by correcting him.

My reply

There is a precept about brotherly correction. The reason is that we are obliged by precept to love our neighbour. Love, though, in itself includes wishing the good of the person who is loved: to love someone is to want what is good for him, as Aristotle says [*Rhet* 2.4, 1380b35]. Since the absence of what is bad has the character of something good, as Aristotle also says [*NE* 5.1.5, 1129a18], it follows that it is also part of the character of love that we should want those we love not to have within them what is bad. However, our wills are neither effective nor true if they are not proved in what we do. It follows that it is also part of the character of love that we should do good for our friends and protect them from what is bad, as Aristotle says [*NE* 8.13.2, 1162b6]. 1 John 3:18 also says, 'Let us not love in words or speech, but in deeds and truth.'

There are three kinds of good for human beings, along with three kinds of evil opposed to these:

(i) One consists in *external* things, and this is the least valuable. Here, we are obliged to assist our neighbours by distributing alms in the physical sense. 1 John 3:17 says, 'If anyone has sufficient of this world's goods and sees that his brother is in need and closes his heart against him, how can God's charity remain in him?' By parallel reasoning, we are obliged to assist our neighbours in the face of the loss of temporal goods. That is why Deuteronomy 22:1 says, 'You shall not see your brother's ox or sheep straying and ignore it, but you shall take it back to your brother.'

(ii) The second is the good of the *body*: here again we owe one another help to achieve this and help to protect each other against any harm that opposes it: Proverbs 24:11 says, 'Rescue those who are being led to their death, and do not cease from freeing those who are being dragged to destruction.'

(iii) The third is the good of *virtue*: that is the good of the soul, which is contrary to the evil of sin. We are, though, obliged by charity to help our neighbour to achieve such good and avoid such evil more {than we are in the case of (i) and (ii)}, insofar as this sort of help is more closely related to the reason why we love out of charity.[6] That is why Aristotle says [*NE* 9.3.3, 1165b19] that someone ought to help a friend avoid sins more than loss of money, to the degree that virtue is closer to friendship. That is also why the precept of love binds us to assist our neighbours in acquiring virtue by counselling and helping them to act well, in keeping with Isaiah 35:3–4, 'Strengthen feeble hands and make firm weak knees, and say, "You of faint heart, be strong and do not be afraid".' For this reason the precept of love obliges someone to draw a brother who is in sin away from sin by correcting him, in accordance with 1 Thessalonians 5:14, 'Rebuke the troublesome, console the faint-hearted.' That is also why the Lord commanded in Matthew 18:15, 'If your brother has sinned against you, rebuke him.' Hence there is a precept about brotherly correction.

However, we need to note that virtuous actions are required of us by *positive* precepts, while vicious actions are forbidden by *negative* ones. Now something that is sinful and *vicious* in itself is bad, in whatever way it is done, since even single flaws can give this result, as Dionysius says [*DivNames* 4.30]. Therefore such things are prohibited by a negative precept, because they must not be done at any time nor in any way.

Virtuous actions, on the other hand, are required by a positive precept, and many circumstances together contribute to their correctness. This is because goodness arises from one complete cause as Dionysius says [*DivNames* 4.30].[7] That is why when something falls under a positive precept it does not need to be followed at every time and in every way, but

---

[6] Cf. *DQChar* 7 rep.
[7] See the Introduction, p. xxvi.

rather when the appropriate conditions are present regarding persons, places, reasons, and times. For example, 'Honour your parents' does not need to be put into practice at every time and place and in every way, but where the appropriate circumstances are present. Similarly, the precept about brotherly correction, because it is a virtuous action, takes effect in appropriate circumstances. It is not possible to provide a discourse that defines these circumstances, because judging them must take place in individual cases. This is the job of practical wisdom, whether acquired by experience and over time, or, better still, infused: as 1 John 2:27 puts it, 'Anointing will teach you concerning everything.'

Replies to objections

(1) Among other circumstances that are needed for virtuous action, the most important seems to be that the action corresponds to the end at which the virtue is aiming. When correcting an offender, charity aims at reforming him. The action would not be virtuous if the offender were corrected in such a way as to make him worse. That is why the wise man says [Prov 9:8], 'Do not reprove someone who scoffs.' As the gloss explains, 'You should not fear that the scoffer may insult you if he is reproved, but rather you should take care not to push him into hatred, which will make him a worse person.'

(2) There are two ways of correcting an offender. (i) The first is by simply *admonishing* him; this is brotherly correction, and it has a place only among those people among whom it is accepted that they agree to such admonition of their own free will. (ii) The second sort of correction uses *compulsion* by inflicting a punishment, as Aristotle says [*NE* 10.9.10, 1180a9]. This sort belongs to superiors, who ought to make an effort to free from the danger of sin even those who are scornful, just as a doctor makes an effort to heal someone who is mad, even by binding or beating him.

(3) We should not ignore a divine precept for fear of scandalising someone else. However, brotherly correction comes under a divine precept only to the extent that it reforms the brother. For this to happen, it must not scandalise him, for the reasons already given in my reply.

(4) As has already been said, evils must be avoided in every way whatsoever. That is why they should never be done in order that good should come of them. But we do not have to do good in every way whatsoever,

which is why on occasion some good actions can be interrupted, in order to avoid serious evils. Moreover, correcting one's neighbour is not a good unqualifiedly, unless the appropriate circumstances are present, as has been said.

(5) Moral goods presuppose natural goods. That is why God did not have to omit to infuse in us our souls – which are one of the goods of our nature – for the sake of avoiding the stain of sin. In the same way, people ought not to deprive themselves of vital sustenance in order to avoid sin. However, from time to time one may refrain from a morally good action in order to avoid some more serious moral evil.

(6) Augustine says [*CG* 1.9] that those put in charge of the churches and appointed to them 'have a far more serious cause, to castigate sins and not spare them'. For it is their responsibility to correct others not only with *charity*, but also with *force*. The Lord is addressing people of that sort through Ezekiel in this passage, which is why a little earlier it says, 'Children of men, I have given you an overseer over the house of Israel.'

(7) The judge in punishing has the common good as his principal intention, because the punishment of one person benefits the general public, even if he or she is not reformed. As Proverbs 19:25 says, 'If you beat the troublemaker, the fool will become wiser.' Brotherly correction is quite different, because its purpose is reforming the person who is rebuked.

(8) As I said in my reply, there is a precept about brotherly correction that applies when the appropriate circumstances are present with regard to persons, places, and times, just as with almsgiving for the body. Moreover, we ought to bestow acts of kindness, whether spiritual or bodily, on our neighbours in a certain order: that is, first on those who are closer to us, on the grounds that it has fallen to our lot to provide for them, as Augustine says [*CT* 1.28.29]. Next, we ought to provide for others further from us as the opportunity arises. In this way it is clear that the precept about brotherly correction does not oblige us to do something impossible, any more than the precept about giving alms for the body.

(9) As Augustine says [*Serm* 82.1], 'Our Lord warns us not to overlook one another's sins, not by looking for things to criticise, but by seeing what to correct.' Therefore, the precept about brotherly correction does not bind us to seek out other people's sins so that we can correct them, or we would turn into spies on other people's lives, in contradiction of Proverbs 24:15, 'Do not search for impiety in the house of the just, and do not destroy their rest.' The reasoning is different from that in the case of

a physical debt, because there something specifiable is owed to a specific person, and at a specific time. This is not true with brotherly correction, as I have said in my reply.

(10) There are three possible ways of failing to provide brotherly correction:

(i) *Without sinning* at all: for, as Augustine says [*CG* 1.9], 'If someone spares wrongdoers from castigation and rebuke because he is waiting for a more suitable moment, or because he is afraid that this will make the offenders worse, or else hinder other, weak, people who need to be trained for a good and devout life, and will oppress them and turn them from the faith, this does not seem to be an instance of selfishness, but a policy based on charity.'

(ii) Secondly, for example when 'a smooth tongue and "the human day" [1 Cor 14:2–4] give pleasure, and the judgement of the crowd and torture and the destruction of the flesh bring fear' [*CG* 1.9] – then, if this sort of thing dominates our mind in such a way as to overwhelm charity towards our brothers, that is a *mortal sin*.

(iii) Thirdly, it can be *venially sinful*, for example when such considerations move the mind not so as to take the place of charity towards our neighbour, but so as to make us forget to consider the circumstances and opportunities in which we are obliged to offer correction.

(11) When someone sins mortally, he sins directly against charity, because he does something that is contrary to charity. However, he does not always sin directly against charity in a strict sense, but only when he intends to act against charity, as happens with those who sin out of ill-will.

(12) Precepts about bestowing kindness on certain of our neighbours are derived from the precept about honouring parents. However, honouring parents is mentioned explicitly, because this comes immediately into anyone's reasoning; the same is not true of other sorts of kindness.

(13) A warning speech is not sufficient, according to Aristotle [*NE* 10.9.10, 1180a7], for those who are hard and have slavish souls. These are the people who get worse when they are admonished, and who need to be controlled by the forcible correction of superiors. That sort of correction too is inadequate without divine assistance.

(14) It is not up to us to judge whether to *forgive* sins against God, but it is up to us to judge whether to *reprove* them.

(15) We are not absolved from the duty of offering correction because of our sins. Rather, what renders us unworthy of correcting someone else

is failing to correct ourselves. This need not cause perplexity,[8] since we ought to forgive sins and offer correction in the manner of Matthew 7:5, 'First remove the plank from your own eye, and then you will be able to see to remove the speck from your brother's.'

(16) Every time we are in sin ourselves when we rebuke someone else, we also in a way condemn ourselves, that is, pronounce our own damnation. However, we do not always heap damnation on ourselves: for example, if we are sinful in a small way, and reprove a greater sin, or if we are sinful in secret and reprove a public sin; and also when in public we simultaneously reprove ourselves too, not condemning, but rather criticising, ourselves at the same time. Gregory says [*MorJob* 5.33] that, since we ought to love our neighbours as ourselves, we are therefore obliged to correct someone else's sins and be angry at them as we are at our own. But if we reprove someone else arrogantly, as if we do not acknowledge our own sin, then we bring damnation on ourselves. That is why Matthew 7:3 says, 'Why do you see the speck in your brother's eye, and you do not see the plank in your own?' Again, if because one's own sins are obvious, correcting someone else will cause scandal, then such correction will not be a virtuous act.

(17) Correction by *force* is the duty of superiors, but correction through *charity* the duty of all.

(18) Since our superiors are also our neighbours, we ought to correct them, but in a humble and reverent way, without impudence, to avoid making them angry; indeed, St Paul says this in the same place [1 Tim 5:1], 'Someone senior to you beseech as a father.' That is why Demophilus the monk was criticised, because he corrected an errant priest by insulting him and hurting him, beating him and throwing him out of the church.

(19) If correction is offered when the circumstances are appropriate, such disturbances will not follow, but rather peace and stability, as the causes of disharmony have been removed.

Article 2: Whether the order for brotherly correction laid down in Matthew 18:15–17 counts as a precept

Objections

It seems not, because:

---

[8] 'Perplexity' is Aquinas's term for what some philosophers call a 'moral dilemma': a situation in which, whatever one does, one acts wrongly.

(1) 1 Timothy 5:20 says, 'Reprove the sinner in the presence of every-one.' However, Matthew 18:15 says, 'Accuse him between the two of you alone', that is, admonish him in private. Now, St Paul's words cannot conflict with a precept of Christ's. Therefore it seems that there cannot be a precept that we should first admonish a brother in private and then publicly denounce him in the church.

(2) *Rejoinder*: St Paul's words should be understood to refer to *open* sins, which have to be reproved in public. The words of the Lord, however, refer to *secret* sins. *On the other hand* no one should make secret sins public; that would be betraying an offence rather than correcting a brother. But the Lord instructs us in Matthew 18:16–17 that if our brother does not listen to the warning given in private, we should bring in one or two witnesses, and then tell the church. That, surely, is making the sin public. Therefore it seems that the Lord's precept should not be understood as referring to secret sins.

(3) As Augustine says [*Trin* 8.1.2], all standards of truth are derived from the law of eternal truth. But the law of eternal truth holds that God does not only punish people for secret sins, but also sometimes punishes them without first giving any warning in private. Therefore it seems that a human being too, who ought to imitate divine truth, may publicly denounce someone even without first giving him a warning in private.

(4) As Augustine says [*Ly* 15.26], we can understand from the deeds of the saints how we ought to interpret the precepts of holy scripture. But what we sometimes find the saints doing is publicly denouncing a secret sin, without giving any private warning first. We can read this in Acts 5:1–11, where Peter publicly denounced Ananias and Sapphira for secret dishonesty concerning money from the sale of a field, without first warning them in private. Therefore we are not bound by Christ's precept to warn someone in private before denouncing him in public.

(5) Every action of Christ is there to instruct us; he himself said in John 13:15, 'I have given you an example; you should do just as I have done.' But we are not told that Christ warned Judas in private before he denounced him. Therefore it seems that we too can publicly denounce a brother's sin without first warning him in private.

(6) Just as denunciation happens in public, so also does indictment[9]. But someone can proceed to indicting someone else without warning him

---

[9] For the legal significance of these terms, see the reply to this argument, below.

privately first. The only prerequisite for an indictment is a written challenge, as the Decretal states [*Decretals of Gregory IX* 5.1.24]. Therefore it seems that we are also permitted to denounce someone publicly without first warning him in private.

(7) If in every case one is free to omit a certain act, then there is no precept requiring that act. And it does seem that in every case one is free to omit a private warning. For in each and every sin, one might be aiming at the common good of justice and therefore proceed to an indictment without first giving a private warning. Therefore it seems that the precept does not require that a private warning should be given first.

(8) It does not seem to be plausible that something that is a general custom among members of religious orders is against the precepts of Christ. But it is the custom among religious that specific sins of specific people are declared in the chapter meetings without any private warning being given first. Therefore it seems that the precept does not require that one gives a private warning prior to a public denunciation.

(9) Augustine says [*CT* 4.18.22] that just as roundness has the same character whether the circle in question is large or small, so justice has the same character in both great and small matters. Therefore, if for small sins there is no need for a private warning prior to a public denunciation (as was being argued), then neither, it seems, is there for big sins.

(10) If a public denunciation ought to be preceded by a private warning, it is necessary for there to be some delay between criticising the sin and publicly denouncing it. Sometimes, however, such a delay could be dangerous in that afterwards it would not be possible to cure the problem adequately. Suppose, for example that someone has had dealings with an enemy about betraying the city, or that there is a heretic within the flock seducing people from the faith. Then it does not seem as if a private warning should be given first.

(11) An agent can function in three types of way: (i) natural; (ii) artificial; (iii) acting through grace or charity (in this case, rebuking a brother out of charity). (i) But a *natural* agent does everything as well as it is able; (ii) the same is true of an *artificial* agent. (iii) Therefore, someone who rebukes a brother out of *love* ought to do this as well as possible. But this would be done better if done publicly, for it is more beneficial to the majority in that way, and the good of the majority is better than the good of one person. Therefore it seems that it is better to reprove a brother in public straight away, without a prior warning in private.

(12) A sinner in the church is like a gangrenous limb in a natural body. It does not matter *how* a doctor chooses to amputate a gangrenous limb in order to prevent the whole body being infected. Therefore it seems that it does not matter how a brother who sins is rebuked, whether in public or privately.

(13) Subordinates are under an obligation to obey their superiors. But sometimes superiors order their subordinates to tell them whatever they know about someone else's sinning. Therefore, even if these sins were committed in secret, the subordinates are obliged to reveal them, without giving the sinner a prior warning.

(14) The gloss comments on Matthew 18:15, 'If your brother has sinned against you', that you ought to reprove your brother out of a zeal for justice. From this it seems that brotherly correction is an act of justice. However, justice ought to be done openly. For Aristotle says [*NE* 5.1.15, 1129b28] that justice is a virtue that is brighter than the morning or evening star. Therefore brotherly correction ought to be carried out in public not in private.

(15) It is the role of justice to pay people what they merit. But sinners by sinning are dishonoured before God. Therefore it seems that they ought also to lose their reputation among human beings, as they merit, by being corrected publicly.

(16) None of God's precepts are contrary to a counsel or another precept. But the Lord says in Luke 6:30, 'If anyone takes what is yours, do not ask for it back', and this saying must be either a counsel or a precept. Therefore it seems that where you cannot give a warning without asking for your things back, especially in a case where someone has made off with your goods, the precept cannot require a private warning.

(17) At any time and in every way we are allowed to return good for evil. But Augustine says [*GrFC* 17.34] that when we rebuke troublesome people, we are returning to them good for evil. Therefore it seems that we are allowed to rebuke them publicly at any time without a prior private warning.

(18) Laws are passed to deal with common rather than rare events. But it happens only rarely that someone actually becomes a worse person through losing his reputation. Very often, however, people are checked from sin through its being exposed. Therefore it seems that there is no precept of God's law which tells us to warn someone privately before denouncing him in public.

(19) The order for brotherly correction includes the stipulation that the sin should only be denounced to the church or to a superior when the brother refuses to listen when he is first reproved. But if a person commits a sin with the knowledge of someone else and then promises to correct himself, it seems that he has therefore listened to the brother who reproved him. However, it still seems that the sin should be denounced to the relevant superior, so that the discipline of justice is maintained. Therefore it seems that the order of brotherly correction given by the Lord is not a precept.

(20) Jerome comments on Matthew 18:15, 'If your brother has sinned against you', as follows: 'If he has sinned against God, then it is not up to us to judge' (*CommMatt* 3). Therefore it seems that this system of correction does not apply to all sins.

(21) The Lord says in Matthew 18:15, 'If he listens to you, you have gained your brother.' But you do not gain your brother if he merely listens to someone reproving him and desists from sin when he has already committed serious sins. It needs a lot more than this for him to reach salvation, to which 'gaining your brother' refers. Therefore it seems that this order of brotherly correction does not apply to serious sins.

(22) Ecclesiasticus 19:10 says, 'Have you heard words against your neighbour? Let them die inside you, trusting that they will not harm you.' Therefore if we catch our neighbour sinning, we ought not to report him to anyone else.

(23) We should treat a brother more gently in the case of other sins than in the case of the perverse sin of heresy. But with the perverseness of heresy, we should warn someone two or three times, according to Titus 3:10, 'Avoid a heretical person after his second or third warning.' Therefore it seems that rebuking someone once before denouncing him, as the words of the Lord seem to imply, is not enough.

(24) According to Augustine [*Serm* 82.5.8–8.11], this order of giving correction is observed in the case of secret sins. But in such a case it does not seem possible to prove anything through witnesses. Therefore it is inappropriate to include in the order of giving correction the calling in of witnesses.

(25) We ought each to love our neighbours as ourselves. But no one is obliged to bring in witnesses to make his own offence public. Nor, then, should this be done in order to reveal a brother's offence.

(26) Augustine says [*Rev* 3.23] that one should reveal such things to whoever is in charge before one does so to witnesses. But to reveal them to whoever is in charge, as to a superior, is to tell them to the church. Therefore witnesses do not have to be brought in before telling the church. Consequently, it seems as if the order that the Lord gives cannot be a precept.

But on the other hand

(1) Augustine when explaining 'Rebuke him between the two of you alone' says [*Serm* 82.4.7] the following: 'Be eager to correct but spare people's shame. For someone might begin to defend his sin out of shame. Then you will make worse the person you want to make better.' Therefore the reason for preserving this order when correcting a brother is to spare his shame so that he does not get worse. But we are obliged to do this by the precept of charity. Therefore there is a precept about the order for brotherly correction.

(2) The gloss comments on Matthew 18:15–17 'If he has sinned against you' etc. as follows: 'We ought to avoid scandal by using this order.' But there is a precept about avoiding scandal, as is clear from Romans [14:13]. Therefore there is a precept about the order for brotherly correction.

My reply

Just as we said above, there is a precept about brotherly correction insofar as it is an act of virtue; it is an act of virtue insofar as it is clothed in the appropriate circumstances. Among these, being ordered towards the end seems particularly important; moreover, this ordering should have a common standard in everything that is to be done.[10] Now the purpose of correcting a brother is to reform him, as has been said. That is why the Lord wanted brotherly correction to be given in this order, because it is suitable for reforming a brother, whom we want to free from sin.

Sin threatens a person with a double danger – to *conscience* and to *reputation*. These two, i.e. conscience and reputation, are related in such a way that conscience should be put before reputation: for the witness of

---

[10] That is, the proper end for a given sort of action provides a general rule or standard governing all the actions of that sort.

conscience happens in the sight of God, whereas the witness of reputation is part of human responsibility. They also differ in that people need a conscience for their own sake, but they need reputation both for their own sake and for that of others. Therefore, the Lord wanted brotherly correction to be offered in an order that first, as far as possible, provides for conscience without injuring reputation. This happens by means of a private warning. Next, since conscience is to be preferred to reputation, the Lord ordained that if a brother cannot be reformed except by losing his reputation he should in the end be publicly denounced, so that when more people castigate him, this might be the cure that saves him.

However, if one were to proceed straight away to denouncing the brother publicly, he would lose his reputation; this ought to be avoided (i) for his sake, and (ii) for all those others who also have need of his reputation.

(i) *For his sake* for two reasons: (a) because good reputation is the most important of the exterior goods, in accordance with Proverbs 22:1, 'A good name is better than great wealth'; and also because a good reputation renders someone fit for carrying out the human duties that are a part of human social life. That is why Ecclesiasticus 41:12 says, 'Take care to keep a good name; for this will last longer for you than a mass of great and precious treasures.' Therefore, if it is a sin to deprive a neighbour of his wealth where that is not necessary, it is far more of a sin to deprive him of his reputation where that is not necessary, by making his sin public where that is not necessary; (b) because frequently people refrain from sinning in order to keep their reputation. Consequently, those who see that they have already lost their reputation may think nothing of sinning, in accordance with Jeremiah 3:3, 'Your face has become like a prostitute's, and you have forgotten how to blush.' That is why Jerome comments on the passage from Matthew as follows: 'You ought to rebuke your brother away from others in case he once loses his sense of propriety and of shame and then remains in sin' [*CommMatt* 3, on 18:15].

(ii) Again, there are two dangers from the point of view of *others*: (a) people may hear about someone's sin and be scandalised and then begin to scorn not only the sinner, but many other innocent people too. Hence Augustine says [*Let* 78.6], 'When it is rumoured falsely or revealed truly that someone who has a reputation for holiness has committed a crime, immediately people busy themselves in trying to believe the same of everyone'; (b) if one person's sin is publicised it can provoke many others to sin; as 1 Corinthians 5:6 puts it, 'Do you not know that a little leaven can spoil the whole lump?'

That is why there is a precept that we should not proceed to a public denunciation before correcting someone in private. However, one goes from one extreme to another via a mid-point. Therefore, the Lord included a middle level: after the private warning and before denouncing someone publicly to everyone else, one should bring in two or three witnesses, so as to correct the offender more privately without telling everyone, as Augustine says in his *Rule* [4.9]. Consequently, there is a precept about the order of brotherly correction, just as there is about brotherly correction itself; in both cases, though, you need to preserve proper distinctions, observing appropriate times, places, and other circumstances, and do everything that you see to be helpful for reforming your brother, which is the purpose and standard of brotherly correction.

Replies to objections

(1) As Augustine explains [*Serm* 82.5.8–7.19], we should understand St Paul to be talking about *public* sins. The Lord's words, though, should be taken to refer to *secret* sins, as is clear from his very form of expression. For he says, 'If your brother has sinned against you.' But someone who has sinned publicly has sinned not against you alone, by insulting or harming you, but also against everyone who see this. The Lord signifies this in the parable at Matthew 18:31, when describing the worthless servant: when he beat his fellow-servant, 'his fellow-servants on seeing what was happening became very distressed'. Again, 2 Peter 2:8 says, 'They tormented the soul of the just man by their wicked deeds.'

(2)(i) Some people understand the order of brotherly correction that we should observe as follows: first the brother should be rebuked in private; if he listens, all is well. If he does not listen, they say, you need to make a distinction: (a) if the sin is completely secret, you should go no further; (b) if it is already beginning to be noticed by more people, you should continue the procedure in accordance with the Lord's instructions.

However, this does not seem to be correct, for Augustine says [*Rule* 4.8], 'If your brother has a wound in his body which he wants to hide because he is afraid of being operated on, would it not be cruel of you to remain silent, but merciful to point this out? How much more ought we not to keep secret wounds in the heart, in case they fester and get worse?'

(ii) Therefore we need a different distinction: (a) if we can consider it likely that by proceeding further we will get somewhere with reforming him, then we ought to proceed further by calling in witnesses and denouncing him; (b) if we reckon it likely that making the sin public in this way will make him worse, then we ought not to proceed any further. If this is the case, we ought completely to leave off correcting the brother, as we said above.

(3) The entire truth of human justice is regulated by divine truth. However, the deeds of human beings are not related in the same way to divine and to human judgement. From the point of view of *human* judgement some sins are secret, and therefore here we ought not to proceed immediately to the public forum. But no sin is related to *divine* judgement in this way, because 'everything is naked and open in the eyes of God', as Hebrews 4:13 says. That is why there is no need for a secret warning first with respect to divine judgement; however, normally sinners do receive a sort of private warning when God reproves them through the inward remorse of their conscience and through inward inspiration, whether when they are awake or when they are asleep. For Job 33:15–17 says, 'In sleep and in dreams at night, when slumber overwhelms us, then he opens men's ears and teaches, instructs and trains them, to turn them away from what they have done.'

(4) Peter did not find out about Ananias's and Sapphira's sin in a human way, but through divine revelation. For this reason, he acted in the case of this sin according to the procedure for divine rather than human judgement, on the grounds that he was in this case God's agent.

(5) The Lord also recognised Judas's sin by divine power insofar as he knew what was hidden. That is why, as God, he could have proceeded immediately to making the sin public. However, he did not actually make it public, but gave Judas a warning about the sin in coded language.

(6) The rationale is different for indicting and for denouncing someone. A *denunciation* aims to reform the brother, which is why it ought to be done in an order suitable for reforming him. An *indictment*, however, aims at the good of the church, to keep the community free from the infection of sin. That is why an indictment does not always need to be preceded by a denunciation.

(7) We ought not to proceed to an indictment for every sin, but only for those sins which easily cause either spiritual or physical danger to the mass of people. Then someone can proceed to an indictment without

giving a prior warning, if this is needed to help the community. This is because the common good should be put before the good of an individual.

(8) The declarations in the chapter-meetings of religious are *reminders* rather than denunciations or indictments. They are there to make the brother mindful of the fault from which he ought to cleanse himself, without this damaging his reputation. For declarations of this sort deal with minor faults. However, it would be unlawful and against Christ's precept to make a public declaration of a serious fault, which could harm someone's reputation, without a prior warning.

(9) A poor reputation is not created by minor sins, as it is by serious ones. Therefore the reasoning is different in the two cases.

(10) In cases where it would be dangerous to delay a denunciation, we ought not to wait and warn the offender first, but proceed straight to the denunciation. This is not against Christ's precept, for two reasons: (i) because the sin that risks endangering a lot of people is not against you alone, but also against a lot of others. But the Lord's words were, 'If your brother sins against you'; (ii) because the Lord was not speaking about taking precautions against future faults, but about past faults that had already been committed.

(11) It is far better both for the brother whom you are aiming to reform, and for the mass of people, if you manage to reform him privately, as is clear from what has been said. That is why someone who is offering correction in accordance with charity ought to proceed in the manner we have described.

(12) If a doctor were to proceed to amputating gangrenous limbs immediately, he would be acting rashly, and would often amputate limbs when they could have been healed. A wise doctor will begin with less drastic remedies, and only amputate a limb as a last resort, after discovering that it cannot be healed. We should act similarly as regards brotherly correction.

(13) We ought not to obey a superior in contradiction of Christ's precept, as Acts 5:29 tells us: 'You ought to obey God rather than human beings.' The superior who gives an order that is contrary to the instruction of Christ is not exonerated from sinning. Therefore, if a superior commands someone to tell him anything he knows about where correction is needed, or about someone else's sins, we surely ought to interpret the command in accordance with the order established by Christ (in a case, that is, where he has the right to give this command). If he gives a command that is

expressly against this order, it ought not to be obeyed. However, in those cases where a secular or ecclesiastical judge is able to require an oath, in the process of denunciation or of investigation or of indictment, there a religious superior too is allowed to bind his subordinates under a precept of obedience.

(14) Justice is said to be the brightest of the virtues because of the beauty of its order; a part of this is that secret things are kept secret.

(15) Those who sin in secret merit losing their reputation, but they can only be punished in a way that repays what they merit by the one who is judge of what is secret, that is God; as 1 Corinthians 4:5 puts it, 'He who will illuminate what is hidden in the darkness and reveal the plans of our hearts.'

(16) (i) 'Do not ask for your own things back' counts as a *precept* if it is taken to refer to an attitude of preparedness not to do this, as Augustine explains [*SermMount* 1.19.59]. For we are obliged to be prepared not to ask for our own things back in cases where that is required by faith or by charity; we are also obliged in such a case to give in the first place out of what is ours.

(ii) In cases apart from this, however, 'Do not ask for your own things back' can be a *counsel* applicable in appropriate circumstances, just as it is a counsel that we give what is our own to whom, and when, we should.

Now brotherly correction does not contradict either the counsel or the precept in question. For someone can warn a brother who has taken what is someone else's in order to make him ashamed of his sin and ready to make up for it, even where the other person is willing to give up what is owed, thinking that expedient.

(17) Someone who rebukes an offender in the proper manner and order returns good for evil. Someone who overlooks the proper manner and order by rebuking hidden sins in public does not return good, but evil, for evil.

(18) It happens only rarely that secret sins are made public, and that is why it is rare for this to be dangerous. But if secret sins were frequently made public, then we would discover through experience that dangers would arise from this.

(19) Where the sin is secret and there seems to be no immediate reason for publicising it, and where the sinner has promised to reform, one would

be violating the Lord's precept by reporting an errant colleague, whether to a superior or to anyone else.

(20) It is not up to us to judge whether to forgive the penitent who has sinned against God, but it is up to us to judge whether to preserve the order established by Christ when we correct such sins.

(21) We should take it that the sinner has listened to the rebuke when he stops doing what he was doing and does anything else he needs to do for his salvation, such as confessing or making up for his sins. Then, however serious the sin was, you will have gained your brother, if he listens in that sense of the word.

(22) When we hear a word against a brother, it ought to die in us in the sense of not escaping from us to damage his reputation. However, we are not forbidden from proceeding further in order to reform him.

(23) When the Lord says, 'Rebuke him between the two of you alone', we should not take this to mean only once, but two or three times, or even more, as long as there is still plausible hope that he may be corrected in private. However, when we can take it that it is no longer likely that he can be reformed in this way, then we can consider that he has failed to listen.

(24) Witnesses are brought in either (i) to show that what someone is being reproved for actually is a sin, as Jerome says [*CommMatt* 3, on 18:16]; or (ii) to provide evidence about their actions if they repeat them, as Augustine says [*Let* 211.11; *Rule* 4.8]; or (iii) to witness that the brother who gives the warning has done what he can, as John Chrysostom says [*CommMatt* 60].

(25) We do not need witnesses to reform our own sins. We may, however, need witnesses to reform someone else's, in the three ways just mentioned. That is why the reasoning is different in the case of one's own sin and of that of a brother.

(26) When Augustine says that you should tell a superior before you tell witnesses, he is thinking of the fact that a superior has a specific role, which enables him to help even more than others can. In this sense telling a superior is not the same as telling the church. That would only be the case if you told him publicly, say, when he was sitting as a judge.

On Hope

The first question is whether hope is a virtue.
The second is whether hope is found in the will as its possessor.
The third is whether hope is prior to charity.
The fourth is whether only those on the journey possess hope.

Article 1: Whether hope is a virtue

Objections

It seems not, because:

(1) Virtue does not relate to both what is good and what is bad, but only to what is good. That is why Augustine says [*FC* 2.18, 19] that no one uses a virtue in a bad way. But hope is related to both good and bad, as some people have good hopes and some have bad hopes. Therefore hope is not a virtue.

(2) God works virtue in us without us, as I have already said. From this it is clear that virtues precede, and do not result from, merit. But hope is a result of merit, because it means 'a confident expectation of future blessedness that flows from grace and merit', as Peter Lombard says [*Sent* 3.26.1]. Therefore hope is not a virtue.

(3) *Rejoinder*: hope does not presuppose meritorious *activity*, but only a meritorious *disposition. But on the other hand* the disposition that is the basis of merit is charity. Now hope precedes charity rather than presupposing it. For the gloss says on Matthew 1 that hope produces charity. Therefore even the disposition of hope does not presuppose merit.

(4) Virtue is a tendency of something perfect, according to Aristotle [*Phys* 7.3, 246b2]. On that basis, he proves elsewhere [*NE* 4.9.1, 1128b10] that shame is not a virtue, because it affects those who are imperfect. But hope is also a tendency of those who are less than perfect, because they are still separated from what is good. Therefore hope is not a virtue.

(5) No emotion is a virtue, since we are neither praised nor blamed for emotions, as Aristotle says [*NE* 2.5.3, 1105b32]. But hope is one of the four principal emotions.[1] Therefore hope is not a virtue.

(6) *Rejoinder*: the type of hope that is an *emotion* is not a virtue, only the hope that is a feature of the *mind*. *But on the other hand* all the emotions of the sensory desire possess some analogue in the mind. For both the sensory and the intelligent desires contain not only hope and love, but also longing and pleasure and so on. However, apart from love, the other emotions do not give their name to virtues. Therefore neither should any virtue be called hope.

(7) There are three classes of virtue: (i) moral, (ii) intellectual, and (iii) theological. (i) But hope is not a *moral* virtue, because it is not traced back to any of the cardinal virtues. (ii) Nor is it an *intellectual* virtue, because it does not belong to the power of cognition, but rather to that of desire. (iii) Nor is it a *theological* virtue, because it is a characteristic of a theological virtue to consist in an extreme rather than a mid-point, according to Deuteronomy 6:5, 'You shall love the Lord your God with your whole heart.' Hope, however, holds a middle position between presumption and despair.

(8) Virtues, in particular theological ones, are a supernatural gift, divinely infused into us. But we do not need any supernatural gift to hope for eternal blessedness, because since what is good naturally attracts our desire, the highest good, which is blessedness, will naturally attract our desire to the greatest degree. Therefore hope is not a virtue.

(9) The activity of charity is more perfect than the activity of hope. But a created nature is capable of acting with charity without any gift of grace, according to the view of those who say that human beings and angels, in their natural created state, loved God above themselves and above everything else. Surely that seems to be acting with charity. Therefore far more are we capable of acting in hope without the gift of grace. Therefore hope is not a virtue.

---

[1] The four principal emotions are joy, sadness, hope, and fear. These concern, respectively, a present good, a present evil, a future good, and a future evil. See *ST* 1a2ae 25.4.

(10) According to Aristotle [*NE* 1.10.10–11, 1100b11 ff.], we can be more certain about virtue than about any skill. But that is not true of hope, since it derives from grace and merit, about which we cannot be certain, according to Ecclesiastes 9:1, 'No one knows whether he is worthy of hate or love.' Therefore hope is not a virtue.

(11) Every virtue can coexist with charity. But hope cannot coexist with charity, because it involves separation, while charity involves union; Dionysius says [*DivNames* 4.12] that love is a force that unites. Therefore hope is not a virtue.

(12) The whole fullness of grace and virtue was found in Christ, according to John 1:14, 'We have seen him full of grace and truth.' But hope was not found in Christ, because anyone who sees does not hope, as Romans 8:24 tells us. Therefore hope is not a virtue.

(13) Virtue gives us pleasure in doing things. Hope, by contrast, brings us suffering, according to Proverbs 13:12, 'Hope that is postponed troubles the soul.' Therefore hope is not a virtue.

(14) Virtue is pleasurable *per se*, as Aristotle says [*NE* 1.8.10, 1099a7]. However, neither hope nor memory is pleasurable in itself, as Aristotle also says.[2] Therefore hope is not a virtue.

(15) No virtue makes an action bad. But hope can make an action bad, in the sense that it can make an action difficult. Therefore hope is not a virtue.[3]

(16) Hope is a kind of expectation, as I have said. Expectation, though, involves separation. Therefore the greater the hope, the greater the separation from the good you hope for, which is blessedness. But the greatest virtue will not be the furthest separated from blessedness; rather it brings us as near as possible to it. Therefore hope is not a virtue.

(17) Memory is of past things in the way that hope is of future things. But the memory of the past is not a virtue. Therefore neither is hope for the future.

But on the other hand

(1) The virtues lead us to blessedness, for happiness is the reward of virtue, as Aristotle tells us [*NE* 1.9.10, 1100a3]. Hope, though, does lead

---

[2] This is most likely a loose reference to *NE* 9.7.6, 1168a19.
[3] This objection trades on an ambiguity in the Latin words, which an English translation inevitably clarifies, between 'makes an action bad' and 'makes a bad action'. Aquinas's reply disentangles the ambiguity.

us to blessedness; for, as Hebrews 6:19 puts it, 'we have hope that moves forward' and moves us forward 'to within the veil', which, as the gloss explains, means the blessedness of heaven. Therefore hope is a virtue.

(2) 1 Corinthians 13:13 says, 'Now, though, there remain faith, hope, and charity, these three.' But faith and charity are virtues. Therefore so is hope.

(3) Gregory says [*MorJob* 1.27] that the three daughters of Job signify the three virtues of faith, hope, and charity. Therefore hope is a virtue.

(4) The precepts of the law we are given are about acting virtuously. But we are given several precepts about acting with hope. For example, Psalm 37:3 says, 'Hope in God and do good.' Therefore hope is a virtue.

My reply

We understand dispositions from their related actions and actions from their related objects. Therefore if we want to understand whether hope is a virtue, we need to think about the character of its actions.

Now it is clear that hope involves some movement directed towards the good by a power of desire; the good in question, however, (i) is not something *already* possessed, as in the case of joy or pleasure, but (ii) is *still* to be attained, as in the case of longing for or lusting after something. There are two differences between hope and longing. (iia) Longing can be for any good in general, and therefore it is located in the sensual desire. Hope, though, is for a *hard* good, i.e. one difficult to obtain. For this reason it is located within aggression. (iib) Longing is simply for something good, without reference to whether it can be obtained or not. Hope, though, focuses on a good as something that *can be obtained*. Its very meaning includes a certain confidence about acquiring the good.

Hence we need to bear in mind four aspects of the object of hope: first, that it is a *good*; that distinguishes hope from fear; secondly, that it is *a future* good; that distinguishes hope from joy and pleasure {cf. (i)}; thirdly, that it is a good that is *hard* to obtain; that distinguishes hope from longing {cf. (iia)}; that it is a good that *can* be obtained; that distinguishes hope from despair {cf. (iib)}.

There are also two ways in which we can possess something: (i') through our own power; and (ii') through someone else's assistance. For we sometimes say that things are possible when we mean 'possible through our friends', as Aristotle makes clear [*NE* 3.3.13, 1112b27]. Accordingly, we can sometimes hope to attain something through our own power, and sometimes through someone else's help. Hope of the second sort involves expectation inasmuch as one looks to the help of another. Then, indeed, hope must be directed towards two objects: (ii'a) the good we want to obtain; and (ii'b) the person on whose hope we are relying.

The supreme good, which is eternal blessedness, is something that we can only only obtain with God's help, according to Romans 6:23, 'Eternal life comes by the grace of God.' Therefore the hope of obtaining eternal life has two objects, i.e. eternal life itself, which we are hoping for {cf. (ii'a)}, and God's help, through which we hope to get it {cf. (ii'b)}. Similarly, faith has two objects, i.e. the things that we believe and the first truth to which these correspond.

Faith, however, only has the character of a virtue insofar as it holds on to the witness given by the first truth, believing whatever that reveals. As Genesis 15:6 tells us, 'Abraham believed in God and it was counted to him as righteousness.' Consequently, hope possesses the character of a virtue precisely when someone holds on to the help provided by God's power in order to acquire eternal life. Indeed, if one were to rely on human help, whether one's own or someone else's, and try to obtain the fullest good without divine assistance, that would actually count as a vice, according to Jeremiah 17:5, 'A curse on those who put their trust in human beings, and make mere flesh their arm.'

Now the *form* of the object of faith is the first truth, and we assent to the content of faith through this, as if through a mediator; the *matter* of the object of faith is just that content of faith. In the same way, then, the form of the object of hope is the help that comes from God's power and compassion, since our hope is stirred by these towards the goods for which we hope; the matter of the object of hope is just those goods.

Again, everything that is the matter of faith is referred to God, even though some of these things are created things – for example, when we believe that all created things come from God, or that the flesh[4] of Christ was assumed by the Son of God in a personal union. In the same way, everything that is hoped is also ordered towards the ultimate, single, thing for which we hope, which is to enjoy God. For with an eye to that enjoyment, we hope for God to help us not only in spiritual, but also in physical, ways.

---

[4] That is, the human nature.

Replies to objections

(1) Hope cannot be related to something bad insofar as it holds on to God's help. For no one can hope too much concerning God. But when people hope in a bad way, this happens because they do not hold on to God, but to their own virtue or false opinions: for example, when people take it for granted that they are going to be saved even if they continue to sin.

(2) The description of hope as 'the expectation of future blessedness that flows from grace and merit' can be understood in two ways. The expectation can be understood (i) to 'flow from merit' with reference to the *person* doing the expecting, in the sense that his expectation is caused by his previous merits. The objection holds against this interpretation: it makes the description false; or (ii) to be 'from merit' with reference to the *thing* he is expecting. In this sense, the description is true: for he is expecting that he will acquire blessedness through the grace of God and through merit.

(3) In the sense just explained, meritorious activity and dispositions are not a necessary prerequisite for hope. They are a prerequisite for achieving the *object* of hope, i.e. blessedness. That is why it is possible for us to hope even without meritorious activities or dispositions, having merit only as our aim.

(4) With reference to the *matter* of the object, hope is a tendency of someone who is imperfect, because he does not yet possess what he hopes for. However, with reference to the *form of the object*, i.e. to divine help, hope is a tendency of someone perfect: for human perfection consists in holding on to God. The same is true for faith: it is imperfect in that one does not yet see what one believes, but perfect in that it holds on to the witness of the first truth. That is how it can be a virtue.

(5) Hope is an emotion when it means a movement of the sensory desire, which cannot aim at God. That is why that sort of hope is not called a virtue. It is only the movement of the *mind*, which has the potential for God, that is called a virtue.

(6) The only virtues that can take their names directly from an emotion are the theological ones. This is because the *intellectual* virtues relate to the power of knowledge, while the emotions are found in the power of desire. The *moral* virtues, on the other hand, establish a mid-point in the emotions, and so they cannot take their name straight from the

emotion, but only from their being moderated; hence we get 'temperate-ness', 'courage',[5] and so on.

However, when the movements of the human mind touch God in any way, then they are connected with virtue. That is why the names of these movements, or emotions, can be given directly to the *theological* virtues. Moreover, since the object of the theological virtues is God, i.e. the supreme good, it is clear that the emotions that have a bad object can-not give their names to theological virtues. Similarly, since the theological virtues are needed for the period of our journey, when we are still aim-ing at God, the emotions that have as their object a good that is actually present, such as pleasure or joy, are not the names of virtues; rather they are actually part of blessedness. For this reason 'pleasure' is classed as one of the gifts of blessedness. Finally, longing involves a movement towards the future, but without at the present time holding on to God himself or having any spiritual contact with him. That is why no virtue gets its name from longing. Hence only hope and love are left to provide names for theological virtues.

(7) The reason that *moral* virtues are found in a mid-point is that they have to observe the standard of reason in respect of their distinctive and *per se* object, i.e. human emotions and behaviour. But everything that is mea-sured by a standard has to that extent the character of a mid-point, because it can fail to match the standard by being either too much or too little.

Again, *intellectual* virtue means hitting the truth, which is the good of the intelligence. However, the truth of the human intelligence takes its standard and measure from what the thing is that it understands. Therefore opinions are true or false depending on whether the thing is so or not. That is why intellectual virtue too lies in a mid-point with regard to its own distinctive object, i.e. one grasps just what is the case about something, neither more nor less.

On the other hand, *theological* virtue has for its object the first standard itself, which is not measured by another standard. Consequently, all that is needed here to possess the character of a virtue is to reach the standard in some way or another. Because of this, a theological virtue does not lie in a mid-point with respect to (i) the *form* of its own distinctive object. It can lie in a mid-point with respect to (ii) the *matter* of its object. This happens, for example, when the catholic faith about God takes a middle line between

---

[5] *fortitudo*, literally 'strength'.

the heresy of Sabellius, which confounds the persons of the Trinity, and the heresy of Arius, which divides their substance.[6] In the same way, the object of hope with respect to its *matter*, consists in a mid-point insofar as someone can hope to acquire blessedness in different ways {cf. (ii)}; with respect the *form* of its object, which is the help of God, it does not lie in a mid-point: for no one can rely too much on God's help {cf. (i)}.

(8) The goods that move the desire are suited to us, for we do not naturally desire things that are not so suited. The fact that eternal blessedness can be a good that is suited to us derives from the grace of God. For that reason, hope, which focuses on that good as something that is, in this way, suitable for us to possess, is a gift that is infused in us by God.

(9) To love God above everything else can be understood in two ways.

(i) In one sense, the goodness of God is the beginning and end of everything that exists by nature. It is in this sense that not only rational animals, but also non-rational animals and even inanimate things love God above all else, at least to the extent that they are able to love. This is because each thing loves the *good of the whole* of which it is part more than it loves its own good; that is why it is natural for a hand to risk being wounded in order to protect the whole body. In human beings, this natural love of God is corrupted by sin. But in their original, undamaged, natural state they were able to love God above all things in the way I have explained.

(ii) Someone can love God above all things as the *object of blessedness*, by sharing a sort of fellowship with God in having a mind endowed with reason, and can be united with him in a spiritual way. Love of this kind is something that no creature can engage in without grace.

(10) Virtue makes us incline towards our own activity in a moderate way, as Cicero tells us [*Inv* 1.56]; that is why the certainty of hope, as with other virtues, characterises the reliability of our inclination when we act, rather than our awareness of an object or of its distinctive principles.

(11) It is in *feeling* that we are united by charity; thus, if you love a friend, you think of him as 'another yourself', while if you love God, you think of him as more than yourself. This can still happen, however, when there is an actual distance between you and the thing you love. That is how charity can coexist with hope.

---

[6] Sabellians held that Father, Son, and Holy Spirit were simply different manifestations of an utterly unitary God. Arius denied the divinity of Christ.

(12) Hope possesses both a kind of incompleteness and some completeness. Insofar as it is *complete*, it has the character of a virtue. Christ possessed hope utterly in this sense, since he held utterly on to God's help. However, he did not possess hope insofar as it is something *incomplete*, just as he did not possess faith in that sense either.

(13) Hope does not cause the soul distress; rather it brings it pleasure, in that it makes the thing one hopes for present in some sense insofar as one is confident of achieving it. That is why St Paul talks in Romans 12:12 of 'rejoicing in hope'. But the delay in acquiring the thing you hope for can sometimes cause distress.

(14) Pleasure comes from two things: (i) the object of the activity; (ii) the activity itself. (i) The first type of pleasure is not distinctive of virtue, because some virtues involve grieving about their *object*, for example, repentance. (ii) The second type of pleasure, from the *activity*, is distinctive of virtue, because anyone who possesses a virtue gets pleasure from doing whatever is in accordance with the relevant disposition. That is how someone who is repentant can rejoice to be grieving. In this way hope, when it gives us pleasure in the thing we hope for, does not give pleasure in itself, but in something else, in the sense that it makes us think of the thing as present. But it also gives us pleasure in itself to the extent that it gives us pleasure in our own activity.

(15) We can understand 'do a difficult action' to mean two different things: (i) *cause* the difficulty in the action. On this interpretation, the objection would hold. However, hope does not make an action difficult in that sense, because it does not introduce, but rather reduces, the difficulty of an action; (ii) *carry out* a difficult act, i.e. the act is already difficult. In this way, hope can perform a difficult action, because it makes us attempt to do difficult things.

(16) The gap between a finishing-point and a starting point is covered by some kind of movement. The type of movement it is, though, depends upon the end, not upon the gap. That is why from the fact that something moving must be separated from its destination, it does not follow that the more separated it is, the more movement there must be. That method of argument[7] only holds for things that are qualified *per se*. With a natural movement, we can see that the nearer it gets to its conclusion, the more intensive it becomes. The same is true for hope.

---

[7] *scientia arguendi*: the text is problematic.

(17) Memory does not, while hope does, involve holding on to anything that might give it the character of a virtue. Therefore the comparison does not hold.

Article 2: Whether hope is found in the will as its possessor

Objections

It seems not, because:

(1) The object of hope is a good hard to get. But whatever is hard is the object of the aggressive part. Therefore hope is found in the aggressive part, not in the will.

(2) Charity is the most complete of the virtues; therefore it is sufficient to bring any given capacity to completion. But charity is found in the will. Therefore hope is not found in the will.

(3) We are not able to have several things in our understanding at exactly the same time, because our understanding cannot be informed at the same time by a lot of different concepts, just as a body cannot at the same time take on several different shapes, as Al-Ghazali says. Therefore, by parallel reasoning, one capacity cannot be actively informed at the same time by different dispositions, in the sense of actively doing things in accordance with each of them. But we can at the same time act with hope and act with charity. Therefore charity and hope cannot coexist in the same capacity. But charity is found in the will; therefore hope is not.

(4) Hope is an expectation marked by certainty. But certainty belongs to the power of cognition. Therefore hope is found in the power of cognition and not in the will.

But on the other hand

Hope 'flows from merits'. But merits belong to the will. Therefore hope is found in the will.

My reply

As I have said, hope is a theological virtue, and so its object is God. No sensory power, though, can include God as one of its objects, because the senses cannot go beyond physical things. For this reason, hope cannot be located in any of the sensory powers. It is obvious, though, that hope belongs to one of the powers of desire, because its object is the good, as

I have said above. It follows that it must be found in the desiring power of reason, which is the will, according to Aristotle [*Soul* 3.10, 433a23]. Hence, hope is found in the will as its possessor.

This power of desire, i.e. the rational one, is not divided into an aggressive and a sensual part, as some hold;[8] the reason is that the object of the will is something good under the general description of good, and the intelligence, rather than the sense, is able to grasp this. Conversely, the sensory desire, which has as its object something good under a particular description, is divided between aggression and sensual desire, in accordance with the different descriptions of the goods perceived by the senses. For some of these give sensory pleasure, and sensual desire deals with these; others possess a certain loftiness that lifts them above any obstacles that pleasure may put in their way; aggression deals with those. That is why aggression and sensory desire are not located in the higher faculty of desire {i.e. the will}.

In this way, then, hope is possessed not by the aggression, but by the will.

Replies to objections

(1) The hope that we are discussing is for an intelligible good that is hard to get. That is not the object of any capacity related to the latter specifically; rather the will inclines towards it *qua* good in general.

(2) Charity completes the will fully in respect of one of the will's movements, i.e. loving. But it lacks some completeness in respect of another of its movements, i.e. hoping.

(3) When many things are ordered towards one thing, they can be grasped by the intelligence at the same time. In a similar way, a movement of hope can coexist with a movement of charity, because they are mutually interconnected.

(4) The certainty possessed by hope stems from the certainty possessed by faith: hope shares to some extent in the certainty of faith insofar as the movements of a power of desire are guided by a cognitive power.

Article 3: Whether hope is prior to charity

Objections

It seems not, because:

---

[8] See *ST* 1a 82.5.

(1) Ambrose comments [*CommLuke* 8.30] on Luke 17:6, 'If you had faith equal to a grain of mustard, etc.' as follows: 'Charity comes from faith and hope from charity.' Now faith is prior to charity. Therefore charity is prior to hope.

(2) Augustine says [*Hand* 2.8] that faith without charity is of no benefit; hope, though, cannot exist without charity. But if hope were prior to charity, it would be able to exist without it, just as faith can, even if it were of no benefit. Therefore hope is not prior to charity.

(3) Augustine says [*CG* 12.9] that movements and feelings that are good come from love and from holy charity. Hoping, insofar as it is an activity of the virtue of hope, is a praiseworthy movement and feeling. Therefore it stems from holy charity. Thus charity is prior to hope.

(4) Hope involves longing, as I explained above. But longing can only be for a good that is loved. Therefore hope presupposes love. Therefore hope comes after charity.

(5) Love is first among the feelings in the soul. For everything done or felt by the soul is a result of love, as Dionysius makes clear [*DivNames* 4.10]. But hope involves certain feelings in the soul. Therefore charity, which is love, is prior to hope.

(6) Hope and longing are only for one's own good. But a good becomes one's own when one seeks it through love. That is what makes it suitable for one. Therefore hope and longing both presuppose love.

(7) Augustine says [*CG* 14.7] that a rightly ordered will is charity. But hope presupposes that the will is rightly ordered. Therefore hope presupposes charity.

(8) When two things are simultaneous, one is not prior to the other. But faith, hope, and charity are simultaneous, because, as Gregory says [*HomEzek* 2.10.17], someone possesses them all equally. Therefore hope is not prior to charity.

(9) A thing cannot be prior to itself. But hope and charity seem to be the same thing, for they both have the same object, i.e. the supreme good. Therefore hope is not prior to charity.

(10) Peter Lombard says [*Sent* 3.26.1] that hope flows from merits, and these precede not only the thing that we hope for, but also hope itself, which charity precedes. Therefore hope is not prior to charity.

(11) Despair is opposed to hope. Every mortal sin, though, is opposed to charity. But people fall into mortal sin before they fall into despair. Therefore charity is prior to hope.

(12) The ordering of dispositions and actions follows that of objects. But goodness, which is the object of charity, comes before what is hard, which is the object of hope, because what is hard includes something on top of the goodness. Therefore charity is prior to hope.

(13) If something that is an incomplete specimen of its class has a given standing, then something that is a complete specimen of that class will have as much standing. But it is clear that sometimes an incomplete love can come before hope. Therefore far more will complete love, which is charity, come before hope.

But on the other hand

(1) The gloss comments on Matthew 1:2, 'Abraham begot Isaac, and Isaac begot Jacob', as follows: 'That is, faith begot hope and hope begot charity.' But what begets is prior to what is begotten. Therefore hope is prior to charity.

(2) The gloss comments on Psalm 37:3, 'Hope in God and do good,' as follows: 'Hope is the gateway to faith and the beginning of human salvation', and this seems to show that hope is prior to faith. But faith is prior to charity. Therefore so is hope.

(3) St Paul says in 1 Timothy 1:5, 'The end of the precept is charity from a pure heart and a pure conscience.' The gloss comments, 'That is, hope.' Therefore hope is prior to charity.

(4) Augustine says [*Trin* 10.1.1] that you never love anything unless you hope that you will be able to attain it. If you are not hopeful of getting something, then you will love it at most in a lukewarm way. Therefore love presupposes hope.

(5) A is prior to B if B implies A but not vice versa. But hope is like this: for while we are on our journey, anyone who has charity has hope, but not vice versa. Therefore hope is prior to charity.

My reply

'Prior' is predicated of something with respect to some principle; in other words, if A is prior to B, A is nearer to that principle than B. But each thing possesses two intrinsic principles, matter and form. 'Before' means different things with respect to these two different principles. (i) A can be prior to B in terms of completeness, as actualisation is prior to capacity, or as the complete to the incomplete. This sort of priority corresponds to *form* as principle. (ii) A can be prior to B in the process of coming into being, i.e. in time. In this sense, within the same specimen capacity is prior to actualisation, or what is incomplete to what is complete. (Speaking simply and in general, of course, what is complete is also prior in time, because incomplete things are changed only by something complete that already exists.) This sort of priority corresponds to *matter* as a principle.

According to (i), then, charity is naturally prior to hope. However, according to (ii), within a single person, hope precedes charity, because hope is what then leads someone on to charity. To show this, we need to know that all those feelings of the mind that are movements of desire correspond to a natural movement. This is because natural movements arise from a natural inclination that is known as a desire of nature; in a similar way, the movements of the soul's feelings come from an inclination in the soul, that is, a desire of the soul.

What we find in *natural* movements is the following: (i') a *principle* of the movement itself, where the natural form that belongs to something changeable gives it form, as, for example, when something heavy or light is brought into being; (ii') the natural *movement* flowing from such a form, for example, rising or sinking. (iii') The third stage is *resting* in the thing's own place.

The case is similar with desire in the soul. The desire is formed in a certain way by something good, and the result is love, which unites the one who loves to the thing that is loved {cf. (i')}. From this it follows next that, if the good that is loved is at a distance, desire tends towards it through a movement of longing or hope {cf. (ii')}. The third stage then follows, i.e. joy or pleasure, when one attains the thing one loves {cf. (iii')}.

Just as natural change and rest flow from the form, so every feeling in the *soul* flows from love. We ought, then, to identify distinctions among the other feelings in the soul in accordance with distinctions within love. Love, though, can be of two sorts, either (a) imperfect or (b) perfect. (a) You have *imperfect* love for something when you love it because you want to have what is good about it for *yourself*, rather than wanting in itself what is actually good for *it*. Some people call this sort of love sensual desire. An example would be when we love wine in that we want to savour its taste, or when we love some other person because we can get some benefit or pleasure through him. (b) The second sort of love, *perfect* love, is found when you love in itself what is someone's good – for example, when I love someone and want him to possess whatever is good even if that will not affect me in any way. This sort is called the love of friendship, and it makes you love your friend in himself. That is why it is also the perfect form of friendship, as Aristotle says [*NE* 8.3.6, 1156b7].

Now charity is not just any sort of love of God, but only the perfect sort, in which God is loved in himself {cf. (b)}. However, we are led to love the goodness of God in itself by the good things that come from God, which we want to have for ourselves, and by the bad things that we might avoid by holding on to God. Because of avoiding such evils, fear is a part of this love of oneself; because of pursuing such goods, hope is a part of it, and this, as I have explained, is a movement tending towards getting something. Both fear and hope, then, in their own character flow from our love for God in the imperfect sense {cf. (a)}. Because of this, within time and coming into being, i.e. on our journey, fear precedes charity and leads us to it, as Augustine tells us [*TEpJn* 9.5], and, in the same way, hope leads us to charity, provided that whoever hopes to acquire some good from God is led by this to loving God for himself.

Replies to objections

(1) Ambrose adds in the same place that these all flow back into one another in a virtuous circle, because when you have been led from hope to charity, then you are able to hope more completely and fear more devoutly, just as you also believe more firmly. So when he says that hope flows from charity, he is not talking about the initial arrival of charity, but the *second* wave of it, since once it is established in us, it makes us both hope and believe more completely.

(2) The hope that flows from existing merits cannot exist without charity, which is the basis of merit. But unformed hope, which has no merit in its actions, but depends upon merit in its aim, is without charity in its actions, but not without charity in its *aim*.

(3) Augustine is speaking there about *good* movements and *meritorious* feelings; things of that sort do have charity as their cause.

(4) The reasoning proves that hope presupposes some sort of love. However, it need not presuppose love in the sense of charity, but rather love of oneself, which may make one choose divine goodness.

From this the answers to (5) and (6) are clear.

(7) A rightly ordered will is described as 'charity' with reference to its cause, since the will cannot be rightly ordered in the complete sense

except through charity. But the will does not have this sort of completeness before it possesses even an unformed hope.

(8) The authoritative text from Gregory should be understood to refer to faith, hope, and charity as being *virtues*; but this is the case for faith and hope only if they are given form by charity. As for the *unformed* versions of faith and hope, they can sometimes appear earlier than charity.

(9) The goodness of God as something *loved in itself* is the object of charity; as something *to be gained*, however, it is the object of hope. For this reason, charity and hope are different.

(10) If we mean hope that is *unformed*, then merit does not come before it, but rather before the thing we hope for. If, though, we mean hope that is *formed*, then merit comes before hope too. In this case charity also naturally comes before it.

(11) Stages that come later when something is being built up, come earlier when it is being broken down. That is why in the process of *acquiring* the virtues hope precedes charity, but in the process of *losing* them, the opposite happens: the wrongdoing that causes the loss of charity comes before the despair that causes the loss of hope.

(12) This reasoning shows that *love in general* exists before hope, because the good understood generally is the object of love. That does not mean that *charity* has to be prior to hope.

(13) Coming first in the process of coming into being is not a mark of completeness; this is because in this context, incomplete things come before complete ones.

Article 4: Whether only those on the journey possess hope

Objections

It seems not, because:

(1) Just as hope is for something we do not possess – which seems incongruous with the situation of the blessed – so also is longing. But the blessed do experience longing, according to 1 Peter 1:12, 'On whom the angels long to look.' Therefore hope too can be found in the blessed.

(2) Hope, which has good things as its object, is something more perfect than fear, which has bad things as its object. But some fear is found in the blessed, according to Psalm 19:9, 'The holy fear of the Lord will remain for ever.' Therefore some hope is also found in the blessed.

(3) Just as it is a good but hard thing to obtain blessedness, so it is good but hard to continue possessing it. But before people actually attain blessedness, they hope to attain it. Therefore even after they have attained it, they can hope to continue possessing it.

(4) Hope and despair are found with respect to the same things. But we can despair about someone else, which is why we are commanded not to despair about anyone who is still on the journey. Therefore we can also have hope for someone else. It is in this way that the saints, who are already in our homeland, are able to have hope for other people who are still on the journey, that they will reach blessedness.

(5) *Rejoinder*: hoping for blessedness for someone else is not part of the *virtue* of hope. *But on the other hand* charity, like hope, is a theological virtue. But one and the same virtue of charity makes us love ourselves and our neighbour. Therefore one and the same virtue of hope makes us hope for eternal life for ourselves and for others. In this way, when the blessed hope that other people will have eternal life, they seem to be possessing the virtue of hope.

(6) Prayer flows from the virtue of hope, according to Psalm 37:5, 'Show your path to the Lord and hope in God and he will act.' But it is appropriate for the saints who are in our homeland to pray, and we ask them to do so when we say, 'Pray for us, all saints of God.' Therefore hope can also be found in them.

(7) It is the same principle that makes something both move to its finishing-point and rest there. But hope is the principle which moves us towards blessedness, as Hebrews 6:19 tells us: 'We who have hope that moves forward' (i.e. makes us go forward) 'to within the veil'. Therefore hope must also be the principle of resting in blessedness, and so the blessed ought to possess it.

(8) Isidore says [*Sent(Is)* 2.4.2] that justice flourishes with faith and hope. Augustine, too, says [*Hand* 31.117] that anyone who lives rightly will also believe and hope rightly. But in our homeland, people will possess justice and live rightly, as Isaiah 60:21 tells us: 'Your people shall all be just.' Therefore there will also be faith and hope in our homeland.

(9) Blessedness requires being certain that one will remain for ever in blessedness. It is because they lacked this certainty that the angels were not completely blessed before they either were established or fell, as Augustine tells us [*CG* 11.11]. But being certain about the blessedness to

which one is looking forward is part of the virtue of hope. Therefore the blessed do possess hope.

(10) According to Aristotle [*Top* 2.9, 114b24], whatever is destroyed by something good must itself be bad. Therefore if the hope we have on our journey were destroyed by blessedness, which is the greatest good for a human being, it would seem as if hope were something bad. That is wrong, since hope is a virtue, as I have said.

(11) Virtuous activity seems to consist not only in doing or wanting to do whatever is relevant to the virtue when one is *able* to, but also in wanting to do this even when one is *unable* to. For behaving justly would mean wanting to return some money you owed even if you were not actually able to raise the relevant amount. But the attitude of the saints in our homeland is such that they would be wanting to look forward to blessedness even if they did not have it. Therefore they are actively hoping. But activity flows from the relevant disposition. Therefore they possess the virtue of hope.

(12) Anselm[9] says in *On Likenesses* that the saints after the resurrection will be strong enough to move the earth. He does not mean that they *will* move it, or do anything similar (since everything will always be in the best possible place), but that that is how perfect they will be. Therefore in a similar way, the disposition of hope, which is one of the perfections of the soul, will be able to exist in the blessed even though there is no opportunity there for them actively to hope.

(13) The goodness of God is not greater than his majesty. But charity, which has God's goodness as its object, will remain when we are in our homeland. Therefore so should hope, which has God's majesty as its object.

(14) If you destroy the foundations and the walls, you will destroy the roof. But faith is the foundation of our spiritual building, and hope, which raises up, functions like a wall. Therefore if faith and hope are taken away from the blessed, charity, which works like the roof, will not be able to stay. That must be wrong, because 'charity never fails', as St Paul says in 1 Corinthians 13:8.

(15) Those who are looking forward to something that will satisfy their desire once they get it seem to hope for that thing. But the souls of the blessed are looking forward to their bodies being glorified, as

9 Actually a collection of Anselmian sayings.

Augustine says [*LCG* 12.35.68]. Therefore they do possess the virtue of hope.

(16) Christ had full possession of blessedness from the first moment of his conception. But Christ also had hope, since the words of Psalm 71:5, 'I hoped in you, Lord', are said in his person, as the gloss explains. Therefore the blessed can possess hope.

But on the other hand

(1) Romans 8:24 says, 'Who hopes for what he can see?' But the saints are already enjoying the full vision of God. Therefore they do not possess hope.

(2) St Paul in 1 Corinthians 13:13 proves that charity is greater than faith and hope on the grounds that charity does not fail, while faith and hope will vanish, with the arrival of 'what is complete'. But 'what is complete' refers to the condition of blessedness. Therefore faith and hope do not remain in the condition of blessedness.

(3) Augustine says [*GMarr* 21.25], 'A disposition enables us to act when we need to: if we do not act, we are still able to act.' From this we can see that a disposition cannot exist where it is not possible to engage in the relevant activity. But it will not be possible actively to hope in our home-land, because that would involve focusing on a blessedness we did not yet possess. Therefore we cannot possess the disposition of hope there either.

My reply

Once you remove whatever gives a thing its type, it follows that it will no longer be of that type. For example, if you remove the substantial form from a natural body, then its type will change. But just as a *form* gives a natural thing its type, so the *object* gives a moral act, and therefore also a moral disposition, its type. Therefore if you remove the principal object of some disposition, it will not be possible for the disposition to remain. The object of hope *simply speaking*, is a future good that is hard, but possible, to get, as I have already explained. That is why if the object ceases to be good, or future, or hard, or possible to get, then hope will disappear, in accordance with its general character. The object of hope *as a theological virtue*, however – that is, its formal object – is the help of God, to which it holds on. It is true that the formal object embraces

235

several different material elements in the things that we hope for, but the former is principal and the latter are secondary or additional.

We can understand this last point in two ways: (i) with respect to the *thing* we hope for; and (ii) with respect to the *person* doing the hoping. (i) Here the principal object of the theological virtue of hope is the full enjoyment of God, which makes its possessor blessed; other things that we hope for, whether spiritual or temporal, are ordered towards this end. (ii) Here the principal object is that one hopes for blessedness for oneself; secondarily, one may hope for other people to possess it insofar as they are in some way united with one, and one desires and hopes for their good as one's own.

As long as this principal object remains, then – i.e. as long as the good of blessedness, which is hard to get, remains in the future and as long as it is still possible for the person hoping for it to get it – then the virtue of hope can remain. Then, through this virtue of hope, we hope not only for blessedness in the future, but also for the other things that are ordered towards this. The same virtue of hope enables us to hope for blessedness for other people and for whatever else is ordered towards that. But if we remove the principal object of the theological virtue of hope by making eternal blessedness something already possessed rather than something in the future, then this virtue will no longer be of the same type. That is why the blessed cannot possess the sort of hope that is a theological virtue.

However, the saints can hope for other things, by holding onto God's help, in connection with either themselves or others; they do this, though, according to the general character of hope, rather than according to its character strictly as a theological virtue. We can give a parallel example from the opposite situation, i.e. among the wicked, as follows. The primary object of charity is God; hence as long as one loves God, one also loves one's neighbour in God, through the same virtue of charity. But if one ceases to love God, one will still be able to love one's neighbour in a natural way, though not through the virtue of charity; for charity, as such, will disappear once its primary object has been removed.

Replies to objections

(1) The word 'longing' is not used here in a strict sense, of something that is in the future, but simply to mean 'not weary of', in the way that Ecclesiasticus 24:21 says, 'They who eat me will hunger for more.'

(2) Fear is related to something bad. Every limitation can be included under the description 'bad'. Human beings, though, have three limitations:

(i) that they incur *punishment*, and 'slavish' fear particularly focuses on that;

(ii) that they incur *guilt*, and 'filial' or 'devout' fear particularly focuses on that; as long as we are on our journey, where we are still able to sin.

Neither of these types of fear will exist in our homeland, when we will have lost our ability to incur guilt or punishment, according to Proverbs 1:33, 'They will enjoy plenty, once the fear of bad things has been taken away.'

(iii) The third type of limitation is part of our *nature* and comes from the infinite distance between God and every creature, and this can never be removed. The 'reverential' fear we will have in our homeland will focus on this; it will make us show reverence to our creator in the light of his majesty, glancing back from this to our own little selves. But the object of hope, which requires blessedness still to be in the future, will be removed once we acquire blessedness; that is why hope will not remain.

(3) The continuation of blessedness does not have the character of something future, because insofar as a person is blessed, he participates in eternity, in which there is neither past nor future. That is why in the context of blessedness we talk of 'eternal life'. Even if we granted that it could possess the character of something future, it still does not have the character of being something hard to get, at least not for someone who has already attained it. For blessedness brings with it not just the possibility but also the necessity of never sinning and of always abiding in it. For this reason, hope, as we have characterised it, must wholly disappear.

(4) The reasoning is based on things that are included in hope not primarily, but only secondarily.

(5) As long as the principal object of hope remains, those who hope for what is good for themselves and for others will do so through one and the same virtue of hope. Once the primary object of hope has gone, one can have hope for other people in a different way, but not through the virtue of hope.

(6) It is appropriate for the saints to pray just as it is for them to hope, but not through the virtue of hope understood as a *theological virtue*.

(7) If you take the *first* principle that moves something towards its finishing-point, then it is true that the principle of movement towards the finishing-point is the same as the principle of resting in it. But if you take some *secondary* and instrumental principle, then there will be principles of movement that cease when the thing reaches its finishing-point, just as a ship stops when it reaches harbour, and so does the driving-force of the wind. In this way, charity, which is the primary mover, remains when we reach the finishing-point of blessedness; however, hope, which is a secondary principle appropriate to the process of getting there, does not.

(8) Those authorities are speaking about justice and living rightly in the context of the *present* life, where we are moving towards living rightly.

(9) The blessed are certain that their condition will never change; such certainty, though, does not come from something future to which they are looking forward, but comes from something that they have *already* received. Therefore it is not part of the character of hope.

(10) As Aristotle says [*Phys* 5.1, 224b30], in the context of change we use 'more' and 'less' to stand for contraries, so that instead of 'black' and 'white' you have just 'less white' and 'whiter'. Similarly, you have 'better' and 'less good' instead of 'good' and 'bad'. In this way, then, when blessedness arrives and makes hope disappear, it is not a case of good driving out bad, but of better driving out less good, just as youth does to childhood.

(11) The object of a virtue can be missing in two ways: (i) while the possibility of having it remains; in this way even if you do not possess the object you can have the virtue and act virtuously, on condition that you have the ability to get it; (ii) when it is impossible to possess it, and then you can no longer either have the disposition or engage in the activity, for they would both always be pointless. It is in the latter way that the object of hope cannot exist in our homeland, because blessedness could not at any subsequent time become something future.

(12) The strength that the saints will possess will be a result of a pre-existing principle, that is, their holding on completely to God, who is all powerful. This will not be ordered towards an end, but will rather *follow* the end in question, as I have said. That is why the reasoning works differently for hope, which is given to us only for moving towards the end.

(13) Although the majesty of God is not less than his goodness, the relation between charity and goodness is different from that between hope and majesty. Charity of its own character includes *union*, and that is why

it comes to completeness in our homeland, while hope includes *distance*, and that is incompatible with the condition of being in our homeland.

(14) Faith and hope have the character of foundation and wall respectively with reference to the *complete* element in each, i.e. insofar as faith holds on to the first truth, and hope to the supreme majesty of God. They do not have this character with reference to the *incomplete* element in each, i.e. for faith the things not yet seen and for hope the things not yet possessed. That is why in the condition of complete blessedness, when charity (which includes in its own character no element of incompleteness) will be complete, faith will be succeeded by a more complete foundation, i.e. clear vision, and hope by a more complete wall, i.e. full possession, in accordance with 1 Corinthians 9:24, 'Run so that you will possess.'

(15) The bodily glory of the saints is a result of the glory of their souls. That is why when they already have glorified souls, which is a more powerful thing, bodily glory no longer has the character of something hard to get.

(16) The hope that Christ exercised was hope in its *general* sense. He did not possess the theological virtue of hope, because for him blessedness was not future, but present.

On the Cardinal Virtues

The first question is whether the cardinal virtues are practical wisdom, justice, courage, and temperateness.

The second is whether the virtues are connected in such a way that if you possess one of them you possess them all.

The third is whether all the virtues within a person are equal.

The fourth is whether when we are in our homeland the cardinal virtues will remain.

Article 1: Whether there are four cardinal virtues, i.e. practical wisdom, justice, courage, and temperateness

Objections

It seems not, because:

(1) If things are not distinguished from one another, they ought not to be counted up together, since distinctions are what make it possible to have numbers, as John Damascene tells us [*OrthF* 2.1]. But the virtues in question are not distinguished from one another, since Gregory says [*MorJob* 22.1.2], 'Practical wisdom is not true unless it is just and temperate and courageous; temperateness is not complete unless it is courageous and just and has practical wisdom; courage is not whole unless it has practical wisdom and is temperate and just; justice is not true unless it has practical wisdom and is courageous and temperate.' Therefore these ought not to be described as four *distinct* cardinal virtues.

(2) These virtues seem to be known as 'cardinal' because they are more fundamental than others: hence some people describe as fundamental

what others call cardinal, as Gregory makes clear [*MorJob* 22.1.2]. But since an end is more fundamental than whatever contributes to that end, the *theological* virtues, which have as their object the ultimate end, seem to be more fundamental than the virtues in question here, which concern whatever contributes to that end. Therefore the virtues in question ought not to be called 'cardinal'.

(3) Things that come from different classes ought not to be included within a single system of ordering. But practical wisdom comes in the class of intellectual virtues, as is clear from Aristotle [*NE* 6.3.1, 1139b15]. The other three, however, are moral virtues. Therefore it is wrong to count the four virtues in question as cardinal.

(4) Among the intellectual virtues, wisdom is more fundamental than practical wisdom, as Aristotle proves [*NE* 6.6.7, 1141a21], because wisdom deals with questions relating to God and practical wisdom with those relating to human beings. Therefore if it were right to include an intellectual virtue among the cardinal virtues, it ought rather to be *wisdom*, as the more fundamental.

(5) The other virtues ought to be traced back to the cardinal virtues. But Aristotle distinguishes [*NE* 2.7.4–13, 1107b10 ff.] several other virtues on a par with courage and temperateness, e.g. liberality and magnanimity, without tracing them back to the former. Therefore the virtues in question are not cardinal virtues.

(6) Something that is not a virtue ought not to be included in the cardinal virtues. But *temperateness* does not seem to be a virtue, because you can possess the other virtues without having it, as is clear from St Paul, who possessed all the other virtues, but not temperateness. For he still had disordered sensual desire in his limbs, according to Romans 7:23, 'I see another law within my limbs, in conflict with the law in my mind.' The temperate person differs from the self-controlled in that the former does not have disordered sensual desires, while the latter does have them, but does not obey them, as is clear from Aristotle [*NE* 7.9.6, 1151b35]. Therefore it is wrong to number the cardinal virtues in question as four.

(7) One is ordered to one's neighbour through virtue in the same way that one is ordered to oneself. But two virtues are given, i.e. courage and temperateness, which order one to oneself. Therefore there should be two virtues, and not only justice, for ordering one towards one's neighbour.

(8) Augustine says [*MorCath* 15.25] that virtue is the ordering of love. Graced love, though, is included under the two precepts about loving God and neighbour. Therefore there should be only two cardinal virtues.

(9) If matter is varied by extending it, it only makes more things. If it is varied by receiving different forms, then it makes things of different classes. That is why, as Aristotle says [*Met* 10.10, 1058b26], destructible and indestructible things differ in their class. But the virtues in question differ because their respective matter varies in that the way that it receives its form is differently characterised, e.g. with temperateness as *restraining* the emotions, and with courage as *striving towards* something when emotion is pulling one away from it. Therefore the virtues in question differ in their class; therefore they should not share a single ordering as cardinal virtues.

(10) The character of a moral virtue comes from its connection with reason, as is clear from Aristotle [*NE* 2.6.15, 1107a1], who defines virtue as following right reason. But right reason is a standard that is measured by the first standard, i.e. God, and it takes from there its power of measuring. Therefore the moral virtues possess the character of a virtue in particular insofar as they touch on the first standard, i.e. God. But the theological virtues, which concern God, are not called cardinal. Therefore neither ought the moral virtues to be called cardinal.

(11) Reason is the principal part of the soul. But temperateness and courage are not found in the reason, but belong to the non-rational parts of the soul, as Aristotle says [*NE* 3.10.1, 1117b24]. Therefore they ought not to be classed as cardinal virtues.

(12) It is more praiseworthy to give of what is yours than to return, or not to take, what is someone else's. But the former is part of liberality, the latter part of justice. Therefore *liberality* rather than justice ought to be counted as the cardinal virtue.

(13) If a virtue provides a foundation for the others, then it seems to be more of a cardinal virtue. But humility is of this sort: for Gregory says that someone who piles up the other virtues without humility might as well be carrying straw in a gale. Therefore *humility* ought to be counted among the cardinal virtues.

(14) Virtue is a sort of perfection, as Aristotle says [*Phys* 7.3, 246b2]. But as James 1:4 says, 'Endurance does what is perfect.' Therefore as something perfect, *endurance* ought to be included among the cardinal virtues.

(15) Aristotle says [*NE* 4.3.14–16, 1123b26 ff.] that magnanimity does great things among the virtues, and is a sort of embellishment of the other virtues. But that would seem to be the role of a principal virtue. Therefore *magnanimity* seems to be a cardinal virtue. Therefore it is wrong to number the cardinal virtues as four.

But on the other hand

Ambrose says [*CommLuke* 5.62 on Luke 6:20, 'Blessed are the poor in spirit']: 'We know that there are four cardinal virtues: temperateness, justice, practical wisdom and courage.'

My reply

'Cardinal' is derived from *cardo*, a hinge, which allows a door to turn, as Proverbs 26:14 puts it: 'Just as a door turns on its hinge, so do the lazy on their beds.' That is why those virtues that are the basis of human life are called 'cardinal', because we enter through the door of human life.

Human life, though, corresponds to human beings. In human beings, the first thing we find is (i) a *sensory* nature, which is shared with non-rational animals; then (ii) *practical reason*, which is distinctive of human beings according to their own level; then (iii) the *theoretical intelligence*, which is not found in human beings in the full way that it is in angels, but only through their participating in something else. That is why the life of contemplation is not, strictly speaking, human, but above what is human. The life of sensual pleasure, though, which clings to the things we perceive through the senses, is not human, but suited to animals {cf. (i)}. Therefore the life distinctive of humans is the active life, which consists in exercising the moral virtues {cf. (ii)}. That is why the virtues known strictly as cardinal are those on which the whole moral life in a sense turns and is based, as if they are a sort of principle of this life. For that reason, this sort of virtue is also called 'principal'.

We need to consider, though, that there are four elements of the character of a virtuous act, as follows: (i') The substance of the act itself, in the way that it is, in itself, qualified: an act is described as 'good' from this, when it relates to the appropriate matter and is accompanied by the appropriate circumstances. (ii') The fact that the act is related in the appropriate way to the subject, i.e. that it is firmly rooted in the subject.

(iii') The fact that the act corresponds in the appropriate way to some-thing external, as to its end. These three elements are aspects of the act that is being directed by reason. (iv') The fourth is awareness, which is an aspect of the reason that is doing the directing.

Aristotle touches on these four when he says [*NE* 2.4.3, 1105a30] that it is not enough for virtue to do something justly or temperately, which refer to how the act is qualified (i'). The other three elements are also needed on the part of the person doing the thing. Firstly, they need to know what they are doing (iv'), which relates to the awareness which directs the action. Then they need to choose, and to choose on account of something, i.e. the appropriate end (iii'). This is what makes the act right in the way that it is ordered to something external. Finally, (ii') they need to be firm and unshakeable and to act in the same way.

These four elements, then, i.e. *awareness* that directs (iv'), *correctness* (iii'), *steadiness* (ii') and being *properly qualified* (i') are needed for every virtuous action, though each one of them may have a kind of priority when particular types of matter or action are in question.

Three things are required from the point of view of *practical awareness* (iv'). The first (a) is counsel, and the second (b) judgement about what has been proposed by counsel. (In the same way, in the area of theoretical reason, we find 'discovery' or 'inquiry' and 'judgement'.) But because practical intelligence tells us to pursue or avoid things (which theoretical reason does not), as Aristotle says [*Soul* 3.9, 432b7], it is, thirdly, the role of practical reason (c) to tell us what to do. The other two elements are ordered primarily towards this.[1]

The virtue of thoughtfulness, i.e. taking counsel well, perfects someone in respect of the first element (a); *synesis* and *gnome*[2] perfect them in respect of the second (b), by making one good at judging, as Aristotle says [*NE* 6.11.1, 1143a24]. It is, though, the virtue of practical wisdom that makes our reason good at telling us what to do {cf. (c)}, as Aquinas explains in the same place. Therefore it is clear that *practical wisdom* has the chief role within the awareness that gives us direction. That is why it is counted as the cardinal virtue within this area.

Similarly, the *correctness* (iii') of an act in relation to something external has the character of something good and praiseworthy even in those things

---

[1] For the three elements of practical reasoning, see the Introduction, p. xx.

[2] These are technical terms, which Aquinas leaves in Greek. For an explanation, see the Introduction, p. xx.

that relate to oneself.[3] But it is particularly praised in cases that concern someone else, when one makes what one does right not only in matters that concern oneself, but also in things that one shares with others. For Aristotle says [*NE* 5.1.15, 1129b32] that many people are able to exercise virtue in what belongs to them, when they do not manage this in what concerns other people. That is why *justice* is classed as the principal virtue in this area; for it allows us to become properly adapted in a fair way to other people who are there for us to share with. That is why things that are adapted in the appropriate way are called in common speech 'just'.

Moderation or restraint (i') is praised and has the character of goodness especially when emotion is particularly forceful and reason needs to restrain it in order to meet the mid-point of virtue. Emotion, though, is most forceful in pursuing the greatest pleasures, which are those of touch. That is why *temperateness* counts as the cardinal virtue in this area, as it holds in check sensual desires for what is pleasurable to the senses involving touch.[4]

Firmness (ii') is praised and has the character of goodness especially in cases where emotion most pushes us to flee. This happens above all in very great dangers, where there is a risk of death. That is why *courage* counts as the cardinal virtue in this area; for it holds us steadfastly to the good of persevering while there is risk of death.

Of these four virtues, practical wisdom is found in the reason, justice in the will, courage in the aggressive part, and temperateness in the sensual desire. These four capacities alone can act as principles of human, i.e. voluntary, activity.

From all this, it becomes clear that the character of the cardinal virtues comes partly from the way in which they are virtues, i.e their formal character, and partly from their domain, and partly from the capacity which possesses them.

Replies to objections

(1) People speak in two different ways about the four cardinal virtues in question. (i) Some use the four names in question to signify *general*

---

[3] The text reads *ad unum secundum se ipsum*. It is not clear exactly what it means, or ought to read, although Aquinas clearly intends a contrast between self-directed and other-directed actions. Perhaps *unum* is a mistake for *hominem* or *aliquem*.

[4] Including taste, which Aquinas regards as an extension of the sense of touch.

ways of being a virtue, for example, labelling every sort of awareness that gives direction as 'practical wisdom'; every sort of correctness in making human actions fair as 'justice'; every sort of moderation that restrains the human appetites from temporal goods as 'temperateness'; and every sort of firmness of character that holds us steadily to what is good in the face of attack from any type of evil as 'courage'. Augustine seems to use the names in this way in *On the Morals of the Catholic Church* [1.15.25]. We can interpret the passage from Gregory in this way, to the effect that satisfying one of the relevant criteria is not enough for the true character of a virtue, if the other criteria we have given are not also present. On this interpretation, the four things in question are called four virtues not because they are different *types* of disposition, pursuing different objects, but in respect of different formal characters.

(ii) Other writers, such as Aristotle in the *Ethics*, discuss the four virtues in question as *particular* virtues directed towards their own distinctive domain. In fact, we can also corroborate Gregory's words even when interpreted in this way: because of a sort of abundance, the virtues in question operate in those domains where our four general criteria for virtue are exceptionally commendable. In this sense, then, courage is temperate and temperateness courageous, in that someone who can restrain his appetite from pursuing his sensual desires for pleasure (which are dealt with by temperateness) will be even more capable of restraining the impulse to act rashly in danger. Similarly, someone who can stand firm when at risk of death, will be even more capable of standing firm against the enticements of sensual pleasure. On this interpretation, the quality that primarily belongs to temperateness transfers also to courage and vice versa. The same reasoning holds for the others.

(2) Human desire comes to rest when it reaches its end. That is why the way in which the theological virtues, which concern our ultimate end, are fundamental is not compared to a hinge, which moves, but rather to a foundation or root, which are both stable and still, as Ephesians 3:17 puts it, 'rooted in and founded upon charity'.

(3) According to Aristotle [*NE* 6.5.4, 1140b5] practical wisdom is right reason in doing things. The things we do are called moral deeds, as is clear from what he says there. That is how practical wisdom shares its domain with the moral virtues, and is numbered with them for that reason, even though with respect to its own being and to its possessor, it is an intellectual virtue.

(4) Wisdom does not share its domain with the moral virtues, because it treats not human, but divine, matters. That is why it is not numbered among the moral virtues in such a way as to be called 'cardinal' along with them. Indeed, the character of a 'hinge' is incompatible with contemplation, for the latter is not like a door through which we enter to get somewhere else. Rather, it is moral activity that is the door through which we enter to reach the contemplation in which wisdom engages.

(5) (i) If the four virtues in question are understood from the point of view of the *general* criteria of virtues, then all the particular virtues treated by Aristotle in the *Ethics* can be traced back to these four, as types belonging to a class.[5]

(ii) On the other hand, if they are understood as *particular* virtues dealing with specific principal domains, the other virtues can be traced back to them as something secondary to something primary. For example, playfulness, which moderates our pleasure in fun, can be traced back to temperateness, which moderates our pleasure in the things we touch. That is why when Cicero [*Inv* 2.53.159–54.165] classes the other virtues as part of these four, we can understand this in two ways: as *subjective* parts, if you interpret the virtues in the first way {cf. (i)}; or as *potential* parts, if you interpret the virtues in the second way {cf. (ii)}. In this same way the sense-faculty is a potential part of the soul, since it does not mark out the whole of the soul's power, but only something belonging to the soul.

(6) It does not belong to the character of temperateness to remove distorted sensual desire completely; rather the temperate person does not suffer from strong and forceful desires of this sort, in the way that people do who have not practised restraining their sensual desires. Therefore St Paul did suffer from disordered sensual desires, because of the corruption of *fomes*,[6] but these were neither strong nor forceful, because he had practised restraining them by chastising his body and making it his servant. That is why he was truly temperate.

(7) Justice, which orders one towards another person, does not deal with one's own emotions, but with whatever one does that involves sharing with other people, such as buying and selling and so on. Temperateness and

---

[5] That is, all the particular virtues treated by Aristotle will be species or types of the four general classes of virtue.

[6] *fomes*: literally, kindling or tinder. The word was used to describe the proneness of fallen human beings to sin. Metaphorically, the idea is that it takes only a small spark of temptation to ignite full-blown sin.

courage, though, deal with one's own emotions. That is why, just as human beings have one power of desire unrelated to the emotions, i.e. the will, and two involved with the emotions, i.e. sensory desire and aggression, so they have one cardinal virtue that orders them to their neighbour and two that order them towards themselves.

(8) Every virtue can be described as 'charity' not because every virtue consists essentially in charity, but because every virtue is caused by charity, since charity is the mother of the virtues. However, there are always more effects than there are causes. That is why there ought to be more kinds of other virtues than there are of charity.

(9) The characterisation of the way that something is received can differ either (i) from the point of view of the *matter*, which is able to receive form; that sort of difference makes a difference in class; or (ii) from the point of view of the *form*, which can potentially be received by the matter in different ways; that sort of difference makes a difference in type. The second type of difference is at issue here.

(10) The moral virtues relate to reason as their *proximate* standard, but to God as their *primary* standard. Things receive their type from their proximate standard, not from their primary principles.

(11) The principal part of a human being is the rational part. But something can be rational either (i) in its own being or (ii) through participating in something else. That is why practical wisdom is more fundamental than the other virtues, just as reason is more fundamental than the powers that participate in reason.

(12) The cardinal virtues are described as more fundamental than the others not because they are more perfect than all the others, but because human life turns on them in a more fundamental way, and the other virtues are then founded on them. It is clear, though, that human life turns more on justice than on liberality, for we exercise justice in relation to everyone, but liberality only to a few people. Furthermore, liberality itself is based on justice, because a gift would not be a liberal one if you were not giving what was your own; it is justice, though, that allows you to distinguish what is yours from what belongs to someone else.

(13) Humility supports all the virtues *indirectly* by removing the things that lie in wait for, to destroy, whatever good the virtues do. However, the cardinal virtues support the other virtues *directly*.

(14) Endurance is included within courage, as courageous people possess the essence of endurance, which is not to be made anxious by evils that

threaten us. But they also possess something more than this, which enables them to drive out the evils that threaten, in whatever way they ought to.

(15) It is obvious from the fact that magnanimity is an embellishment of the other virtues that it presupposes, and so is based on, the other virtues. From this it is clear that the other virtues are more fundamental than it.

Article 2: Whether the virtues are interconnected in such a way that if you possess one of them, you possess them all

Objections

It seems not, because:

(1) Bede comments [*CommLuke* 5] on Luke 17:10 that the saints are more humbled by not having certain virtues than they are elated at having those they do have. Therefore they possess some and not others. Therefore the virtues are not all interconnected.

(2) After repentance, people are in a condition of charity; however, they still find it difficult to do things in a given area[7] because of their previous habits, as Augustine tells us [*AJ* 5.4]. This difficulty seems to come from a disposition contrary to the virtue, which has been acquired through bad habits, and which cannot coexist with the virtue to which it is contrary. Therefore it is possible for someone to possess one of the virtues, i.e. charity, while lacking the others.

(3) Charity can be found in all the baptised. But some of the baptised do not possess practical wisdom, as is especially clear in the case either of people who are half-witted or of the young, who according to Aristotle [*NE* 6.8.5, 1142a13] cannot have become practically wise. It is also the case in adults who are rather simple, who do not seem really to have practical wisdom, since they are not good at taking counsel, which is one of the jobs of practical wisdom. Therefore someone can possess one virtue, i.e. charity, and not all the others.

(4) Aristotle says [*NE* 6.5.4, 1140b5] that practical wisdom is right reason in doing things just as skill is right reason in making things. But it is possible to possess right reason in making one sort of thing, for example tools, but not for other types of artefact. Therefore it is possible to possess practical wisdom in one class of things that one does, for example, just

---

[7] *de his*: the text is difficult at this point.

things, and not in another, for example, courageous things. Therefore someone could have one virtue without the others.

(5) Aristotle says [*NE* 4.2.3, 1122a26] that not every person who is liberal with money is also a magnificent benefactor. But both liberality and magnificence are virtues. Again, some people are moderate without possessing greatness of spirit. Therefore some people possess one virtue without possessing them all.

(6) St Paul says in 1 Corinthians 12:4, 'There are distinctions among gifts', and then adds, 'The Spirit gives some the gift of speaking with wisdom, others of speaking with knowledge' (and these are intellectual virtues) 'others the gift of faith' (and that is a theological virtue). Therefore someone may possess one virtue and not another.

(7) Virginity is a kind of virtue, as Cyprian says [*Virg, passim*]. But many people who do not possess virginity have other virtues. Therefore someone may have one virtue but not all of them.

(8) Aristotle says [*NE* 6.7.5, 1141b5] that we call Anaxagoras and Thales wise but not practically wise. But both wisdom and practical wisdom are intellectual virtues. Therefore someone can possess one virtue and not others.

(9) Aristotle says in the same book [*NE* 6.13.1, 1144b4; 6.13.6, 1144b34] that some people have an inclination towards one virtue and not another. Therefore it can happen that someone engages in activities characteristic of one virtue but not in activities characteristic of another. But we acquire certain of the virtues by practising the relevant activity, as is clear from Aristotle [*NE* 2.1.4, 1103a32]. Therefore at least the acquired virtues are not interconnected.

(10) Even if a natural aptitude for virtue comes (i) from *nature*, the completeness of virtue does not, as Aristotle says [*NE* 2.1.4, 1103a27]. It is also clear that it does not come (ii) from *fortune*, because matters of fortune are outside our choice. Therefore the remaining possibility is that we acquire virtue (iii) through our own undertaking, or (iv) from God. If (iii) by our *own undertaking*, however, it seems that we can acquire one virtue without another, because someone can aim to acquire one virtue and not another. Similarly, even if we acquire them (iv) from *God*: we can seek one virtue from God and not another. Therefore in each of these ways one virtue can exist without another.

(11) The relation between an end and virtuous activity in the area of morals is comparable to the relation between the principle and the

conclusions in the area of demonstrable knowledge. But someone can know one conclusion and not another. Therefore one can have one virtue and not another.

(12) Augustine says [*Let* 167.3.10] that when it says, 'Whoever has one virtue has them all', this is not a divinely inspired opinion; someone can have one without another, e.g. mercy without self-control, just as one of the limbs of the body, but not another, may be lit by beauty or health. Therefore the virtues are not interconnected.

(13) When things are interconnected, this is by reason (i) of a principle, or (ii) of a subject, or (iii) of an object. But here it is not (i) by reason of the *principle*, which is God, because in this sense *all* good things, which come from God, are interconnected. Nor is it (ii) by reason of the *subject*, which is the soul, because in this respect the virtues are not all interconnected. Nor is it (iii) by reason of their *object*, because it is their objects that distinguish the virtues, and the same thing cannot be the principle of both distinguishing and connecting things.

(14) The intellectual virtues are not connected with the moral virtues, as is particularly clear from the fact that it is possible to have understanding of principles without having moral virtues. But practical wisdom is an intellectual virtue, and is counted as one of the cardinal virtues. Therefore it does not have a connection with the other cardinal virtues, which are moral virtues.

(15) In our homeland we will not have faith and hope. We will, however, have charity there. Therefore the virtues will not be interconnected when we are in our most perfect condition.

(16) The angels, who do not possess sensory powers, and similarly the separated souls,[8] possess charity and justice, which lasts forever and does not die. However, they do not possess temperateness and courage, because these virtues belong to our non-rational parts, as Aristotle says [*NE* 3.10.1, 1117b24]. Therefore the virtues are not interconnected.

(17) The body possesses virtues just as the soul does. However, the virtues of the body are not interconnected: for example, some people can see but not hear. Therefore neither are the virtues of the soul.

(18) Gregory says [*HomEzek* 2.3.3] that no one becomes 'supreme' suddenly. Psalm 84:7 says, too, 'They will go from virtue to virtue.' Therefore

[8] The souls of the dead, which are separated from their bodies.

people do not acquire all the virtues at the same time, but one after the other. Therefore the virtues are not interconnected.

But on the other hand

(1) Ambrose says [*CommLuke* 5.63], 'The virtues are interconnected and interlinked, so that someone who has one seems to have them all.'

(2) Gregory says [*MorJob* 22.1.2] that if someone possesses one without another, then it is either not a virtue, or it is imperfect. But perfection is part of the character of a virtue: for a virtue is a sort of perfection, as Aristotle says [*Phys* 7.3, 246b2]. Therefore the virtues are interconnected.

(3) The gloss comments on Ezekiel 1:11, 'The two wings of each were joined', as follows: 'The virtues are interconnected, so that someone who lacks one lacks another.'

My reply

We can speak about the virtues in two ways: (i) about the virtues as imperfect; (ii) about them as perfect. The *perfect* virtues are interconnected, but the *imperfect* virtues are not necessarily interconnected.

To show this we need to know that since virtue is something that makes a person and what he does good, *perfect* virtue is something that makes a person and what he does perfectly good. *Imperfect* virtue, though, makes a person and what he does good not unqualifiedly, but in some respect. Good is found unqualifiedly in human activities when they match up to one of the standards that govern human activities: one of those corresponds strictly to human nature, and this is right reason; the other, though, is the first measure, which transcends us, so to speak, and this is God. It is through *practical wisdom* that we attain right reason, because it is, precisely, right reason in doing things, as Aristotle says [*NE* 6.5.4, 1140b5]. It is through *charity*, though, that we attain God, in accordance with 1 John 4:16: 'Those who remain in charity remain in God, and God in them.'

In this way, then, there are three levels of virtue. (i) Virtues which are *wholly imperfect* exist without practical wisdom, and so do not achieve right reason, for example, the inclinations that some people have even from when they are born to act in a way characteristic of a certain virtue, as Job 31:18 tells us: 'Since I was a baby my compassion has grown with me, and it left the womb together with me.' Inclinations of this sort are not found all together in everyone; rather some people have an inclination of one sort, others of another. These inclinations do not possess the character of a virtue, because no one can misuse a virtue, according to Augustine [*Rev* 1.9]. Someone can, though, misuse this sort of inclination even in a harmful way, if one uses it without discernment, just as a horse that is blind bangs into things harder the faster it runs. That is why Gregory says [*MorJob* 22.1.2] that unless the other virtues do in a practically wise way whatever they are aiming to do, they cannot be virtues. That is why such inclinations, when they lack practical wisdom, do not possess the character of a virtue in a perfect way.

(iia) The second level of virtue consists in virtues that achieve right reason, but do not reach God himself through charity. These are *perfect in one way*, in relation to human good, but not unqualifiedly perfect, because they do not attain the first standard, which is our ultimate end, as Augustine says in *Against Julian*. That is why they fall short of the true character of a virtue, just as moral inclinations without practical wisdom fall short of the true character of a virtue.

(iib) The third level consists of virtues that are *unqualifiedly perfect*, and these are combined with charity. For such virtues make a human action unqualifiedly good, in that it is something that attains our ultimate end.

We need to consider further that just as the moral virtues cannot exist without practical wisdom, for the reason given, so *practical wisdom* cannot exist without the moral virtues: for practical wisdom is right reason in doing things. But right reason concerning any class of things requires someone to make a correct evaluation or judgement about the principles on which the reasoning is based. For example, in geometry no one can make a correct evaluation without possessing right reason concerning the principles of geometry. In actions, though, the principles are the ends, and we can take our reasons for acting from them. But it is through the disposition of a moral virtue that we can evaluate ends correctly, because, as Aristotle says [*NE* 3.5.17, 1114b1], how the end appears to a person depends upon what that person is like. Thus a good in keeping with virtue seems a desirable end to a virtuous person, as does one in keeping with vice to a wicked person. This is like healthy or infected taste. That is why anyone who possesses practical wisdom needs the moral virtues as well.

Similarly, anyone who possesses *charity* ought also to possess all the other virtues. Charity is infused into us by God, according to Romans 5:5, 'The charity of God is poured into our hearts through the Holy

Spirit, who has been given to us.' Now when God gives a thing A an inclination towards something B, he also gives A certain forms, which are the principles of acting and moving towards whatever God is making A incline to {i.e. towards B}. In this way, he gives fire its lightness, which enables it to rise up quickly and easily. That is how, as Wisdom 8:1 tells us, 'He prepares everything in a way that brings delight.' Therefore in a similar way it is appropriate for other forms to be poured into us, along with charity, as dispositions that are readily able to do the things towards which charity makes us incline. Now charity inclines us towards all sorts of virtuous activity, because it commands the activities of all the other virtues, since it is concerned with the ultimate end: for a skill or a virtue that includes a certain end, also governs whatever concerns that end, just as military skill commands horsemanship and a horseman's skill that of the saddler, as Aristotle says [*NE* 1.1.4, 1094a10]. That is why the dispositions of all the other virtues are infused into us along with charity, because God's wisdom and goodness does whatever is fitting. For this reason, 1 Corinthians 13:4 says, 'Charity is patient and kind', etc.

If, then, we take the virtues as (iib) unqualifiedly perfect, they are connected because of *charity*, because no virtue can be of this sort without charity, and once you possess charity you possess all the virtues. However, if we take the virtues as (iia) perfect at the second level, with reference to the human good, they are connected through *practical wisdom*, because no moral virtue can exist without practical wisdom and we cannot possess practical wisdom if any of the moral virtues are lacking.

On the other hand, if we take the four cardinal virtues as implying certain *general* criteria for virtues, they are interconnected in that one of these criteria alone is not enough for any virtuous action: all need to be present. This seems to be Gregory's grounds for connecting them [*MorJob* 22.1.2].

Replies to objections

(1) Anyone may be inclined by nature or by the gift of grace more to one sort of virtuous activity than another; therefore anyone may turn out to be readier for one sort of virtuous action than another. In this sense, where the saints are quicker to act virtuously in one specific way, they are said to possess the related virtue. They are said not to possess the virtue relevant to the actions they are less quick to perform.

(2) A disposition in itself makes us do things readily and with pleasure; however, some additional factor can interfere with this. For example, someone who possesses the disposition of knowledge can be hindered from using it by being sleepy or drunk or whatever. In this way, those who repent receive charity, along with the grace that makes them pleasing to God, and also the dispositions of all the other virtues. However, they can still find it difficult to exercise the virtues which they have received as dispositions, because the tendencies resulting from their earlier sinful activity remain with them. This does not happen with virtues that are acquired through engaging in virtuous activity, because through such activity the opposing tendencies are removed at the same time as the dispositions of the virtues come into existence.[9]

(3) Someone who is baptised receives practical wisdom and all the other virtues along with charity. But it is not necessary for practical wisdom that someone is good at taking counsel in every area, e.g. commerce or war, but only in those matters that are necessary for salvation. Those who are dwelling in grace do not lack that, however simple they are, in keeping with 1 John 2:27: 'Anointing will teach you about everything.' Of course, some of the baptised could be prevented from acting with practical wisdom because of the bodily limitations due to their age, as with children, or to a deformed condition, as with people who are half-witted or crazy.

(4) The products of *skill*, where they fall under different classes, are based on totally unconnected principles. That is why nothing stops us possessing a skill to do with one class of things and not with another. *Moral* principles, on the other hand, are mutually ordered, so that a failure in one leads to failures in others. For example, those who fail to hold to the principle, which is part of *temperateness*, that they should not chase after sensual desires, will from time to time, by doing just that, end up acting unjustly and therefore violating *justice*. Similarly, within one and the same skill or branch of knowledge, e.g. geometry, a mistake in one principle leads to mistakes throughout the discipline. That is why no one can have practical wisdom to a satisfactory degree in the domain of one virtue if they do not have practical wisdom in respect of all the virtues.

(5) With respect to *activity*, it is indeed possible to say that someone is liberal with money, but not a magnificent benefactor: for if you are not

---

[9] As throughout, 'disposition' here translates *habitus*, and 'tendency' *dispositio*.

very wealthy, you can be liberal with what you have, but not magnificent. Perhaps, however, you possess the *disposition* that would enable you to give with magnificence if you had the means. We can say the same about moderateness and greatness of spirit. This response holds good generally for all the *infused* virtues. However, with the virtues that are *acquired* through activity, one can say that those who have acquired the disposition of liberality in making use of their modest possessions have not yet acquired the disposition of magnificence; rather, by possessing the disposition of liberality, they are well prepared for acquiring the disposition of magnificence through a small amount of activity. Whatever[10] we are near to possessing, then, we already seem to possess, since when only a little is lacking, it seems as if nothing is, as Aristotle says [*Phys* 2.5, 197a28].

(6) In the verse from St Paul, wisdom and knowledge should not be taken as the intellectual virtues of that name, which are not interconnected, as I said above; nor as gifts of the Holy Spirit, which are interconnected through charity; but rather as graces freely given, such that someone may overflow with knowledge or wisdom in such a way as to be able to support others in their faith and awareness of God and to refute those who argue against these. That is why St Paul did not say, 'Some are given wisdom and others knowledge', but rather, 'Some are given the gift of speaking with wisdom and others of speaking with knowledge.' For this reason also Augustine says [*Trin* 14.1.3] that most of the faithful are not well endowed with this sort of knowledge, even though they are well endowed with faith. We should not take 'faith' there to refer to unformed faith, as some do, because the gift of faith is shared by everyone; we should take it to mean a certain steadfastness or certainty of faith, with which sometimes even sinners can be full to overflowing.

(7) (i) According to some people 'virginity' is not the name of a virtue, but of a particular state of perfection of a virtue. Now to possess a virtue, you do not need to possess it to a perfect degree. That is why you can possess chastity and the other virtues without virginity.

(ii) Or else, if you grant that virginity is a virtue, this will be true in so far as it involves a disposition of mind that allows someone to choose to preserve virginity for the sake of Christ. This disposition can also exist in someone who is not a virgin in the physical sense, in the way that someone can possess the disposition of magnificence without being very rich.

---

[10] Reading *quod* for *quia*.

(8) The intellectual virtues are not mutually interconnected. This is for three reasons:

(i) because they concern different classes of things, and therefore are not mutually coordinated, as we have already said in the case of crafts;

(ii) because in branches of knowledge, principles and conclusions do not mutually imply one another such that whoever possesses the principles also possesses the conclusions. I have explained, though, that that is the case with moral matters;

(iii) because intellectual virtues are unrelated to the charity that orders us towards our ultimate end. The virtues of this sort are ordered to particular goods, for example, geometry to diameters, metaphysics concerning abstract things, physics concerning things that change, and so on.

That is why, by the same reasoning as with the imperfect virtues, these virtues are not interconnected, as I said above.

(9) (i) Certain virtues, for example, temperateness, justice, and gentleness, order us in ordinary areas of human life. In this area, while one is engaged in one type of virtuous activity one must either (a) also be actively engaged in exercising the other virtues; thus one will acquire the dispositions of all the virtues at the same time; or else (b) do well in respect of one and badly in respect of the others. In the latter case, one will acquire a disposition that is contrary to one of the virtues, and therefore destructive of practical wisdom. But without practical wisdom the tendency acquired through acting in accordance with the other virtues will not have the distinctive character of virtue, as I have explained.

(ii) However, when we have acquired such dispositions in ordinary areas of human life, then we possess other virtuous dispositions – those of the virtues that are not often actually exercised in ordinary social life – in a virtual way, by possessing tendencies that are close to them, as I have said about magnificence and greatness of spirit.

(10) (i) The *acquired* virtues are caused by what we undertake. It must also happen that if someone undertakes to acquire one of them, this will cause all of them to exist at the same time: the one will only be acquired if practical wisdom too is acquired at the same time, and all the others are possessed along with that, as I have argued.

(ii) The *infused* virtues, though, are caused directly by God, and are also caused by charity, as their shared root, as I said in my reply.

(11) In theoretical areas of knowledge, principles and conclusions do not mutually imply one another as does happen in the area of morals, as

I have said. That is why someone who knows one conclusion need not know another one. That would be necessary if someone who knew the principles had to know the conclusions, as is true in the present case.

(12) Augustine is speaking there about *imperfect* virtues, which are particular tendencies to act in a way characteristic of the virtues. That is why he himself elsewhere [*Trin* 6.1.6] can prove the interconnectedness of the virtues.

(13) The virtues are interconnected by reason of their *proximate* principle, i.e. something in their own class, that is, practical wisdom or charity, and not by reason of a distant or general principle, i.e. God.

(14) Practical wisdom is unique among the intellectual virtues in being connected with the moral virtues, by reason of the domain with which it deals, i.e. moral matters.[11]

(15) In our homeland, when hope and faith pass away, they will be replaced by something more perfect, i.e. vision and possession, which are indeed interconnected with charity.

(16) The angels and the separated souls do not possess temperateness and courage for the same activities for doing what they do in this life, i.e. for moderating the emotions of our sensory part, but for doing other things, as Augustine makes clear [*Trin* 14.2.9].

(17) The capacities of the soul and its essence do not reciprocally imply the existence of one another; for although no capacity can exist unless the soul does, the soul can exist without some of its capacities, e.g. without sight or hearing, if those organs which are specifically for actualising the capacities in question are destroyed.

(18) A person is not 'supreme' just through possessing all the virtues, but through possessing them to a supreme degree.

Article 3: Whether all the virtues within a person are equal

Objections

It seems not, because:

(1) 1 Corinthians 13:13 says, 'Now, however, there remain faith, hope, and charity, these three; but the greatest of these is charity.' There being a greatest, however, rules out equality. Therefore the virtues in one person are not equal.

---

[11] Reading *moralia* for *mobilia*.

(2) *Rejoinder*: charity is greater in its actualisation, but not as a disposition. *But on the other hand* Augustine says [*Trin* 6.2.8] that in the case of things that are not great in respect of size, 'greater' means the same as 'better'. But the disposition of charity is better than the dispositions of the other virtues, because it is in closer contact with God, as 1 John 4:16 tells us: 'Those who remain in charity remain in God.' Therefore charity is greater than the other virtues also as a disposition.

(3) Whatever completes something is prior to that thing. But charity makes the other virtues complete, according to Colossians 3:14: 'Have charity on top of everything else, for it is the bond of completeness'; 1 Timothy 1:5, too, says: 'The goal of the precept is charity.' Therefore charity is greater than the other virtues.

(4) Something that has no incompleteness attached to it is more complete and greater, just as something is whiter when it has no black mixed in with it. But the disposition of charity has no incompleteness mixed in with it. Faith and hope do have some incompleteness mixed in them, because faith is about things that are not seen, and hope about things that are not possessed. Therefore charity, even as a disposition, is more complete and greater than faith or hope.

(5) Augustine says [*CG* 19.25], 'If the virtues are not related to God, they are vices.' From this we can take it that the character of a virtue is completed by being ordered towards God. But charity orders us more closely to God than do the other virtues, because it unites us to God, according to 1 Corinthians 6:17: 'Whoever clings to God is one spirit with him.' Therefore charity is a greater virtue than the others.

(6) The infused virtues originate with grace, which is what makes them complete. But charity shares more completely in grace than the other virtues do, for grace and charity accompany one another inseparably, whereas faith and hope can both exist without grace. Therefore charity is greater than the other virtues. Therefore the virtues are not all equal.

(7) Bernard says [*Cons* 1.9] that practical wisdom is the mother of courage, because without practical wisdom courage is over-hasty. But if one thing is the principle and cause of another, it must be greater and more powerful than it. Therefore practical wisdom is greater than courage. Therefore the virtues are not all equal.

(8) Aristotle says [*NE* 5.1.19, 1130a10] that justice is the whole of virtue; the other virtues, though, are parts of it. But the whole is greater than the

part. Therefore justice is greater than the other virtues; therefore not all the virtues are equal.

(9) Augustine proves [*LCG* 11.8.10] that if all the things in the universe were equal, they would not be 'all'. But the virtues are all possessed together, since they are interconnected, as I have shown above. Therefore not all the virtues are equal.

(10) Vices are the opposite of virtue. But not all the vices are equal. Therefore not all the virtues are equal.

(11) Virtuous activity ought to be praised. But certain people receive more praise for one virtue than for another. That is why Cassian can say [*MonInst* 5.4], 'One person is adorned with the blossoms of knowledge, another is more strongly fortified by reason of his discernment, another possesses as a foundation endurance in all its solidity, yet others are preeminent in the virtues of humility or restraint.' Therefore within one person not all the virtues are equal.

(12) *Rejoinder*: that sort of inequality relates to activity, not to dispositions. *But on the other hand* Aristotle says [*Cat* 7, 8a35] that the thought of a relative thing includes the thought of that to which it is relative. But the distinctive character of a disposition relates it towards activity, since it is a disposition that enables you to act when the opportunity arises, as Augustine says [*GMarr* 21.25]. Therefore if the same person is more active in one virtue than another, it follows that the respective dispositions are also unequal.

(13) Hugh of St Victor says that activity makes dispositions grow. If, then, we perform different types of virtuous actions unequally, our virtuous dispositions must also be unequal.

(14) In the area of morals, virtuous dispositions are related to their distinctive activity in the way that in natural things form is related to their distinctive changes or actions. But in natural things, the more that something is characterised by a form, the more powerful the relevant behaviour or change. For example, the heavier something is, the quicker it falls, or the hotter it is, the more it heats. Therefore in moral matters too, the activities of different virtues can only be unequal if the related dispositions are also unequal.

(15) Whatever completes something corresponds to that thing. The virtues, though, complete the capacities of the soul, which are unequal because reason is superior to the lower powers, which it governs. Therefore the virtues too are unequal.

(16) Gregory says [*MorJob* 22.20.26; *HomEzek* 2.3.3], 'Blessed Job described as "steps" the increases in virtue that he saw were given as a gift from above differently to different people; this was because by means of them we ascend to reach and gain the things of heaven.' But when there are increases and steps, there is no equality. Therefore the virtues are not equal.

(17) Things that are related such that when one increases the other decreases, must be unequal. It seems, though, that when charity increases, faith decreases, because the situation of our homeland, where charity will be complete, is opposed to the situation on our journey, where faith has a place. When one of two opposites increases, though, the other decreases. Therefore charity and faith cannot be equal. Therefore not all the virtues are equal.

But on the other hand

(1) Revelation 21:16 says that the sides of the city are equal. The gloss comments that these sides signify the virtues. Therefore the virtues are equal.

(2) Augustine says [*Trin* 6.1.6], 'If two people are equal in courage, they are also equal in practical wisdom and temperateness. For if you say that A and B are equal in courage, but A is superior in practical wisdom, it will follow that B's courage has less practical wisdom. But then they will not be equally courageous, since A's courage will have more practical wisdom. You will find the same with the rest of the virtues, if you run through them all with the same thing in mind.' Now it would not be right to say that those who are equal in one virtue are equal in the others, unless all the virtues were equal in one person. Therefore within one person, all the virtues are equal.

(3) Gregory says [*HomEzek* 2.10.17] that faith, hope, charity, and activity are all equal. Therefore by parallel reasoning all the other virtues are equal.

(4) Ezekiel 46:21 says that the four little courts were of the same measure, and the gloss comments: 'By which we advance to virtue.' But things that are of the same measure are equal. Therefore they are all equal.

(5) John Damascene says [*OrthF* 3.14], 'The virtues are natural and they exist equally in everyone.' But the being of an accidental quality

consists in being *in* something. Therefore the virtues are equal according to their own being.

(6) A greater reward is due to the activities of a greater virtue. Therefore if within one person one virtue were greater than another, it would follow that both a greater and a lesser reward were due to the same person. That makes no sense.

(7) If B follows from A, then more B follows from more A. But it follows from the fact that one possesses one virtue that one possesses them all, because they are interconnected, as I have argued. Therefore if someone possesses one virtue to a greater degree, one must possess them all to a greater degree. Therefore all the virtues must be equal.

My reply[12]

Things are described as 'equal' or 'unequal' with respect to quantity: something that is one in quantity is equal, just as something that is one in quality is similar, and something that is one in substance is the same, as Aristotle makes clear [*Met* 5.15, 1021a10]. Quantity, though, includes the idea of measure, which is found primarily (i) in numbers, secondarily (ii) in sizes, and thirdly (iii) in some sense in all the other classes, as Aristotle also makes clear [*Met* 10.1, 1052b20]. For in every class the thing that is most simple and most perfect is the measure of all the other things, e.g. whiteness among the colours or daily motion among kinds of movement. That is because a thing is more perfect the more nearly it attains the first principle of its class. From this it is clear that the degree to which something is perfect, measuring this with reference to its first principle, can be described as its 'quantity'. This is what Augustine means [*Trin* 6.8.9] when he says that in things that are great but not in size, 'greater' means the same as 'better'.

In the case of a form that does not exist independently, its being consists in *being in* its subject or its matter; we can, therefore, consider its quantity or perfection under two aspects: (1) according to the character of its distinctive *type*; (2) according to its *being in* its matter or subject.

(1) According to the character of the distinctive type, (1°) the forms of *different* types are unequal, while of the forms of a *single* type some (1b)

---

[12] Aquinas's very precise and complex reply draws heavily on Aristotle's *Categories*, especially 6, 6a 25–35 and 8, 10b26–11a14.

can be *unequal*[13] and some (1a) cannot. This is because the principle that governs the type has to be indivisible; anything that makes a difference to this principle will change the type. For this reason, if anything is added to or taken away from this principle, the type will necessarily change. That is why Aristotle says [*Met* 8.3, 1043b33] that types are like numbers, since if you add or take away a unit you change the type.

(1a) Certain forms acquire their type through something that is *a part of their essence*; this is true of all absolute[14] forms, whether they are substantial or accidental. In this sort, it is impossible to find one form greater than another (in the sense under consideration) within the same type. For example, one whiteness, considered in itself, is not more of a whiteness than another.

(1b) Other forms acquire their type from something *extrinsic* towards which they are ordered, in the way that movement acquires its type from its termination. That is why one movement is greater than another depending on how far it is from its finishing-point. Similarly, we can find certain qualities which are tendencies ordered towards something, in the way that health is a balance of the humours[15] ordered towards the nature of the animal that is described as healthy. For this reason, the level of balance of the humours that would count as health for a lion would count as sickness for a human being. Health, then, does not acquire its type from the absolute level of the balance of humours, but from the nature of the animal towards which it is ordered. Consequently, it is also the case that the same animal can be healthy to a greater or lesser degree, as Aristotle says [*NE* 10.3.3, 1173a24] – insofar, that is, as there can be differences in the levels of the balance of the humours consistent with the requirements of the animal's[16] nature. The same situation can be found with a branch of knowledge, which receives its unity from the unity of the subject: that is why knowledge of geometry can be greater in one person than in another, in that the one knows more of the conclusions that are ordered to awareness of the subject-matter of geometry, which is magnitude.

---

[13] Reading *inaequales* for *aequales*.

[14] Absolute forms are those that are what they are without reference to anything extrinsic to themselves, as contrasted with the relative forms discussed under (1b).

[15] According to ancient medical theory, health required an appropriate balance among four bodily fluids called 'humours': phlegm, blood, black bile or gall, and yellow bile or choler.

[16] Omitting *humanae*.

(2) Similarly, with respect to the quantity of perfection which forms of this sort possess insofar as they *exist in* their matter or subject, some forms of a single type (b) can be unequal insofar as they exist in these to a greater or lesser degree; others, though, (a) cannot exist in them to a greater or lesser degree.

(2ai) If a form gives its subject its type, then it cannot exist in it to a greater or lesser degree, because, as I have said, we ought to think of the typifying principle as indivisible. From this it follows that no substantial form admits of more or less. (2aii) Similarly, if a form acquires its type from something that is indivisible in its own character, then it cannot be spoken of as more or less. It follows that 'being two', or any other type of numerical value, which gets its type from the addition of units, cannot admit of more or less. The same reasoning holds for figures which are specified through numbers, such as a triangle or square, and for specific quantities, such as two or three cubits, and for numerical relations such as double or triple.

(2b) Forms that do not give their subject its type, and do not acquire their type from something that is indivisible in its own character, can exist in something to a greater or lesser degree, as, for example, with whiteness or blackness.

From all this, it is clear that different forms are related in two ways to each of equality and inequality:

(I) There are some forms that do not admit of inequality within the same type, neither in themselves – i.e. one of them cannot be greater than another of the same type – nor in the way that they exist in something else – i.e. they cannot be in the subject to a greater or lesser degree. The substantial forms are all of this sort {cf. (1a), (2ai)}.

(II) Other forms, such as whiteness or blackness, do not admit of inequality in themselves, but do so only in the extent to which they are found in their subjects {cf. (1a), (2b)}.

(III) Others do admit of inequality in themselves, but not in the extent to which they are found in their subject: for example, one triangle can be bigger than another, because its lines are longer than the other's, even though both sets of lines are ordered towards a single thing that gives them their type. However, one surface cannot be more triangular than another {cf. (1b), (2aii)}.

(IV) Other things, such as health and knowledge and movement, admit of inequality both in themselves and in the way they exist in their subjects.[17] For example, movement is unequal either if it crosses a greater distance, or because the moving thing moves faster. Similarly, one person's knowledge is greater than another's either because he knows more conclusions, or because he knows the same, but more securely. Similarly, health can be unequal either because the level of balance in one creature is nearer to the appropriate complete equality than it is in another, or because one of them is more steadily and better related to that level of balance than is another {cf. (1b), (2b)}.

Once we have seen all this, we must say the following about the equality and inequality of the virtues.

(1') If we take the inequality of the virtues with reference to what they are *in themselves*, then (1'°) virtues of *different types* can be unequal. For since virtue is the tendency of something complete to what is best, as Aristotle says [*Phys* 7.3, 246b2], a virtue that is ordered towards a greater good will be greater and more complete. Accordingly, the theological virtues, whose object is God, are superior to the others; and among these, charity is the greatest, because it joins us most closely to God. Again, hope is greater than faith, because hope moves our feelings in some way towards God, whereas faith makes God present in us in the form of awareness. Next, among the other virtues, practical wisdom is the greatest, because it moderates the others; and after this justice, because it enables us to be what we should be not only in ourselves but also in relation to others. Next comes courage, which enables us to scorn the danger of death for the sake of something good. After this comes temperateness, which enables us to scorn the greatest of pleasures for the sake of what is good.

(1'a) *Within one type* of virtue, however, this sort of inequality cannot be found, in the way, for example, that it is found within one type of knowledge {cf. (1b)}. That is because it is not part of the character of knowledge that if you possess one sort of it you will know all the conclusions belonging to that. By contrast, it is part of the character of virtue that someone who possesses one of them will be in a good state in relation to everything relevant to that virtue.

(2'b) With respect to the perfection or quantity of the virtue from the point of view of *its being in* its subject, there can be inequality even

---

[17] Aquinas never quite comes out and says explicitly that virtues belong in this fourth category. The remainder of his reply is devoted to showing exactly how both sorts of inequality are found in virtue.

within one type of virtue, in that one of those who possess it can be better disposed than someone else to whatever comes under that virtue; this might be through a better natural tendency, or more practice, or better rational judgement, or the gift of grace. This is because virtue does not give its subject its type {cf. (2ai)}, nor is there anything indivisible in its essential character {cf. (2aii)} – unless, of course, we agree with the Stoics, who said that no one possesses a virtue without possessing it supremely, and consequently that everyone who possesses a specific virtue possesses it equally. But in fact it does not seem to follow from the character of a virtue, because there is such a variety of ways in which people share in a virtue, following from the factors I have discussed; none of those factors characterise any particular virtue such as chastity.

In this way, then, in *different* people the virtues can be unequal, i.e. in themselves, with respect to *different types* of virtues {cf. (1'°)}; and in the way they exist in their subject, even with reference to *one type* of virtue {cf. (2'b)}.

In *one and the same person*, on the other hand, according to the quantity or perfection which each virtue has *in itself*, the virtues can be unequal {cf. (1'°)}; according to the quantity or perfection in the way each *exists in* its subject, simply speaking all the virtues must be equal, for the same reason that they are all interconnected: for equality is a sort of connection with respect to quantity. (That is why some people attribute the character of equality to them because they interpret the four cardinal virtues as general ways of being virtuous.[18] This is the reasoning Augustine uses in *On the Trinity* [6.4.6]. In another way, one can attribute this to the dependence of the moral virtues on practical wisdom and of all the virtues on charity. That is why where charity is equal, all the virtues must be equal in terms of the formal perfection of virtue. The same reasoning will hold for practical wisdom in comparison with the other virtues.)

However, the virtues can be unequal in one and the same person, just as they can also be unconnected, *in a relative sense*, in terms of the inclination of the capacity to be actualised, which comes from nature or some other cause. That is why some people say that the virtues are unequal with respect to their actions; however, we should interpret this only in accordance with this sort of inequality of an inclination to be actualised.

[18] See *DQCard* 1 ad 1.

Replies to objections

(1) The argument depends on the inequality that refers to the virtues *in themselves*, not the inequality related to their existing *in something else*, which we are speaking about now. For charity, as I have said, is greater in itself than the other virtues; however, when it grows, the other virtues also grow in a correlative way in one and the same person, just as the fingers on a hand are different lengths, but they grow at a correlative rate.

We can give a similar reply to objections (2) to (6), and even (7), which proved that practical wisdom[19] was greater than the other virtues only in this same way.

(8) We can make a similar reply, namely that it argues in the same way about justice – even if you mean the justice that is defined as the whole of virtue, rather than that which is counted as one of the cardinal virtues.

(9) Similarly, we can reply that all the virtues exist in a person in such a way that they can be distinguished according to the greater or lesser degree of perfection possessed by each type.

(10) Similarly, the vices are also unequal in this way.

(11) People are praised for one virtue rather than for another because they are quicker to act in accordance with it.

(12) Those who possess a greater disposition should act more in accordance with the inclination of that disposition. However, sometimes someone can have in him something contingently related to the disposition that either hampers him from, or makes him tend to, an action; so, for example, drunkenness can prevent someone from activating the disposition of knowledge that he possesses. Thus, through helps or hindrances to action of this sort, one can sometimes increase one's activity without increasing the related disposition.

(13) In the case of acquired dispositions, more exercise makes the disposition increase. However, dispositions that have already been acquired through repeated activity can be hindered contingently, so that they do not succeed in being actualised, as I have said.

(14) In natural things, where a form is equal, there can be inequality in the resulting action because of some contingent obstacle.

(15) The capacities are unequal in themselves, insofar as one capacity is more perfect than another in its own character. We have agreed that the virtues too are unequal in this sense.

---

[19] Reading *prudentiam*, which is needed for the argument.

(16) The virtues exist in a person correlatively, as I have said. That is why it does not follow that they are possessed in an unequal way.

(17) The situation in our homeland is opposed to faith because of the clear vision we will have, which is not achieved through an increase of charity. That is why faith need not diminish as charity increases.

Replies to objections under 'But on the other hand'

(1) to (4). The replies to these are clear from what has been said.

(5) John Damascene understands virtues to exist in every one equally, meaning generally[20].

(6) The reward in its essence is a response to the root, which is charity. For this reason, even if we grant that all the virtues are not equal, still only one reward will be due to one person, because his charity will be one and the same.

We accept objection (7).

Article 4: Whether when we are in our homeland the cardinal virtues will remain

Objections

It seems not, because:

(1) Gregory says [*MorJob* 6.37] that what we do in our active life will pass away together with the body. But the cardinal virtues complete us for what we do in our active life. Therefore the virtues will pass away along with the body. Therefore they will not remain in our homeland.

(2) When you have achieved your end you no longer need whatever contributed to that end; just as you no longer need the ship when you have reached harbour. But the cardinal virtues are distinguished from the theological virtues by the fact that the latter have the ultimate end as their object, while the former have whatever contributes to that end. Therefore once we have reached our ultimate end in our homeland, we will not need the cardinal virtues.

(3) When you remove an end, whatever contributes to the end disappears too. But the cardinal virtues are ordered towards the civic good,

---

[20] This means: it is equally true of everyone that he or she shares in the virtues, not: everyone shares in the virtues to an equal degree.

which will not exist in our homeland. Therefore neither will the cardinal virtues exist in our homeland.

(4) If something remains not according to its own distinctive type, but only according to the general character of its class, then it is said to 'pass away' rather than to remain in our homeland. In this way, faith is said to 'pass away' even though awareness remains, which is the class to which faith belongs. But in our homeland, the cardinal virtues will not remain in accordance with those distinctive types that distinguish them; for Augustine says [*LCG* 12.26.54] that there virtue will be wholly and only loving what you see. Therefore the cardinal virtues will not remain in our homeland but will pass away.

(5) The virtues derive their types from their objects. But the object of the cardinal virtues will not remain in our homeland. After all, practical wisdom deals with doubtful matters, which need counsel; justice deals with agreements and judgements; courage deals with the danger of death; while temperateness deals with sensual desires for food and sex. None of these will exist in our homeland. Therefore the cardinal virtues will not exist in our homeland.

(6) *Rejoinder*: the virtues will have other things to do in our homeland. *But on the other hand* if any element of the definition of A is altered, A will be altered in type. Now an action is an element of the definition of a disposition, since according to Augustine [*GMarr* 21.25] a disposition is what enables us to act when the opportunity arises. Therefore if there are different activities, there will also be dispositions that differ in type.

(7) According to Plotinus, as Macrobius tells us [*Dream* 1.5–6], the virtues of a purified soul are different from the political virtues. But the virtues of a purified soul seem most to be the virtues that we will have in our homeland. The virtues we possess here, however, are political virtues. Therefore the virtues we have here will not remain there, but will pass away.

(8) The situations of the blessed and of those on the journey are more different than those of master and slave or of man and woman in the present life. Yet according to Aristotle [*Pol* 1.5, 1254b1] the virtues of master and slave are different, and similarly those of man and woman. Therefore the virtues possessed by the blessed and by those on the journey will differ far more.

(9) The dispositions of the virtues are necessary for preparing our capabilities for being actualised. But there this preparation will be adequately effected by glory. Therefore the dispositions of the virtues will not be needed.

(10) St Paul proves in 1 Corinthians 13:8 that charity is more excellent than the other virtues, because it will not pass away. But faith and hope, which do pass away, are nobler than the cardinal virtues, because they have a nobler object, i.e. God. Therefore the cardinal virtues will also pass away.

(11) The intellectual virtues are nobler than the moral, as Aristotle makes clear [*NE* 6.7.3, 1141a20]. But the intellectual virtues will not remain, because 'knowledge will be destroyed', as 1 Corinthians 13:8 tells us. Therefore the cardinal virtues will not remain in our homeland either.

(12) James 1:4 says, 'Endurance possesses a deed that is perfect.' But endurance will not remain in our homeland except as a reward, as Augustine tells us [*CG* 14.9]. Therefore much less will the other moral virtues.

(13) Certain cardinal virtues, i.e. temperateness and courage, exist in the sensory capacities of the soul: for they belong to the soul's non-rational parts, as Aristotle makes clear [*NE* 3.10.1, 1117b24]. But neither angels nor separated souls can possess sensory parts of the soul. Therefore virtues of this sort cannot exist in our homeland either in the angels or in the separated souls.

(14) Augustine says [*CG* 22.30.5] that in our homeland we will be at leisure, we will see, we will love, we will praise. But leisure is an activity of wisdom, seeing an activity of the intelligence, love an activity of charity and praise an activity of worship. Therefore only those will exist in our homeland, and not the cardinal virtues.

(15) In our homeland, human beings will be like angels, as Matthew 22:30 tells us. But human beings do not become like angels through soberness, since angels do not need to consume food and drink. Therefore there will be no soberness in our homeland. Therefore by equal reasoning neither will the other virtues be there.

But on the other hand

(1) Wisdom 1:15 says, 'Justice is everlasting and immortal.'

(2) Wisdom 8:7 says of divine wisdom that 'it teaches soberness and practical wisdom, justice, and courage, which are the most useful things

in human life'. But in our homeland, we will share as fully as possible in wisdom. Therefore the virtues of this sort will exist more fully in our homeland.

(3) The virtues are spiritual riches. But there will be a greater wealth of spiritual riches in our homeland than on the journey. Therefore the virtues of this sort will be in more plentiful abundance in our homeland.

My reply

In our homeland the cardinal virtues will remain, but they will do different things; for, as Augustine tells us [*Trin* 14.9.12], 'The things that at present justice does in assisting the wretched, practical wisdom in avoiding traps, courage in enduring troubles, and temperateness in restraining corrupt pleasures, will not exist there, since there will be nothing evil there at all.' But 'the role of justice will be to be subject to the rule of God, of practical wisdom to treat no other good as equal or preferable to God, of courage to cling to him with utter steadfastness, and of temperateness not to take pleasure in any harmful failing'.

To show this, we need to know that virtue involves the upper limit of a capacity, as Aristotle tells us [*Heav* 1.11, 281a15]. It is clear, though, that different natures have different upper limits to their capacities, because a higher nature has a greater capacity that reaches to more and greater things. For this reason, something that counts as a virtue for one thing does not for another. For example, human virtue is defined in relation to the important things in human life, so that human temperateness consists in a human being's not abandoning reason for the sake of the greatest pleasures, but rather moderating them in accordance with reason; again, human courage consists in standing firm in the face of the greatest danger, i.e. danger of death, on account of the good of reason.

But the upper limit of God's capacity is not found in such things as these, but in something higher, something consonant with the infinity of his power. For this reason, God's courage is his unshakeability, his temperateness is the turning of his mind to himself, his practical wisdom is the divine mind itself, and the justice of God is his eternal law itself.

The next thing we need to bear in mind is that different upper limits can be understood in two ways: (a) as related within the same series of changes; (b) as separate and not mutually ordered.

(a) If, then, we take the different upper limits as *ordered within a single series* of changes, then these different upper limits make the *changes* differ in type. They do not, though, make a difference in type to the *principle of change*, because it is the same principle of change that governs a change from start to finish. We can take as an example the case of building: here the final end-point is the completed form of the house; however, we can also take the completion of individual parts of the house to be other final points; that is why, as Aristotle says [*NE* 10.4.2, 1174a19], the foundation of the house is one type of change, which is completed when the foundation is built, the raising of the columns is another, and a third is the completion of the whole building. However, the skill of building is one and the same, and is the principle of all three of these changes. The same goes for other examples of change.

(b) If, however, we understand the different ends as *separate*, i.e. not as part of a single series of changes, but completely separate, then *both* the changes *and* the principles of change will differ in type. For example, the skill that is the principle of building a house is different from the one that is the principle of constructing a ship.

In this way, then, (i) where the upper limit is the same in type, the virtue will also be the same in type, as will the activity or change resulting from that virtue. For example, it is clear that both in me and in you temperateness attains an upper limit that is the same in type, i.e. moderation of the enjoyments of touch. That is why neither temperateness nor its activities differ in type in you and in me.

(ii) However, where the upper limit attained by the virtue is neither of the same type nor contained within the same series of changes, there must be a difference in type not only in the activities of the virtue, but even in the virtue itself {cf. (b)}. This is clear with virtues that are ascribed to both God and human beings.

(iii) Where the upper limit of the virtue differs in type, but is still contained under a single series of changes, so that it moves from one to another, then the activity will differ in type, but the virtue be the same {cf. (a)}. For example, courageous activities are ordered to one upper limit before the battle, to another during it, and to yet another when victory is secured. Hence, the actions of approaching the battle, standing one's ground courageously during it, and rejoicing at winning a victory are different; the courage, though, is the same. Similarly, the same capacity is actualised in loving, desiring, and rejoicing.

273

It is clear, then, from what has been said that since the condition of our homeland is higher than that of our journey, the virtues in our homeland must attain a more elevated upper limit. If, then, the upper limit attained by virtue on our journey is ordered to the upper limit attained by virtue in our homeland, there will have to be one type of virtue, but different types of action {cf. (iii)}. If, on the other hand, the one is not understood as ordered to the other, then the virtues will not be the same either as activities or as dispositions {cf. (ii)}.

It is clear that the *acquired* civic virtues, which the philosophers discuss, are ordered only to perfecting human beings in civic life, not to perfecting them as ordered towards the winning of heavenly glory {cf. (ii)}. That is why the philosophers held that this type of virtue does not remain after this life, as Augustine tells us was true of Cicero [*Trin* 14.3.12]. On the other hand, the cardinal virtues as given by grace and *infused*, which we are now discussing, perfect us in the present life for being ordered towards heavenly glory {cf. (iii)}. For that reason, it is necessary to say that the dispositions of these virtues are the same here and there, even though their activities are different. For here such activity is suited to those aiming at the ultimate end, and there to those who are resting in it.

Replies to objections

(1) The virtues of this sort complete us for our active life, a sort of journey by which we reach the goal of contemplation in our homeland. For this reason, they remain in the homeland insofar as their activity has been fully realised in the goal.

(2) The cardinal virtues concern things that contribute to the end, but not in the sense that their ultimate end is found *in* them, in the way that the ultimate end of a ship is sailing. Rather, it is *through* the things that contribute to the end that the cardinal virtues are ordered to the ultimate end. For example, grace-given temperateness does not have as its final end moderating the sensual desires for things we touch, but it does this for the sake of the blessedness of heaven.

(3) The civic good is not the ultimate end of the *infused* cardinal virtues, which are under discussion now, but of the *acquired* virtues, which the philosophers discussed, as I explained in my reply.

(4) Nothing prevents one and the same thing from being the end of different virtues or skills. For example, protecting the good of the city is

the end and goal of both military activity and legislation. That is why both of these types of skill or virtue relate their activities to that as the good that is their end. Military activity, on the one hand, looks to protecting the good of the city to the extent that this is achieved through courageous battles; legislation, on the other, rejoices in the same end, to the extent that the good of the city is protected by the legislative order. In this way, then, the enjoyment of God in our homeland is the end of all the cardinal virtues, but each one rejoices in that end in accordance with the end of its own particular activities. For this reason, one can say that in our homeland there will be only one virtue, in as much as there will be one object[21] in which all the virtues rejoice. However, there will be different activities and different virtues in as much as there will be different reasons for rejoicing.

(5) Something can be called the object of a virtue in two ways: (i) as the thing towards which virtue is ordered as its *end*, in the way that the supreme good is the object of charity, and eternal blessedness is the object of hope; (ii) as the *domain* with which it deals, directing itself towards something else on the basis of that; in this sense, the pleasures of sex are an object of temperateness. For temperateness does not aim to cling to pleasures of this sort, but rather to hold them in check so as to direct itself towards what is good according to reason. Similarly, courage does not aim to cling to dangers, but rather by overcoming them to achieve what is good according to reason. The same is true for practical wisdom in respect of issues that are doubtful, and of justice in respect of the necessities of this life. For this reason, the further they have withdrawn from such things in their progress in the spiritual life, the more perfect will the activities of these virtues be. The things mentioned[22] relate to the virtues more as starting points than as finishing points; but the latter is what gives a thing its type.

(6) Not every difference in activity proves a difference in disposition, as I have now explained.

(7) The virtues of a purified soul, which Plotinus defined, are relevant to the blessed. For there the role of practical wisdom is simply to gaze on what is divine, of temperateness to forget selfish desires, of courage to ignore the emotions, of justice to possess a perpetual covenant with God.

---

[21] The text reads, oddly, *erit una virtus, in quantum erit in subiecto, de qua omnes virtutes gaudebunt.* It is tempting to read *in quantum erit una fruitio*: 'insofar as there will be a single enjoyment'.

[22] The text reads *praedicta verba*.

The political virtues, however, which he also mentioned, are ordered only towards the civic good in this present life, as I have said.

(8) The upper limits of the virtues of slave and master, or man and woman, are not mutually ordered in such a way that one passes from one to the other. Therefore the reasoning is different.

(9) The preparation through glory for those virtuous activities that are produced or perfected by means of glory, is a function, precisely, of the dispositions of the virtues.

(10) Faith is ordered towards the truth that is not seen, and hope to something hard to get, not yet possessed, as the objects that determine their type. For this reason, although they are more excellent than the cardinal virtues because their objects are higher, they will still pass away because the thing that gives them their type will no longer exist.

(11) The disposition of knowledge will not be destroyed either; however, it will have different activities.

(12) In our homeland, endurance will not keep the role that it has on our journey, i.e. enduring trials. However, it will have a role suitable to the end, just as I have said for the other virtues.

(13) (i) Some people hold that aggression and sensual desire, where temperateness and courage are found, are located in the *higher* part of the soul, not in its sensory part. This, though, contradicts Aristotle, where he says [*NE* 3.10.1, 1117b24] that they are virtues of the non-rational parts.

(ii) Others, on the other hand, hold that the powers of the sensory part remain in the separated soul either (a) as a *capacity* only; or (b) *actively*. The second (b) cannot be true, because the sensory capacity can only be actualised through the body; otherwise the sensory soul of a non-rational animal would be indestructible, which is false. Now a capacity belongs to the same thing as the related activity; that is why capacities of this sort need to be connected with the body. In this way, after death they will not remain actively in the separated soul, but virtually, as in their root, insofar as the capacities of the soul flow from its being {cf. (a)}.

Moreover, the virtues in question exist in aggression and sensual desire in that they flow through them, but their origins and predispositions are in the reason and will; this is because the principal action of moral virtue is choice, which is an action of the rational desire. But the choice in question is applied by means of temperateness and courage so that it finally reaches the emotions of the aggression and the sensual desire.

(14) All four of those things will be part of a single activity that will be for the cardinal virtues their end, insofar as that will consist of heavenly blessedness.

(15) Soberness does not make us like the angels in what it does on our journey, i.e. dealing with the matter of food or drink, but in what it does in our homeland, which relates to the ultimate end, as with the other virtues.

Terminology and glossary

Terminology

The extent and precision of philosophical and semi-technical words in Aquinas poses a problem for translators, and particularly for those translating into languages such as English which do not contain close equivalents of many of his common terms. The situation is further complicated by the development of English, which has meant that many words, in particular in the field of ethics and psychology, have changed their meaning, often in a way that impoverishes their sense. For this reason, to use what looks like the nearest English equivalent of, say, *habitus* or *temperantia* can be extremely misleading. Scholars and translators working in an age where most of their readers knew Latin often ignored this risk, trusting their readers to recognise that, for example, 'habit' was being used in its 'Latin' rather than its English sense. Wherever possible, I have tried to avoid such near-transliterations, as their collective effect seems to me likely seriously to distort a contemporary reader's impression of Aquinas's ideas.

Glossary

actus: **actualisation, activity, activeness, action, act;** *potentia*: **capacity, potential.**
These two terms encapsulate one of the most fundamental differences between an Aristotelian-Thomist view of the world and a modern one: the idea of directed potential. For Aquinas, each thing has certain capacities or potentialities which are made to be actualised in specific ways, as the

eye has a capacity that is actualised in the act of seeing. The range of senses of *actus* is due to the fact that actions are thought of precisely as *actualisations* of capacities. A capacity is completely actualised when it reaches its *ultimum* or **upper limit**.

perfectus: **complete, perfect, fully developed, elevated**; sometimes the word is translated with a paraphrase using **full**.

The possession of directed capacities is a part of the orientation of each thing towards its natural goal or fulfilment, towards what, in some sense, it is meant to be or become. The participle *perfectus* is used to describe something that is a complete specimen of its kind, which in cases of things that grow and develop means a *mature* specimen. It has nothing essential missing; its potential is fulfilled. In the case of things that change and develop, the word conveys the sense that a *process* has been completed. Unlike the English 'perfect', *perfectus* does not normally convey the sense of 'flawless'. Again, a specimen that is *perfectus* need not be rare or unusual of its type. The word does not imply a relation as in 'perfect for'. For these reasons, 'complete' is often the least misleading translation. 'Developed' is helpful in particular in contexts where the idea of change is important.

The abstract noun *perfectio* can mean (a) the state of being *perfectus*; (b) an element that makes something complete; for example, Aquinas describes the soul as the *perfectio* of a human being. I have used a paraphrase to translate this sense of the word.

The English 'perfect' or 'complete' are normally used by comparison with other things of the same type: an apple is perfect or imperfect *as an apple*, by comparison with other apples. Aquinas, because of his wider philosophical commitments, may also rank different types of thing as comparably 'perfect': a human being, he might argue is more *perfectus* as an animal than a sheep, an apple, maybe, more *perfectus* as a fruit than a gooseberry. We would normally use terms such as 'better' or 'higher' in making comparable comparisons. I have usually translated *perfectior* in this sense as 'more elevated'.

Aquinas also uses the verb *perficere* to mean to make complete or perfect.

ratio: **reason, character**; other translations include **argument, description, meaning, respect**.

Ratio covers a very wide range of senses, including: (a) the faculty or the virtue of reason; (b) the argument or process of reasoning; (c) a reason for something; (d) the definition, or more generally description of the distinctive elements, of a thing;

Aquinas uses *ratio* frequently to refer to (e) the intelligible structure of a thing, that which can be picked out by the definition or, more generally, by a description. Here 'nature' or even 'essence' would often be the most natural translations, but it is best to keep them for *natura* and *essentia*; the English words 'identity' or 'intelligibility' are also sometimes used in a similar sense. I have translated this sense of *ratio* with the word 'character'.

habitus: **disposition**; *dispositio*: **tendency**; *inclinatio*: **inclination**; *inchoatio*: **predisposition**.

Aristotle's *Categories* distinguishes four kinds of 'quality'. One of these kinds includes *habitus* and *dispositio*, which are are distinguished by the fact that a *habitus* is more stable and harder to dislodge than a *dispositio* (for example, knowledge is a *habitus*, but illness a *dispositio*). The English 'disposition' usually refers to something stable in precisely this way, whereas a 'tendency' is weaker and more easily overridden. (It has occasionally been necessary, however, to translate the verb *dispono* with **dispose**.) An *inclinatio* is more temporary still. *Inchoatio* refers to an innate predisposition to develop a tendency or full-blown disposition. A virtue, for example, courage, when fully developed, is a disposition. Someone may be born with a predisposition to act in a brave way, and then develop this through practice until it becomes a tendency to act bravely, and finally a fully developed disposition of courage.

genus: **class, category**; *species*: **type, species**; *differentia*: **distinguishing feature**.

The modern biological categories of 'genus' and 'species' are a relic of a wider, Aristotelian, division, of all types of thing into bigger classes. Different types within a class were distinguished by *differentiae*; for example, sofas might be distinguished within the class of seats by the distinguishing features of 'comfort' and 'capacity-to-seat-more-than-one'. Modern translations often transliterate *species* as 'species', but this seems to me misleading in most cases. Aquinas also uses *genus* to mean 'category' in the technical, Aristotelian, sense.

patria: **homeland**; *via*: **journey**.

The image of the Christian life as a journey or pilgrimage, taken from the New Testament, via Augustine, dominates the structure of Aquinas's ethical thought. In this life we are *in via*, on our journey, towards our homeland of 'heaven' or the enjoyment of the presence of God after death. The saints in heaven are **possessors** (*comprehensores*) of that homeland, for which at present we can only hope. Only Christ himself, as both God and man, was able to be both 'on the journey' and 'in possession of the homeland' at the same time (*DQChar* 10 rep.).

passio: **emotion, passive experience.**
A *passio* is a state of being affected by something or being acted upon, the opposite of an *actio* or 'action'. Often the word refers to those experiences we call 'emotions', which Aquinas categorises under seven main types: love, hate, joy, sorrow, fear, hope, anger.

amor: **love;** *dilectio*: **love, affection;** *caritas*: **charity.**
Amor and *dilectio* are used fairly interchangeably by Aquinas to refer to love in a broad sense. *Caritas* refers specifically to love that involves God: either God's love for himself or his creatures, or human love for God, or human love for other creatures that is ordered towards the love of God. Although the English word 'charity' is often used nowadays with an impoverished sense, it was necessary to keep the word in the translation in order to preserve this fundamental distinction between the two senses of love.

proprium, *proprie*: **distinctive, peculiar, strictly speaking.**
A quality that is *proprium* to a subject is distinctive of it in the sense that it constitutes part of what makes that subject complete as the type or species that it is, in a way that differentiates this from other types of thing. Words are used *proprie* when they are used in a strict sense rather than loosely, that is, when they are used of a thing that possesses all, rather than only some, of the distinctive elements to which the word refers.

principium, *principalis*: **principle, origin, basis; principal, fundamental.**
A *principium* is something that comes first, whether in causality, in authority, or in logic, and which is the source of what follows from it. It is both the beginning or starting point of other things, and thereby more valuable or important than them.

delectatio: **pleasure**; *voluptas*: **sensual pleasure**.
Voluptas refers specifically to the pleasures of the senses. *Delectatio* strictly refers to non-sensual pleasures, but is also used more loosely to include pleasure, delight, or enjoyment in the wide sense.

medium: **mid-point**.
Aquinas uses *medium* to translate Aristotle's *meson*, often rendered in English as 'mean'. I have preferred the more literal and idiomatic 'mid-point'.

subiectum: **subject**.
It has sometimes been clearer to render *subiectum* using the noun **possessor** (of attributes) or the verb **possess**.

materia: **matter, domain**.
The *materia* of a virtue is the area or domain of life with which it deals; the 'domain' of courage, for example, is things that are frightening or difficult.

moveo, motus: **move, movement, change**.
It is important to remember that the Latin makes no distinction between 'move' and 'change'.

virtus: **virtue, power**; *vis*: **power**.
Virtus means both 'virtue' and 'strength' or 'power'. A *vis* is a power in the sense of a capacity or ability; a plant, for example, has a nutritive *vis*, which enables it to acquire nourishment. Aquinas not infrequently uses *virtus* where one would expect *vis*, even in potentially confusing contexts.

Table of parallel questions

DQVirtGen

a. 1   *ST* 1a2ae 55.1; *CommSent* 2.27.1; 3.23.1.3.1.3; *CommEth* 2.5
a. 2   *ST* 1a2ae 55.4; *CommSent* 2.27.2
a. 3   *ST* 1a2ae 56.1; *CommSent* 3.33.2.4.1
a. 4   *ST* 1a2ae 56.4; *CommSent* 3.33.2.4.2
a. 5   *ST* 1a2ae 56.6, 2a2ae 24.1; *CommSent* 3.23.1.4.1, 3.27.2.3
a. 6–7   *ST* 1a2ae 56.3; *CommSent* 3.23.1.4.1
a. 8   *ST* 1a2ae 63.1; *CommSent* 1.17.1.3, 2.39.2.1, 3.33.1.2.1;
        DQTruth 11.1; *CommEth* 2.1
a. 9   *ST* 1a2ae 63.2; *CommSent* 3.33.1.2.2; *CommEth* 2.1
a. 10   *ST* 1a2ae 62.1, 63.3; 2a2ae 17.6; *CommSent* 3.23.1.4.3,
        3.23.1.5, 3.26.2.3.1, 3.33.1.2
a. 11   *ST* 1a2ae 52.1–2, 66.1; 2a2ae 24.4–5; *CommSent* 1.17.2.1–2;
        DQEvil 7.2; *Quod* 9.6
a. 12   *ST* 1a2ae 58.2, 62.1–2; 2a2ae 17.6; *CommSent* 3.23.1.4.2–3,
        3.23.1.5, 3. 26.2.3.1
a. 13   *ST* 1a2ae 58, 60; *CommSent* 3.33.1.3.1–4; *CommEth* 2.6.7

DQChar

a. 1   *ST* 2a2ae 23.2; *CommSent* 1.17.11
a. 2   *ST* 2a2ae 23.3; *CommSent* 3.27.2.2
a. 3   *ST* 2a2ae 23.8; *CommSent* 3.23.3.1.1, 3.27.2.4.3; *DQTruth*
        14.5; *DQEvil* 8.2
a. 4   *ST* 2a2ae 23.5; *CommSent* 3.27.2.4.1

a. 5	*ST* 2a2ae 23.4; *CommSent* 3.27.2.4.2; *DQEvil* 8.2, 11.2
a. 6	*ST* 2a2ae 24.12
a. 7	*ST* 2a2ae 25.3–4 and 12; *CommSent* 3.28.2 and 6–7
a. 8	*ST* 2a2ae 25.8–9, 83.8; *CommSent* 3.30.1–2
a. 9	*ST* 2a2ae 26; *CommSent* 3.29.1–3, 5–7
a. 10	*ST* 2a2ae 24.8; *CommSent* 3.27.3.4
a. 12	*ST* 2a2ae 24.11; *CommSent* 3.31.1.1; *SCG* 4.70
a. 13	*ST* 1a2ae 71.4, 2a2ae 24.12; *CommSent* 3.31.1.1

DQBrCorr

a. 1	*ST* 2a2ae 33.2; *CommSent* 4.19.2.2.1
a. 2	*ST* 2a2ae 33.7; *CommSent* 4.19.2.3.1; *Quod* 1.8.2, 11.10.1–2

DQHope

a. 1	*ST* 2a2ae 17.1; *CommSent* 3.26.2.1
a. 2	*ST* 2a2ae 18.1; *CommSent* 3.26.1.5
a. 3	*ST* 1a2ae 62.4; 2a2ae 4.7, 17.7–8; *CommSent* 3.23.2.5, 3.26.2.3.2
a. 4	*ST* 1a2ae 67.4; 2a2ae 18.2; *CommSent* 3.26.2.5.2, 3.31.2.1.2

DQCard

a. 1	*ST* 1a2ae 61.1–2, 66.4; *CommSent* 3.33.2.1.2–4; *CommEth* 2.8
a. 2	*ST* 1a2ae 58.4–5, 65.1–3; 2a2ae 23.7; *CommSent* 3.36.1–2; *Quod* 12.15.1; *CommEth* 6.10–11
a. 3	*ST* 1a2ae 66.1–2 and 4; 2a2ae 58.12, 123.12, 141.8; *CommSent* 3.36.4
a. 4	*ST* 1a2ae 67.1; *CommSent* 3.33.1.4

Index of scriptural citations

Old Testament

Genesis
2:24 161
15:6 221

Exodus
20:2–17 197
23:4 152

Leviticus
19:17 152
19:18 147

Deuteronomy
5:6–21 197
6:5 166, 171, 182, 218
22:1 200

1 Samuel
16:18 183

Job
22:17 192
31:18 44, 253
31:29–30 152
33:15–17 212

Psalms
6:23 195
11:5 186
19:9 232
27:2 182

34:14 20
36:9 108
37:3 220, 229
37:5 233
55:15 154
58:10 158
69:28 154
71:5 235
83:8 252
139:22 157

Proverbs
1:33 237
3:12 199
9:8 195, 201
13:12 219
19:25 202
22:1 210
24:11 200
24:15 202
25:21 152
26:14 244

Ecclesiastes
1 107
1:15 196
7:14 197
9:1 219
12:12 170

Song of Solomon (Song of Songs)
2:4 162
8:6 138
8:6–7 180

Index of non-scriptural citations

Alcher

SS
11, 45 20
45 20

Ambrose

CommLuke
5.62 244
5.63 253
8.30 228

Anselm of Canterbury

On Truth
12 19

Aristotle

(We have generally given the Bekker number only for the first line of the cited passage.)

Cat
6, 6a25–35 263
7, 8a35 261
8 7
8, 8b29 37
8, 10b26–11a14 263
10, 12a25 94, 193
11, 13b35 181, 187
14, 15b11 53, 72

GA
2.3, 736b14 45

GC
1.5, 320b30 71

Heav
1.11, 281a15 4, 6, 52, 93, 116, 272, 274
2.3, 286a8 6

Int
1, 16a3 75
14, 23b3 98

Met
1.2, 982a14 37
1.9, 991b2 45
2.1, 993b30 163
5.6, 1016b31 129
5.15, 1021a10 263
8.3, 1043b33 264
8.3, 1044a9 76
9.8, 1050b1 57
10.1, 1045b34 63
10.1, 1052a27 75
10.1, 1052b20 263
10.10, 1058b26 135, 243

NE
1.1.4, 1094a10 255
1.1.4, 1094a14 136
1.7.1, 1097a20 88
1.7.15, 1098a16 4, 37
1.13.2, 1102a8 128
1.13.16, 1102b22 44
1.13.19, 1103a4 17, 28

2.53–4 84
2.53.159–54.165 248

Cyprian

Virg
passim 251

Decretals of Gregory IX
5.1.24 206

Dionysius (pseudo-Dionysius the Areopagite)

DivNames
4.3 53
4.10 228
4.12 160, 219
4.13 180
4.18–35 138, 181
4.23 44
4.30 200

Gregory the Great

HomEzek
2.2.8 132
2.3.3 252, 262
2.10.17 228, 262

HomGosp
17.1 146
30.1 161
30.2 179, 180, 183
34.2 158

MorJob
1.27 220
5.33 204
6.37 269
22.1.2 35, 241, 242, 253, 254, 255
22.11.23 158
22.20.26 262

Isidore of Seville

Sent(Is)
2.4.2 233
3.32.1 198

Jerome

CommMatt
2 166
3 196, 198, 208, 210, 215

John Cassian

MonInst
5.4 261

John Chrysostom

CommMatt
60 215

John Damascene

OrthF
2.1 241
3.14 42, 262

Leo the Great

Serm
60.4 190

Macrobius

Dream
1.5–6 270

Origen

CommSS
prol 2.35 144

HomSS
2.8 160

Prin
1.3.8 138, 190

Paul of Friuli (Paul the Deacon)

De salutaribus documentis ad quemdam comitem
7 179

Peter Lombard

Sent
1.17.1.2 75, 109, 183

Index of names and subjects

This index includes references to authors where these are not included in the Index of non-scriptural citations.

CAMBRIDGE TEXTS IN THE HISTORY OF PHILOSOPHY

Titles published in the series thus far

Aristotle *Nicomachean Ethics* (edited by Roger Crisp)

Aquinas *Disputed Questions on the Virtues* (edited by E. M. Atkins and Thomas Williams)

Arnauld and Nicole *Logic or the Art of Thinking* (edited by Jill Vance Buroker)

Augustine *On the Trinity* (edited by Gareth Matthews)

Bacon *The New Organon* (edited by Lisa Jardine and Michael Silverthorne)

Boyle *A Free Enquiry into the Vulgarly Received Notion of Nature* (edited by Edward B. Davis and Michael Hunter)

Bruno *Cause, Principle and Unity* and *Essays on Magic* (edited by Richard Blackwell and Robert de Lucca with an introduction by Alfonso Ingegno)

Cavendish *Observations upon Experimental Philosophy* (edited by Eileen O'Neill)

Cicero *On Moral Ends* (edited by Julia Annas, translated by Raphael Woolf)

Clarke *A Demonstration of the Being and Attributes of God and Other Writings* (edited by Ezio Vailati)

Classic and Romantic German Aesthetics (edited by J. M. Bernstein)

Condillac *Essay on the Origin of Human Knowledge* (edited by Hans Aarsleff)

Conway *The Principles of the Most Ancient and Modern Philosophy* (edited by Allison P. Coudert and Taylor Corse)

Cudworth *A Treatise Concerning Eternal and Immutable Morality* with *A Treatise of Freewill* (edited by Sarah Hutton)

Descartes *Meditations on First Philosophy,* with selections from the *Objections and Replies* (edited by John Cottingham)

Descartes *The World and Other Writings* (edited by Stephen Gaukroger)

Fichte *Foundations of Natural Right* (edited by Frederick Neuhouser, translated by Michael Baur)

Herder *Philosophical Writings* (edited by Michael Forster)

Hobbes and Bramhall on Liberty and Necessity (edited by Vere Chappell)

Humboldt *On Language* (edited by Michael Losonsky, translated by Peter Heath)

Kant *Critique of Practical Reason* (edited by Mary Gregor with an introduction by Andrews Reath)

Kant *Groundwork of the Metaphysics of Morals* (edited by Mary Gregor with an introduction by Christine M. Korsgaard)

Kant *The Metaphysics of Morals* (edited by Mary Gregor with an introduction by Roger Sullivan)

Kant *Prolegomena to any Future Metaphysics* (edited by Gary Hatfield)

Kant *Religion within the Boundaries of Mere Reason and Other Writings* (edited by Allen Wood and George di Giovanni with an introduction by Robert Merrihew Adams)

La Mettrie *Machine Man and Other Writings* (edited by Ann Thomson)

Leibniz *New Essays on Human Understanding* (edited by Peter Remnant and Jonathan Bennett)

Lessing *Philosophical and Theological Writings* (edited by H. B. Nisbet)

CPSIA information can be obtained
at www.ICGtesting.com
Printed in the USA
LVHW022030160820
663337LV00009B/155

9 780521 776615